The Story of Crass

THE STORY OF CRASS

GEORGE BERGER

PM

The Story Of Crass
George Berger

ISBN: 978-1-60486-037-5
Library of Congress Control Number: 2008934200

Copyright © 2008 Omnibus Press
This edition copyright © 2009 PM Press
All Rights Reserved

PM Press
PO Box 23912
Oakland, CA 94623
www.pmpress.org

Cover design by John Yates/Stealworks

Printed in the USA on recycled paper.

Contents

Dedicated to Joanna Markunas

ANOK4U2?

"This time it's for real!" jeered Ronnie Biggs, guest-recording with the remnants of The Sex Pistols on the *Great Rock'N'Roll Swindle* soundtrack, and the paradox was complete. What had seemed like a lifeline to a generation who increasingly felt like the rubbish left out on England's streets was being presented by Malcolm McLaren and his cohorts as nothing more than an elaborate illusion – a rabbit pulled out of the hat, a simple act of misdirection.

The Swindle may have sought to confuse, and certainly succeeded in entertaining, but the lost tribes of England wanted more than that. For people who'd bought into punk as a way of life, 'this time it's for real' was a phrase that could have, *should* have, meant something.

'Helen! Never trust a hippy!' cried McLaren in the *Swindle*. We giggled at the cheek, unsure as to whether there was a tongue in it. Ironic perhaps, that it was to be a group of people emanating from the hippy era that would put the trust back into our lives.

On a more positive, and perhaps relevant note, there was a benign revolution in Nicaragua, when the Sandanistas stormed parliament and seized power. So, in amongst all the despair, always seeds of hope and a sense of possibility. Elsewhere, Astrid Proll is arrested in London and Sid Vicious pogoes off this mortal coil.

"This time it's for real." The irony is complete. London 1978. Punk is dead.

Which leaves a whole generation of punk rockers without a

soundtrack. Because by now, punk is far more than a bunch of alternative music fans. Indeed, it always has been. It starts as a fashion statement screamed out of a shop called Sex (latterly Seditionaries) in the Kings Road and evolves into a lifestyle screaming danger gear and rebellion.

Nature abhors a vacuum. As does capitalism, naming it the 'gap in the market'.

Enter Crass. The rest is, or should be, history. But it is a history so far shamefully under-recorded. Here, then, is the history of Crass. As an early Crass poster cried, hanging tattered and torn outside the corpse of the Roxy Club in Covent Garden: 'Germany got Baader-Meinhoff, England got punk. But they can't kill it.'

They say the past is a different country, but the UK in the mid-seventies was a different continent. Or should that be incontinent – England was a mess when punk exploded into its avenues and alleyways.

In 1974, the miners had gone on strike and brought down the Conservative government. But subsequently the economy, under a Labour Government, had fallen to pieces. They were forced to go cap in hand to the International Monetary Fund to request an emergency loan. By 1976, inflation was running at over 23%, and unemployment had doubled in just three years from just over 2% to almost 6%, the worst since the recession of the thirties. The temporary blip of post war economic boom that peaked in the sixties seemed been replaced by a wider post colonial-exploitation bust that saw Great Britain being put back in her economic post-Empire place by colonies sick of being sucked dry to feed their mother country.

Factor in the long oppressively hot summer of 1976 and you're getting a recipe for anger. A minister for drought – Denis Howell – was appointed and announced everyone had to reduce their water consumption by half or face water rationing. As the heat wave roared on, increasing numbers were admitted to hospital suffering from sunstroke and heart attacks. Motorways had problems with tarmac melting. The drought hardly helped the economy either, as thousands threw 'sickies' from work in order to enjoy the sunshine.

Factor in the mass acceptance of racial bigotry to all this and you're running a serious risk of the anger exploding in a dangerous direction.

This was a time when it was still acceptable for TV to run a comedy (*Love Thy Neighbour*) based on the racial bigotry of a white man towards his black neighbours; a time when Eric Clapton – a musician who had made a fortune from playing the blues – said live onstage that England had "become overcrowded", advising the crowd to vote for Enoch Powell to stop Britain becoming "a black colony". (Rock Against Racism would be set up in late '76 as a direct response to these remarks.) In May 1976, the National Front received almost one in five of the votes at a UK by-election, while summer saw race riots during the annual Notting Hill Carnival as largely black youth declared temporary war on the police.

A time before 'political correctness' had 'gone mad', as the *Daily Mail* might see it.

"I think that the general feeling in society from the mid-seventies onwards was that both main parties had nothing to offer. Till then people thought society would automatically get better." – Dave Morris (London Greenpeace, McLibel Two)

Anarchy In The UK at the time was publicly represented by the Angry Brigade – a loose group of anarchists whose bombing campaign targeted a wide range of fascist and capitalist targets without any loss of life. The targets were usually connected with the state, though interestingly they also targeted hippie boutique Biba, and accompanied by communiqués that sought to explain their actions and encourage the workers to join in. Which, of course, they didn't.

Look backwards and England looks backward. The only spaghetti we had came in a tin (or a junction); our three television channels started at lunchtime and finished before midnight; videos were yet to come into the public arena and foreign holidays were just taking off as Spain became a popular destination. No matter that it was still a fascist dicta- torship – Franco may have died in 1975, but democracy wouldn't happen until 1978. Anna Ford caused a stir by breaking the sexual apartheid to become the first woman newsreader.

England looks backward but was desperately scraping around for something that may point forward. The emphasis on 'new' had percolated through the seventies: slums were pulled down en masse in cities to be replaced by shiny utopian tower blocks. Just twenty years after the end of rationing, the consumer society was rife. People consumed for the sake of consuming: trendy new electrical items, coffee percolators, soda siphons; if it was new you had to buy it, regardless of whether you needed it or would ever use it, and if it was a 'status symbol', all the better. Credit cards and cash machines were introduced to encourage more spending, even if you didn't have the money. The never never. Still you kept buying. New new new. But where was the new music?

In December 1976, The Sex Pistols swore on the teatime family viewing *Today* programme and punk went overground. Anger and anarchy. Outrageous clothes that were statements in themselves. A generation of parents recoiled in horror and a nation of straights were suitably disgusted. Punk jumped from being almost a secret confined largely to London and Manchester, to being tabloid headline news. Depending on who you ask, it was the end of the beginning or the beginning of the end for punk.[1]

Fast forward to 1978 and the initial punk explosion had blown over, particularly in the eyes of the media. The cathartic scream had been screamed and in some ways the dust was settling. Of the initial heroes (in an age of none), The Sex Pistols had been sent to America to die a needless death and The Clash were busy deciding they weren't so bored with the USA after all, and metamorphosing into a successful middle of the road rock band. The music industry was promoting a roster of bands under labels like 'new wave' and 'power pop', doing what it had always done best: taking a movement, watering down its essence and repackaging it for public consumption in a way that kept the accoutrements and readily identifiable ephemera whilst surgically removing the spirit. Bands like The Boomtown Rats leapt up the

---

[1] History – notably the Sex Pistols film 'The Filth And The Fury' – is beginning to record punk as being synonymous with the winter of discontent, where strikes famously saw rubbish and the accompanying stench of decay piling up on the streets. But that wouldn't happen until a little later in our story, in 1979 to be precise.

charts whilst The Jam self-censored the lyrics of *This Is The Modern World*, adding to doubts that they had ever been a punk band in the first place.

But the punk spirit wasn't so easy to brush under the carpet. To a legion of British youth, punk meant more than that. Because, like the great post-war youth movements before it – beatniks, teds, mods, hippies etc – punk gave the individual a route to personal liberation and self-discovery; a place for outsiders, romantics, lovers of outrage, people who sought a life less ordinary. And once discovered, it felt way beyond a simple fashion to be discarded when the forces of attempted control declared that it was time to move on to a soulless mod revival or water down to a soulless power pop tune.

Punk had, to varying extents, preached a dogma of DIY – the idea that anyone could do it. Helped by the supposed rudimentary nature of the music, punks across the land took this onboard to form bands and write fan-magazines. *Strangled* fanzine (not *Sniffin' Glue* as is often credited) emerged with a cover showing finger placements for three chords – "here's three chords – now form a band".

The DIY ethic had, at this point in time, only been a half truth at best. Whilst the rhetoric suggested a new generation emerging from a new, hippie-eschewing, musical Year Zero – "I've just come straight up from nowhere, and I'm going straight back there" as Buzzcocks put it – the truth of the matter didn't quite stand up to the rhetoric. The Pistols and The Clash were both tight, musically competent rock'n'roll bands. The Clash in particular were no spring chickens or first-timers. And, despite the personal posturings of Malcolm McLaren and early Sex Pistols interviews ("I hate hippies, I hate long hair" – John Lydon), the punk movement had at least as much in common with the ideals of the preceding hippie movement as it did apart from it.

That all said, there was a nation out there who had bought the rhetoric and were to slowly turn it into a reality. As the first-wavers of punk scuttled off to get their establishment pay-checks, there was created a vacuum as hordes of punks – ever increasing as waves of younger kids kept joining the furore – were all dressed up craving somewhere to go.

In this context, to be confronted – and confronted really is the only way to describe it – with the first Crass record 'Feeding Of The Five Thousand' was simultaneously a shocking revelation and a feeling of near-salvation. Having been forced to hear Ronnie Biggs cackling 'this time it's for real' almost felt like an insult to the hopes and dreams of a generation. Then Crass came along and you felt that this time, it could very well be for real. Here was a band who, for better or worse, seemed to take 'anarchy' seriously. And maybe even know what it meant.

"If you have embraced a creed which appears to be free from the ordinary dirtiness of politics – a creed from which you yourself cannot expect to draw any material advantage – surely that proves that you are in the right?" – George Orwell

To a bored teenager, 'Feeding Of The Five Thousand' was different and unprecedented in so many ways. Perhaps older generations would have noticed how much was borrowed from the hippie counter-culture or the great art movements of the past, but either way Crass had produced a record – or more accurately a package – that screamed blue murder in your face: screamed its integrity, screamed its love and screamed a scream that defied you to stand up and be counted. It was a record that dared to suggest punk was (or at least could be) part of something bigger and more important than a five-minute fart in the face of authority.

The thought that Crass was different entered the mind before you even had the record. Several specialist record shops of the time advertised their mail-order wares in the back of music weekly *Sounds*. Of these, a shop called Adrians is the most memorable, but the best one for punk records was Small Wonder. Based in Walthamstow in East London and run by a chap called Pete Stennett, Small Wonder also had its own record label, which released a steady stream of fiercely independent punk records from the likes of Patrik Fitzgerald, Menace and Punishment Of Luxury.

At the bottom of their weekly advert, Small Wonder advertised the Crass 'single – 17-track 12 inch. £1.99'. At a time when albums were generally retailing at £3.99, this was little short of a revelation. It seemed equally mysterious that somebody could release a piece of vinyl with seventeen tracks on it yet call it a single. Semantics perhaps, but possibly also the suggestion that here was a band who were taking punk as seriously as the punters who, at this time, were feeling increasingly left out (at best) or sold down the river (at worst) by the big punk bands.

Here was a band who circled the A in their own name. This was a big deal at the time. Whilst many punks littered their copious graffiti with circled 'A's, often bestowing them on bands who would never dream of accepting the honour, this was pretty much the first time an important band had gone along with the concept. It should be remembered that this was a time before arguments about the finer points of anarchism or the reality (or otherwise) of utopian dreaming. No, at this point, it mainly meant simply that Crass was of the people.

The sleeve too was challengingly different. Firstly, it was a 'double-A' side: each side of the sleeve was printed 'upside down' from the other, giving the appearance that either side could be the front. Riding on the coat-tails of a movement that had romanticised all things urban, one of the sides featured simply a ploughed field with a figure in the distance carrying a banner, like some kind of refugee from a Red Square military demonstration, except this banner featured the Crass symbol. The other side featured a more typical collage of inner-city post war decay, with a child mysteriously levitating in the middle of the shot.

The record came with a pull-out crammed with all the lyrics (which was just as well, as many of them were spat out with such phlegmy speed as to be virtually indecipherable), and further mini-collages.

Who were these people? If punks had appeared to 'straight society' to come from a different planet, then planet Crass appeared to be off the radar to most punks. Whatever else it had achieved, 'Feeding Of The Five Thousand' certainly made Crass arrive with a bang and not a whimper.

But somehow it also seemed to be more than the sum of its parts. Down there, in amongst all the swearing and the anger and the outrageous viewpoints … somewhere in amongst the chaotic collage of primal screaming, you could sense something deeper, something that suggested that here was a band who were offering a vision more real, more practical and more achievable to your average Joe Bloggs than the Pistols ever managed. Lydon had been and remained (and often remains) an inspiring role model in terms of having an attitude that equipped you to deal with the ugliness of the world. But it still lacked a real world application inasmuch as his own life was very much that of a musician, and the music business will let you say and do anything as long as you're selling product. Crass appeared, somewhere in their murky depths, to be offering something else – something further out there and yet nearer. More real.

Here was a band that challenged even punk prejudices on many levels – they were a mixture of generations: whilst vocalist Steve Ignorant was clearly of the punk gene, drummer Penny Rimbaud – aside from having a girl's name – was in his mid thirties, which was *ancient*! And the band featured women in uncertain roles – vocalists Eve Libertine and Joy De Vivre were credited on the sleeve but only Joy sang at all on the record and that was only one track . . . what was going on? Already the idea was being subtly presented that here was a band that existed beyond the stage.

Reactions to 'Feeding. . .' split punk down the middle. Crass was easily dismissed with one word by their detractors – hippies. Armed with Malcolm McLaren's clarion call never to trust hippies, many punks would despise Crass with a venom rarely reserved for bands. And other punks – and later other people – would see in Crass a vision paradoxically delicate and beautiful that suggested a better future out there for the sculpting. . .

THE BAND &
SUPPORTING CAST

Gee Vaucher – artwork / radio / piano
Penny Rimbaud – drums / kettle
Eve Libertine – vocals
Pete Wright – bass guitar
Mick Duffield – films and filming
Phil Free – lead guitar
Joy De Vivre – vocals
Steve Ignorant – vocals
Andy Palmer – rhythm guitar

SUPPORTING CAST

John Loder: Sound man for Exit, ran Southern Studios where he recorded most Crass output, and acted as Crass manager.
Dave King: Ex-Dial House resident, designed the Crass symbol
Dave Morris: political activist and free festival veteran who for years was part of the radical London Greenpeace group. Possibly better known as one half of the McLibel Two.
Pete Sutton: old friend of the band who attended art college with Penny Rimbaud and Gee Vaucher. Pete lived in a caravan on a farm near Dial House for ten years.

Bernhardt Rebours: got taught at college by Penny Rimbaud, played In Ceres Confusion and Poison Girls

George Mackay: Professor of Cultural Studies, University Of Salford and author.

Garry Bushell: journalist and sometime TV celeb

Martin Lux: anarchist and anti fascist

Tony D: punk rocker, the man behind Ripped & Torn, Kill Your Pet Puppy and involved in the anarchist centres

Alistair Livingstone: anarchist, also involved in Kill Your Pet Puppy and the anarchist centres

Basil Brooks: member of Zorch, the only band to play at the first Stonehenge festival. www.zorchmusic.com

David Tibet: Current 93 member, ex Sounds journalist, old friend of the band.

Bob Short: punk squatter, writer, guitarist from Blood & Roses

BOHEMIAN RHAPSODY –
THE SIXTIES

"World War Two was neither lost nor won, it simply created a horrific emptiness and within that emptiness there grew a desperation amongst the people of the world, a fear that civilisation had learnt nothing from the tragic lesson of the Nazi death-camps, or the cruel truth of Hiroshima and Nagasaki. It seemed that those in power were setting the planet on a course towards total destruction – the arms race was on, the cold war was on, the third world was starving, but the superpowers looked only to themselves. In the horror of this new world, people turned to bizarre ways of calming their fears.

"To ignore is the greatest ignorance, but ignore became the keyword as individuals buried themselves in mindless materialism. The age of consumerism had been born. If you couldn't find peace of mind, perhaps a Cadillac would do. If life had lost its meaning, perhaps a super deluxe washing machine might give it back. The ownership, this is mine, mine, mine, security boom had started, and you can't have it. Buy, buy, buy. Possess. Insure. Protect. The TV world was upon us, which one's real? This one? That one? Mind-numbing crap to numb crappy minds. Buy this, buy that. Who knows which is which? Layers of shit to hide the awful facts of life in a nuclear reality.

Meanwhile, governments turned to the business of developing nuclear arsenals, nuclear deterrents we were told, and the vast majority of the population, blinded with consumerism and media-junk, was happy to accept the lie. As long as everyone was having fun, no-one would question the behaviour of those in power as they played with their nuclear time-bombs; but all the time the fuse burnt shorter." – Penny Rimbaud – Last Of The Hippies

"The West German state was just following the American model. Their so-called economic miracle was invented as a distraction to stop us thinking about our fascist past. Consumerism put the lid back on history – we were no longer meant to know what our past meant." – A German libertarian remembers the 'libertarian' sixties

Although Crass achieved notoriety as a punk band in the late seventies and early eighties, we must look a lot further back to find the start of the chain of events that led to them doing so. By the time they officially ventured out under the Crass banner(s), the band members had known each other, and creatively worked and lived with each other, for varying amounts of time, often many years.

The epicentre of all this – some may say the reason for all this (though others vehemently disagree) – is a sprawling cottage just outside a small Essex country village called North Weald, near Epping.

Dial House, as the cottage has been known for over a hundred years, was taken over by Crass member Penny Rimbaud in the late sixties and has been functioning as an open house since shortly afterwards. Some might call it a commune – again, others would actively deny the description. Either way, it's through this house that all Crass members came to meet each other and decide to work for a better future, as of course many others were doing in both the arts and the various movements for social change in the sixties and seventies.

The fruits of the sixties were born from the seeds of war. Having featured heavily in the early lives of the older band members, World War Two is a constant reference point: from the family members directly suffering from it to the rationing that lasted right up until the fifties, to the bomb sites that peppered London till the punk years, not forgetting of course the new fears thrown up in its wake by the cold war and the nuclear threat.

But if it's the Second World War that influenced childhood memories, it's during the sixties economic boom it caused where the disparate beings who would constitute Crass started meeting each other.

Some members of Crass refer a lot to 'energy' when referring to these times, and it seems a fair analogy, or even description. When punk rock came along, the energy that had been created in Dial House over the years collided with it and out came Crass, who endeavoured to make up for in ideas and integrity what they plainly lacked in musical talent. To this mixture, they also brought a wealth of artistic creativity and alternative experience, much of which had been centred around activities in Dial House for years.

A fair few of the main players in this book pre-date even Dial House in their coming together however. . .

The first to meet each other did so in the early sixties at art college. Drummer Jeremy Ratter (who would later rechristen himself Penny Rimbaud) and artist Gee Vaucher (also not her real name, but she'd rather keep that private) were both attending the South East Essex Technical College and School of Art (now Barking College of Technology).

This being the days before Dial House, both Penny and Gee were still living with their parents. And this being the early sixties, things were already moving apace all around them in ways that would prove a strong influence on Penny, Gee, and later Crass.

Come the sixties, the rise of The Beatles saw Britain emerge from the shadow of America as style setters. Concurrent with the explosion in pop music, came the explosion in pop art. For the first time, a section of the youth had its own expendable income and began to enjoy a new power and influence accordingly. In an attempt to knit together a generation that was increasingly getting its voice heard, the media came up with the term 'Swinging London'. Though essentially the province of a select band of rich kids in London, the image was to have a disproportionate influence well beyond its habitat. It was against this backdrop of new hopes and births that Gee Vaucher went to art college and changed her life.

Gee Vaucher was born in Dagenham, in the East End of London in 1945, the last of four children, "one of whom died as a result of the war. He'd been evacuated and had got the short end of the straw. As far as I can suss he got bad treatment in terms of not being fed properly, and got very ill. It wasn't treatable; it was a hole in the heart. So when he was 12 and I was four, he died. That hung over the family – it was always there in a funny kind of way, my mother never really got over it." Gee glances away. "She was a very good friend of mine, my mother."

Gee remembers her upbringing fondly, though with an acute awareness of the poverty of the times. "Working class Dagenham was a closed society. It was like a city in itself – you didn't go beyond that area. The upbringing was very poor. Everybody in Dagenham was allied to the Ford factories." Gee's father worked there, cleaning out chemical boilers. "He didn't live that long really," she says, with the sort of nervous laugh that can often turn to tears, "most people in the street didn't live that long."

Despite the poverty, however, they were happy times, as Gee points out: "But yeah, it was a good childhood. My parents were imaginative – they made all our toys. It was very good – I enjoyed it a lot. Even being poor, my mother believed in a holiday every year. It was three miles down the road in a caravan," Gee laughs, "but if you're a child, you could have gone to the moon and back."

Her education was typical of the area and the times, and hardly inspiring for that. Concepts such as choosing which school you went to were yet to come into fruition, at least in this part of the world. "You went to the one at the end of the street, you didn't have a choice. Infants, juniors and seniors were all the same named school. You and your brothers or sisters just trotted after each other, got the same crappy teachers. It was just to keep you off the street really; you didn't have any exams, except for RSI for girls (a sort of typing certificate). There was no uniform or anything either, you were fodder for the factory."

It was an obsession with art ("It's always what I've done – I can't remember not doing it.") that would see Gee attending Art School in Barking from 1961 to 1965, and discovering a new world. Back in the early sixties, as many talented success stories of the time attest to, art school was the saviour of the creative poor – it was a space and an accessible one at that. "You just needed a 'folio of work and your mum and dad to go to the art school to have an interview with the head and if you were good enough you got in."

For Gee Vaucher, it was also a revelation. "Meeting people like Pen, middle-class people . . . up till then, I'd only ever known working class people. There were only two working class people there, me and this girl called Glynis. Of course, we're all 'gore blimey'. I actually couldn't eat in front of strangers, just couldn't do it. I'd never eaten in a restaurant or anything, never actually sat in front of friends and eaten. So I found that quite difficult. I didn't speak either – I didn't know the art of debating. I was quite quiet . . . but that was fine with me because I was besotted with the art."

The Vaucher-Rimbaud axis wasn't initially as bold as love: "I thought he was a complete arsehole! No, that's not fair, I didn't. I thought he was silly, stupid, for not really doing his work. I thought he was good at his work but he was always the entertainer – always up to some jokery or being Jack the lad. I do remember quite vividly having a conversation saying why don't you just do your painting?"

Despite Gee's initial bemusement, the pair soon grew close. Gee remembers: "It was a coming together of very different cultures. We learnt an enormous amount from each other. He didn't have an intimate knowledge of where I'd come from – the sort of people I'd come from and the way people lived and worked together and helped each other. Although he comes from a family that were very generous, very unpretentious. I think there was a very special bond, to do with mutual respect really."

Penny Rimbaud remembers: "We got on very well at art college. We were both very inspired by the Pop Art movement of the day. We were artistic buddies. Also we were at an art school that specialised in commercial art, and both of us very quickly realised we didn't want to do commercial art – we wanted to be artists. So we were buddies in that respect too – we were the bad guys at the college – not behaving ourselves and doing our own thing."

Pete Sutton was a friend from those art school days, and remains so now (indeed, it's striking just how many long term friends are still around). Of Gee, Sutton says: "She rapidly showed she had a talent. She was a very friendly, tomboyish Dagenham girl – she had a naughty side to her. She quickly developed a group of friends – they'd all wear stockings and short skirts . . . very beat. Shy? I wouldn't have said that at all."

Pete Sutton was a year or two younger than Penny Rimbaud when they met at art school, and remembers of him: "He reminded me of a young Paul Jones (from Manfred Mann) – combat jacket, short hair, Chelsea boots. We were just Essex kids and in breezed Penny. He seemed to draw people to him – he was confident, articulate, upper-middle class and cocksure. And always up for a good laugh, good company."

Penny Rimbaud was born Jeremy John Ratter on the outskirts of London in Northwood, Middlesex in 1943, a war child. As has been noted, Penny was from a privileged upbringing, in direct contrast to Gee. He is searingly honest, if somewhat defensive, about it: "I was given everything in my life that a kid could want. My parents gave me what on their terms was a bloody good education. I've got a huge amount of social advantages – I'm a good talker, I'm a charmer. I could have used that the way most people I was at school did – they're all politicians and church people or military or successful lawyers – that sort of stuff. But I didn't want to. I remember my own childhood, finding out about Dr. Barnados and the concentration camps … finding out it isn't a lovely world, it's horribly unequal. So ever since I was a kid I thought that whatever I got I'd share. What else can you do? I don't really believe you can change governments, but you can change your immediate environment. You *can* live a life of sharing and giving and taking."

Perhaps the most noteworthy of Penny's fellow schoolmates, somewhat ironically, was the far-right-wing historian David Irving, who at the time of writing is imprisoned in Austria for Holocaust denial. "He taught me shadowing, he was a very good artist. He taught me how to make things look three-dimensional through shading," remembers Rimbaud, before adding wryly "… and anti-Semitism."

Of course, Rimbaud didn't follow Irving into Fuhrer education. It would be a very different avenue of radical thought that Penny Rimbaud would pursue. Penny first came across radical ideas and different ways of looking at the world via CND (the Campaign for Nuclear Disarmament) as a young teenager: "There was a sweet shop up the road with a garage out the back and it had this display of nuclear war stuff. It just made sense." His parents were literary types, with a wide library. "I read a lot of Hemingway when I was young and it gave me a great sense of the individual, a fairly anarchistic view of the individual and of self-will. Sometimes I wonder what would have happened if there'd been more Steinbeck than Hemingway at my parents ... maybe I'd have become a socialist then!"

A socialist perhaps, but never a fascist. In his book *Shibboleth*, Rimbaud asserts that his father had been one of the soldiers who liberated the concentration camps at the end of the Second Worlds War. So, a minor revelation:

"It's a lie. He was in Africa and Europe and he went up through Italy, blowing up bridges and rebuilding them with the Engineer Corps. He certainly knew about the camps, but he never visited them. I've used it consistently in its existential meaning really. I remember confusions in my own head about how he'd 'liberated Europe'. It didn't look very liberated to me ... it's a useful lie, a metaphor."

Perhaps an example of the old maxim of artists using lies to tell the truth. Whatever the nature of his involvement, Rimbaud Snr, so to speak, soon made Penny aware of the vile reality of fascism: "I remember somebody at school gave me some stickers, Oswald Moseley stuff. I took them home, not knowing what they were and sticking one on the kitchen wall. Dad absolutely blew a fuse about it and I learnt about fascism."

In his teens, Penny Rimbaud was also exposed to the 'angry young men' such as John Osbourne and John Wain. He was particularly influenced by Wain's *The Contenders* and the French existentialists, especially Francoise Sagan. Not to mention good old rock'n'roll, particularly in the shape of The Beatles. John Lennon remains to this day a massive influence on Penny Rimbaud. Whilst Rimbaud was at art school, he got to meet Lennon when he won a competition organised by old *TOTP* predecessor *Ready Steady Go!* with a painting he'd done representing what was then their latest single 'I Wanna Hold Your Hand': "I really got into the Beatles when they first happened. But by the time that actually happened (two years in), I'd gone through that, because they seemed to have sold out..."

Nonetheless, Penny sent off his entry: a board featuring a portrait of The Beatles against a background of Beatles graffiti, bookended by two halves of a guitar. Out of one half stretched a mannequin arm.

Rimbaud recalls, with little humility: "I knew I'd win it if I went in for it, because I was adept at pop-art. Now they've put out the *Ready*

Steady Go! videos, and it's included in those. I was at a friend's house, about fifteen years ago and they showed them. For some strange reason, they'd left in my bit.

"I turned up at the programme. I was meant to do a rehearsal but I didn't want to. I didn't want them to able to make some smart-arsed remark about me, but equally I didn't want to be in the position where I'd make a smart-arsed remark myself. I wanted to go in 'pure'. I was meant to go and meet 'the lads' after the programme and have a cup of coffee in the dressing room. I was so pissed off with it by then that the moment I got my prize I pissed off home.

"Iconically, it was amazing. Peter Blake had done a picture of The Beatles and the only thing left to go on it was their signatures, and he never got them. I think that painting's in the Tate Gallery now, minus the signatures. In the shot, the three of them were standing in front of my picture! That to me was puerile. They were going round scribbling on all the other entries, writing funny things. They were getting round to mine – I didn't want them writing on top of my art! I prevented them from signing mine."

Penny unfortunately lost the painting at a later date when the Rank organisation took it on a tour round the ballrooms of the time, and it got lost or stolen.

Meanwhile, back at college, Gee's obsession with art grew and grew with all the exposure that art school enabled: "That's all I did – I didn't really go to the parties and stuff. I was wanting to keep the college open at night so you could work."

And, of course, this was the sixties and Bob Dylan was pointing out with some accuracy that the times they were a changing. A nation of youth was getting its arse in gear to get out of line in all manner of ways. Penny and Gee were two of them, naturally.

For Gee, 'I was very politicised at art school – it was the sixties for Christ's sake! The heart of revolution! I'd always been a very independent strong-willed kid anyway. The first thing that gave me a really vocal voice was Aberfan."

The Aberfan disaster happened on Friday, October 21st, 1966, when a slag heap, containing from the local coal mine slid down the side of a mountain the in the Welsh village. It demolished almost all of Pantglas

Junior School and part of the separate adjacent senior school. Some 144 people were killed, 116 of whom were children, mostly between the ages of 7 and 10.

Gee continues: "When that happened I was really really angry and sad. Pen was joking about it cos it was his only way of dealing with it. I understand that now. But then as a very young naïve person, I thought it was callous. I do remember that very very vividly . . . in the Robin Hood pub . . . the whole disaster of Aberfan, and the first hint of corruption. They *knew* that was going to happen, and they did nothing. That was a political awakening for me. That and CND."

Another art college friend of the time, Dave King, would later go on to become a resident of Dial House and design the Crass symbol. He describes the college: "The art school occupied one wing of the college, with the rest of the buildings being taken up by people learning trades like welding and painting. The school, for better or worse, was very classical in its approach. For the first year, you just did hours and hours of life drawing. Just sitting there with a pencil, or charcoal, just drawing – eventually you had the idea that if you could see something as it really was, then you could draw it: that it wasn't a big mystery. . . You might have some aptitude, but it *was* a technique, and it did have to do with perception. You could be taught to perceive, to see with a certain amount of clarity."

Dave King throws some light on the textures of the times, art college in 1964, when he had what he describes as "a psychedelic experience without psychedelics. After all this intense drawing, I was in the cafeteria of the college, which was pretty drab, pretty grey. I remember looking at the salt and peppershakers and seeing them light up – they suddenly seemed very bright, and you could see the light passing through them. They started to have this incredible clarity and then it spread from there to the table and the plates, to the room, the people. It was like a grey veil had been lifted, and it never went back. I attribute that to the days, hours, weeks of life drawing, of looking and concentrating. I think those techniques go back hundreds of years – that's why renaissance paintings look the way they do, why they're so intense.

"At the same time, it's the swinging sixties – the first time there was some colour. After the war, there was still rationing for a few years, it was a really grey time. Everyone wore grey, the houses were grey; the only colour that I remember was in little clusters on street corners, where the newsagents had the ads for Wills cigarettes, Senior Service, or Tizer. That's what lead me to design, being desperate for some colour and seeing it only in commercial applications. The swinging sixties were really an economic phenomenon – when we were kids, our playgrounds were literally bombsites. Those bombsites stayed until the early sixties.

"At the same time there was this media explosion, where the visuals were being joined with music, and programmes on television like *Ready Steady Go!* had really interesting graphics. There was a lot of cross-pollination between the arts – it was hard to say where it came from but suddenly everyone was waking up to think things could be done a little bit differently ... things could be brighter, more vibrant, louder, more diverse..."

Despite the times, and the involvement of art schools in the story, this is not leading up to some great rock family tree around the Essex Art School scene; not unless you count a delicate and unexpected web-thread to Kilburn & The High Roads – quite feasibly the UK band with the most legitimate claim to influencing the birth of British punk via their influence on a certain Johnny Rotten. Kilburns vocalist and future star in his own right fronting The Blockheads, Ian Dury was at South West Essex College while Gee was at South-East.

Gee Vaucher: "He was doing painting. One of his best friends – Terry Day – is a jazz drummer (and was drummer of the Kilburns); he was a very good friend of mine. I never saw Ian play." So, not an alliance as such, but nevertheless interesting that the earthy end of pre-punk (that we are told didn't trust hippies as a matter of principle) and the more traditional alternative culture, could smell each others' breath.

Rock music aside – and it was well aside in this case – Gee started thriving at art school, like any hungry working class genius might. Blown away by all the new possibilities opening up to her, she began devouring inspiration and influence like a hungry child: "I progressed in the first two years of art school like a meteor. Two years at art school just doing art 24 hours a day, it was like ... whoosh!"

It would be a mistake, however, to presume that Gee's art was as overtly political as her thoughts. At this stage in her life, nothing could be further from the truth: "My art didn't really get overtly political until Crass, because I was trying to illustrate what we were trying to say. Before that my work was political in the sense that it was an observation of the world or my immediate surround."

Accordingly, when asked about her artistic influences, Gee replies: "Everybody! You name it! I could do pointillism, fauvism, cubism – I tried it all. In the beginning I didn't really know any artists – we didn't have any at home." Indeed, Gee's sole collision with artists at school was when she "got a prize at school, which I've still got, which was a Leonard Da Vinci book. I loved it because it was an art book! I must be an artist to receive it!

"I wasn't very informed about artists till I went to art school, then I was like a sponge – I was soaking it up, trying this, trying that – anything I could grab hold of. I was insatiable. And I didn't want anybody near me – lecturers gave up coming near me in the end. They were very good actually, very respectful – they kept well back."

Gee found herself less isolated but equally inspired when it came to more conventional studies: "We did history of art and I learnt about art from the renaissance and I found my favourites in the mannerists etc – all the way through the periods really, and hitting contemporary stuff. Then obviously there was the explosion of all the sixties people like Peter Blake, Cordair. What I did get into in the end was Hockney, which I really adored. And still do."

The "explosion of all the sixties people" is still something you sense brings a warmth to Gee's heart. As well it might – for any budding artist, particularly a young one, the social and artistic liberations of that decade made them feel like they were taking over the world: the future could be classless.

Gee Vaucher: "It was a very exciting time – it lapped over into fashion – Mary Quant, Sasoon, and then it lapped over into music – The Beatles, The Rolling Stones, and they were all coming out of art school! There was so much going on."

While the young felt they were taking over – or at least Jim Morrison did – they were also doing something else that their parents had never done when they were their age: psychedelic drugs. Industrial amounts of them in many cases. Gee was resolutely not involved and feels no regrets whatsoever: "Of course drugs weren't prevalent then. There were no drugs till the last year at college and that's when purple hearts started to creep in. But before that? Well, not as far as I know – maybe I was naïve but there wasn't much at all. Now it's rife with it and I think it's fucked a lot of people."

Vaucher's views on art are no less forgiving. For her, there are no short cuts.

"A lot of artists don't know their skills. I think if you want to destroy something, you've got to know what it is you've got in your hand to destroy. To confront the world we live in, you've got to know a lot of the craft to turn it in on itself. The jazzers or the avant-gardists, they know how to do all the classical stuff, they know their instrument inside-out, that's why they can make it turn into all sorts of shapes and colours. I think it's the same for me with art."

All good things come to an end – at least they do this side of utopia. At the end of her Essex Art School experience, Gee applied to go to London's highly prestigious Royal College of Art. It all went about as wrong as it could: "Spending a couple of days up in London on my own was too much for me. I thought it was going to be really *really* radical – I didn't understand then why I was so disappointed with the whole set up. I was disappointed with the way you had to apply – there was this one long table, all your 'folio of work laid out and all these people opposite, and you had to sit there. I couldn't handle that. The first question was, 'Why do you want to do illustration?' I remember I said, 'It's something to do.' That wasn't what I wanted to say, but I couldn't handle the situation – I thought it was a pile of shit."

Gee, perhaps unsurprisingly, didn't get in to the Royal College Of Art. Instead, she took to working three days a week in an arts centre in Dagenham, where the work was considerably more fulfilling. "A lot of the schools in Dagenham didn't have art classes, so they used to come to the centre and learn. I really enjoyed it."

Meanwhile, something radical had happened to Penny and Gee: they had fallen in love and become partners whilst at art school, an arrangement which continued as they both left.

For a year after leaving art school Penny tried to make a living as a portrait painter, before getting a job as a teacher in the art department at Loughton College of Further Education. "When I got the job, I started looking round for somewhere to live," he remembers. After a period of searching the countryside, Penny chanced on Dial House. Set a mile or so up at the end of a distinctly unmade dirt track, it was a cottage on a working farm that afforded him the privacy of isolation at an affordable price – the house was so run down when he moved in that he lived there rent free at first as a pay off for doing the place up.

The oldest parts of Dial House date back to the 1400s. Originally a one-up, one down cottage, it was gradually added to room by room over the years. In 1883, Dial House was occupied by one Primrose O'Connell, who wrote a classic textbook on model farming, *The Agricultural Notebook*, still used in agriculture today, and remarkably still available to buy on the internet.

While Penny lived and painted at Dial House, Gee moved from Dagenham to another old farmhouse nearby. "It was independent woman time – I didn't want to live with my lover." So Gee moved to a place called Toot Hill, a ten minute bike ride away. She stayed there for a couple of years until, having "tired of the impracticalities of dragging lawnmowers and hoovers back and forth", Gee moved into Dial House.

Gee Vaucher: "When we first found it, it was a shell really. The kids in the village had been using it a lot to have parties. There was spray on the wall and there'd been a fire in what is now my studio. We made one room upstairs good enough to sleep in. The bloke who had lived here in the previous ten years had just lived in two rooms. We were just working towards the dream really – an open house. I wasn't doing any art – I'd stopped – I got very frustrated by Hockney: every time I went to do something, he'd just done it – it was uncanny! I just got so dejected I put everything down for two years."

The initial years of life at Dial House took a more conventional hew than the alternative lifestyles that the future held. Penny lived there on his own for the first three months, though Gee would be a regular visitor. He was presently joined by two other teachers from his college: Mick Linnister and Pat Collins, the pottery lecturer and storekeeper respectively. They stayed till 1970, when Penny became disillusioned with teaching and straight lines in general.

Penny Rimbaud: "I was forced to resign because they couldn't actually sack me. That summer, I realised that I didn't actually want to live in a traditional shared house anymore. I explained to Mick and Pat what I wanted to do and neither of them wanted to do it. They had their own biscuit tins. I could never quite get that – maybe it's my background, because I was at boarding school, where you shared things naturally."

Penny asked them to leave; a request which wasn't contested. "I loved that idea of somewhere where people could stop to tell their story with a comfortable bed for the night and go on on their journey. My original dream was that if I created one of those, then everyone who visited would then go off and do something similar. That by now, forty years down the line, there would have been hundreds of places all around Britain, so we could wander from place to place, by foot even. Creating a workable community within society."

Shortly afterwards, Richard Le Beau turned up at the house and Dial House became an open house. As Penny put it in *Shibboleth*: "Individual housing was one of the most obvious causes for the desperate shortage of homes. Communal living was the practical solution to the problem. If we are able to share our homes, maybe we could learn to share our world, and that, surely was the first step towards global sanity?"

Pete Sutton: "There was a guy called Richard who was a bit like Pen's manservant."

Another friend from Penny Rimbaud's stint as a teacher at Loughton F.E. was Bernhardt Rebours, who would later play with Penny Rimbaud in the experimental outfit Exit, and later still play bass for Crass stable-mates and touring partners Poison Girls.

Rebours remembers his first encounters with the future Crass folk as something of an enlightenment: "I was living with my mum and dad – very straight. Then encountering Terry (Day – Kilburn & The High Roads), Pen & Gee, then Eve Libertine the next year – it was a culture shock. It was like a completely different shift into another way of looking at the world. Terry & Pen got into doing these art school type projects which were very different from the orthodox way of seeing things. It was such a fantastic period – that time alone was worth a dozen degree courses – it was so influential on me."

Penny Rimbaud is big on the list of Bernhardt Rebours' influences: "I really admired how he managed to feel he was part of us. We did some silly things. We went up into the forest, half a dozen or so of us. Pen would say, 'We're not going to do any drawing today, we'll go into the forest and talk.' We'd make things like fairy villages out of leaf mould, twigs and mushrooms. I was like, 'Gosh, this is art school, is it?' We thought we'd be seeing gold light and pink canvasses. It was a way of shaking us up into finding something unexpected that really makes us tick. Penny needed us to feel passionate about why we did things – we weren't just doing things because he was the tutor – we had to know that we did things because we felt it was genuine. If we didn't have that, he really laid into us, cross-examining why we did things. It was quite intimidating sometimes. Nothing was ever safe – you never knew whether there was another agenda, another motive for doing things or whether you took things at face value."

As Dial House slowly began to develop into an open house on the cusp of the sixties and seventies, Penny Rimbaud & Gee Vaucher started to think about a more multimedia approach to their creativity.

Penny Rimbaud: "I started doing paintings which were a bit like Kandinsky's, which were like music on paper. Then I began to think, why not just make music? Why confine it to canvas?"

Why indeed?

EXIT-STANCE

"Wherever we are, what we hear is mostly noise. When we ignore it, it disturbs us. When we listen to it, we find it fascinating. The sound of a truck at 50 mph. Static between the stations. Rain. We want to capture and control these sounds, to use them, not as sound effects, but as musical instruments." – John Cage on the future of music from a lecture given in 1937

"Tell Idi Amin / tell Idi I'm out / tell that Idi / I am not about" – The K9s – Idi Amin

Penny Rimbaud once described Dial House as a place where people were free to drop in rather than to drop out, and as such it wasn't long before one of the rooms was given over to music. The first creative concern to involve Dial House people, however, was paradoxically named after, and based at, a house nearby – Stanford Rivers Hall. Despite sounding like some kind of stately home, Stanford Rivers Hall was in fact just a house on a farm owned by the Co-Op. It was divided into two halves, one of which was shared by various people central to our story.

The Stanford Rivers Quartet was an experimental outfit consisting of Penny Rimbaud on percussion, Gee Vaucher on stripped down upright piano, Jim Clancey on keyboards, Steve Reeves on flute and trombone and John Loder as recording engineer. Penny was already friends with Jim Clancey from school and had developed a friendship with John Loder previously too. The emphasis was clearly on 'experimental' in the outfit: this wasn't a question of adding art to music, but of attempting to merge the two forms.

Penny Rimbaud: "Inspired by the theories of the Bauhaus artists and composers such as Berio and Varèse, our early work investigated the relationship between sound and visual imagery. Out of this we developed a method of notation, which used markings on graph paper to determine time, pitch and volume, the resultant scores appearing more like painting than music. Equally, by placing a grid graph over any given image, we were able to translate it into sound."

Gee Vaucher: "I started writing music – we did it with colours and shapes. We did it on a regular bar system of music writing but you'd have, say, for the violin, I'd do a red line, that maybe started off thick and maybe end up thin at the end of the bar. And you'd know that red would maybe mean something to that musician – it might be anger or it might be heat. And it would be a very thick sound because it was covering maybe two bars. But the shape would waver. So you'd interpret this and play. . . . So anybody could write music. And then you'd have dots maybe, you could do anything. And then the musician would translate it . . . so then you'd get together with the other musicians and it would all tie-in and you'd get this . . . row! It was really lovely – I used to love it!"

Gee"s prime role in the Quartet was, "voice, and I had a stripped down piano, which I eventually laid down flat. I put an electric pick-up on it and I used to sit in the middle of it and drown everbody out," she chortles.

Jim Clancey's partner of the time, also resident at Stanford Rivers Hall was Bronwen Jones, or Eve Libertine as she's now better known. In what is an increasingly small world, she too had been an art pupil of Penny Rimbaud at Loughton College of Further Education.

Eve Libertine: "I guess it was to do with breaking down the structures of music and sound – the whole John Cage thing. I'd say it was avant-garde, but something people can do for themselves. Similar, I suppose to the punk thing, but totally different at the same time. Just do it and see what happens!"

In the late sixties, Eve was asked to be part of the Quartet, but reflects: "I couldn't do it. I was probably about 18 or 19 and I was too self-conscious to do something that was improvised – I just felt an idiot really! But I remember the scores were very beautiful – more like coloured drawings really."

The Stanford Rivers Hall abode was ended when the occupants were evicted to make way for a farmworker, just before Eve had her baby son. In a scene not unreminiscent of a certain Biblical tale, a pregnant Eve found herself living out of a suitcase while just about to have a child. In need of an address to give the authorities for the birth, there was room at the proverbial inn courtesy of Dial House, and the baby boy Nemo (now a successful musician in his own right) was born there.

Just over 18 months later, in the summer of '74, Eve would move back into Stanford Rivers, this time to the other half of the house, with Jim Clancey, his brother Phil (later to be Free) and Phil's three children. Then came a deja-vu second eviction. This time, according to Eve, it was due to some kind of pensions fiddle and it was necessary to get rid of the farm to make up for the financial shortfall. It was apparently sold to a relative of Idi Amin. Not the most likely of characters to turn up in this story, I'm sure you'll agree.

As time went on, the Stanford Rivers Quartet went the same way of Stanford Rivers Hall (metaphorically, that is, not to Idi Amin's family).

Penny Rimbaud: "For a short time I taught the (Stanford Rivers Quartet) technique in art school, creating interpretations of works as diverse as Vermeer's and Pollock's. Being colourful and easily read, it was a good technique with which to introduce young children to the fundamentals of music. Although our work might well have become schoolroom based, we chose to take to the road, playing the University circuit. By then Steve had left, and we had changed our name to Exit..."

Exit was another avant-garde experimental affair that Penny Rimbaud describes as a fusion of American Free Jazz and European Avant Garde.

Gee Vaucher: "Exit was me & Pen and anyone who turned up and wanted to have a go." By the time Exit started playing the university circuit, the core had spread to include Jim Clancey. "Then came John Loder who ran Southern," remembers Gee. "He was a dear friend of the house. Although he was working in electronics, he started touring round with a reel-to-reel, recording everything. There's some great photos of John (Loder) looking like Frank Zappa!"

Exit (being, according to Rimbaud, the direction he expected the audience to head in droves when they appeared) was almost a musical extension of the open house policy. To call the line-up fluid would be an understatement – people were free to come and go as they pleased, even during performances. Given the improvised nature of the sounds – 'music' might be stretching it, and it certainly bore no truck with rock – the end product of an Exit performance would be totally reliant on the sum of whichever parts had turned up and / or decided to join in that particular day.

A listen to their performance at the ICES '72 festival confirms that this is a band concerned with sound and atmosphere rather than music (and therefore not really a band at all). But there are no new-age sound-scapes, no swirling keyboards or whale songs – it's *way* too avant-garde and 'out there' for that. And it wasn't just the music that was out there, but the whole concept.

Penny Rimbaud: "In Exit, we actually gave up names – there wasn't such a thing as our individual identity. That was another way of saying that anyone belongs here. If anyone wanted to come up and play whilst we were playing, they did. Invariably, you'd start off with a ten-piece playing and end up with a fifteen-piece".

"It seemed like anyone could come and join in," remembers Eve, at that point still choosing not to enlist herself.

Penny Rimbaud: "A lot of what Crass was about was actually developed in the days of Exit. We used to do handouts at Exit gigs, but they were artworks. There might be a little card – a beautiful print that Gee had done, or a packet of seeds. There would always be a gift. The whole idea of the gift was very much a principle of the house, and of Exit."

Also, somewhat remarkably, Exit not only didn't charge an appearance fee, but refused even to take expenses: "We didn't charge, ever," confirms Rimbaud.

This wasn't the only unusual aspect of Exit in their musical incarnation. As Penny Rimbaud explained to Christopher Eamon in the book *Anthony McCall, The Solid Light Films And Related Works*: "We had a policy of starting at least an hour earlier than billed, this being so that the audience would walk into a musical environment which had not been conditioned by their presence. Likewise, finishing times were random, our performances often going on late into the evening (or until we were switched off by uncomfortable management)."

Exit began evolving from a purely sound-based act to incorporating performance. "We started doing a lot of happenings and events – little art pieces which involved us, as bodies, within them. We were a bit of a Gilbert & George in a way," remembers Penny Rimbaud.

It's here that another two future members of Crass join the fold: Pete Wright, the future bass player, and Mick Duffield, the film-maker. Both had been visiting Dial House on a regular basis and both would seal the connection by working with Exit. Ironically, however, Pete never played the bass with Exit and Mick never showed his films.

Mick Duffield had discovered Dial House with a school friend. They'd noticed an unusual house visible from the tube train on their way to school. Intrigued by all the flags flying in the garden, Mick and his friend visited the house and before long Mick found a new and interesting outlet for his photography – photographing what were to him bizarre but intriguing performance art events that were being staged by Penny and Gee. "I hadn't any involvement with art at all at that point – I had quite a technical education," he says. "It was quite an eye-opener … the people in the house weren't weird but the performances definitely were! And very intriguing in that sense."

Pete Wright was born in Peckham but grew up in Surrey. He ended up in London, where he attended Central London University. After university – the only person in the band to have made it, despite popular belief – Pete went travelling with a girlfriend, returning to London in the mid-seventies. It was after splitting up with this girlfriend that he first met Penny Rimbaud. Pete Wright had started going to the house to make use of its music room, where he would play folk music as part of a duo called Friends Of Wensleydale Jasper. Mick Duffield also made a short film of the same name featuring Pete Wright and others talking about their respective partners. "From the Gower Street Rectory, a brief stay in Clapham Common, and on to Dial House. Urbanite, suburbanite, country dweller," as Pete puts it.

"We were all fucked up people," opines Pete, citing his own fucked-upness to "fucked up parents. My father was screwed up and broke down due to the war. My mother had driven lorries in the war, retrieving the

31

injured from the train and she comforted them in hospital. I couldn't understand why she became the way she is. They both had horrible childhoods. All our parents of that generation did."

And like many of their children, Pete tapped into the thinking of the alternative society; the dreaming of the possibility. "It was in the late sixties air. Anyone who felt even slightly discordant could reach out and grab. Whatever happened to R.D. Laing, eh?"[1]

Meanwhile, Exit continued to thrive. Whilst the Exit music gigs were exclusively on the University Circuit, the happenings were more varied. A couple were at the Museum Of Modern Art in Oxford, and "festivals and squats" says Penny. "We did a piece called Santa Meditation on Epping Green, which was actually me & Pete Wright, way before he came back and joined the band. That involved me meditating on a small wooden table dressed as Santa Claus, holding out two oranges; with Pete sitting behind me dressed as a pixie."

Pete Wright: "I had a red dressing-gown. From a great distance I might appear as a pixel."

Penny Rimbaud: "I was meditating for the whole day, and my rule was that I wasn't allowed to react to anyone – I just had to hold out these oranges: the idea being that kids could come along and take them. I remember the police coming along to that one and being very angry, wanting to know who had given us permission. It was quite extraordinary, the aggressive response we got from the local police"

Of course, bizarre behaviour like this doesn't exist in a vacuum. Of particular influence was the Fluxus movement, described on Wikipedia as "an art movement noted for the blending of different artistic disciplines, primarily visual art but also music and literature", and boasting Yoko Ono as its most famous advocate, which may well provide a clue as to Penny Rimbaud and Gee Vaucher's interest. Fluxus was also widely seen as the beginning of 'mail art', as practised by Genesis P Orridge amongst others.

---

[1] He actually ended up releasing an album around the same time as 'Feeding Of The Five Thousand', called 'Life Before Death'. Reviewing it in NME, Crass-sympathiser Graham Lock mercilessly tore it to pieces in a parody of a psychiatric report.

Gee Vaucher: "We were part of the Fluxus movement. And before that we were affected by the Situationists. We were affected by street theatre – by the idea of taking something out of the four walls and off the canvas. Then we started working with (experimental artist) Anthony McCall. We started performing his pieces with him because he needed people to be able to do what he did, which at the time was burning petrol," Gee laughs and makes a face, "which would be outrageous to do now!"

Artist and future Exit-collaborator Anthony McCall remembers: "I'm not sure that I knew what situationism was in those days. But the culture Exit had set up was relatively familiar. This was 1972, we were the same generation; many of us had been through art school in the mid and late sixties, listened to the same music, smoked the same dope, and gone to the same demonstrations. The idea of dropping out to some extent, of living as a creative, independent community, was in the air."

Something in the air. Always the air.

Anthony McCall: "I was surrounded by artists and friends who were involved in Fluxus culture, particularly my partner Carolee Schneemann, artist and publisher Felipe Ehrenberg (who ran the artists press, Beau Geste out of a farmhouse in Devon) and art historian David Mayor, who worked with Felipe and who curated and produced "Fluxshoe", an exhibition that toured England between 1972 and 1974. Involving both "old guard" card-carrying members of Fluxus as well as second cousins twice removed, I found myself surrounded by Flux culture without ever having quite signed on. Carolee and I did a collaborative performance early on in the tour, and as a participant I was included in the accompanying publication."

A young teenage Steve Ignorant attended one of the Oxford performances: "Afterwards we all went into a studio and Anthony McCall showed a short film. And he was also working on was projecting light which created shapes."

Of the audience for such work, Steve remembers: "It wasn't the public so much as people from the arts scene, some Americans – I remember them because this bloke had a fucking big cigar!"

This work with light would evolve into the classic *Line Describing A*

Cone, which wrote Anthony McCall into artistic history and has been described as 'a classic of American avant-garde cinema'.

In 1972, Exit helped organise the ICES '72 festival – an international festival of the avant-garde that lasted two weeks and took place all over London, featuring avant-garde luminaries from all over the world. Wildly ambitious, it remains the biggest avant garde festival ever seen in the UK.

Anthony McCall: "I met Pen and Gee in 1972 a month or two before the August opening of ICES (International Carnival of Experimental Sound) at the Roundhouse in Camden Town. They were designing the poster and programme for the festival, but we came together after they offered to help find a location for performing the piece I had proposed as my contribution to the festival, "Landscape for Fire." They thought that it might be possible to do it on North Weald (airfield), near to Dial House, the farmhouse in which they lived and worked."

Penny Rimbaud: "We got involved with a guy called Harvey Matusow who lived ten or fifteen miles from here. He was married to a New Zealander by the name of Anna Lockwood, an avant-garde composer. He had the original idea for Ices 72. It seemed about as mad as Wally's Stonehenge idea. When we first met him, we thought this bloke's nutty – he was going to get the Roundhouse, do all these gigs and everyone in the world was going to come to them. And would we help? Which we did."

Gee & Penny did most of the artwork for the festival while Penny took care of a lot of the printing, laying out stuff and programming.

Penny Rimbaud: "It was a magnificent festival – I don't think there's ever been an avant-garde music festival to compare with it. Two weeks solid, starting about midday every day – there were events going on all over the place. The great and the not so great avant-gardists worldwide came to it and performed, mostly for nothing. Financially it was a disaster, but it was a fantastic festival. And he was a fantastic character, he was a very interesting character."

Indeed he was, and one with a highly unusual and dubious, background. In fact, the word 'dodgy' leaps up and screams at you. Harvey Matusow had been a communist who, to prevent himself being blacklisted by the House Committee on Un-American Activities, provided evidence against his former colleagues, including giving evidence against folk singers such as Pete Seeger.

Penny Rimbaud: "Then something happened – one never knew with him, he was a *very* complex character. He completely turned tail and exposed MacCarthy. This after having got heaps of people jailed. But he claimed that this was the only way he could really get the dirt on the bloke. He was largely responsible for MacCarthy's downfall – the reason he was living in England was because he was so hated by a) the left because of what they said he'd done and b) by the right because of what *they* said he'd done. His life was probably in danger in America."

In 1955 Harvey Matusow had written a book, *False Witness*, in which he revealed he'd been a FBI agent paid to lie about members of the American Communist Party. Because of this, he was jailed for three years for perjury, with a genuine radical, Wilhelm Reich, in the next cell when Reich died. Matusow found it impossible to get work on his release, moving to England and some years later meeting up with Rimbaud & Vaucher to organise Ices '72. Funny old world.

Enter Phil Clancey (Free – future Crass guitarist), whose brother Jim was a member of Exit. He got involved with the Festival as he was media resources officer at Stoke Newington College F.E. at the time. As such he had access to tape recorders which he borrowed for certain performances that required them.

Phil Free: "One of the guys – John Cage? – was going to do a performance that required 100 tape recorders, of which 30 came from my college. The college didn't know – a little burst for freedom there!"

Anthony McCall remembers of the festival: "For me it was extraordinary. There were some astonishing performances. The two that stick in my memory particularly was Kosugi and the Taj Mahal Travellers, and John Cage's brilliant HPSCHDS. ICES was completely international and for those couple of weeks London was host to dozens of artists and performers from all over the world. It has to be said that this was something of a miracle, for the entire event was funded mostly by smoke and mirrors."

Of Exit themselves McCall recalls: "Their performance at ICES was the first piece of theirs that I had seen, and I admired it. But I had already come to know them, and respect the multi-media situation they had set up in North Weald. It was an extremely creative community that lived together and made art. Their practices included visual art, performance, graphic design, and music."

Despite helping out with lending gear for the festival, Phil Free wasn't actually moved to attend. He did however, receive an oral review from a college workmate: "I remember her saying she'd been to it and it was 'absolute rubbish'! I remember being really intrigued."

Perhaps the best description of an Exit performance can be gleaned from a letter written by Gee Vaucher to Penny Rimbaud's mother in America, describing their Roundhouse performance during the ICES '72 festival: "I think you would have liked our Roundhouse show. To our surprise it started with a distant, mumbled recital of Walt Whitman's 'Mystic trumpeter'. Together with the audience, we looked up to a single light on the balcony where Toby Buxton, wearing a large Corinthian-columned hat, was making his quiet contribution (later on the piece got louder). At that point the band started playing and over the next hour, much action took place. Wearing what looked like an oversized dunce's cap with slits cut for eyes, nose and mouth, Dave King commenced by drawing a curtain around the band who were seated on the stage, thus cutting them off from everything that was going on in the hall and creating a backdrop for the visual performers.

"In front of the stage, Mary Buxton sat on a chair doing whatever she wished, which turned out to be smoking, being nervous and looking incredibly innocent. Next to her were two video monitors, one of them feeding from a camera operated by Malcolm Redding, who was recording her facial expressions, the other showing whatever happened to be on the television at the time. To the left of the stage, Clare Francis threaded large silver tins onto a rope lit by a single blue spotlight and suspended from the very high ceiling. By the time she had threaded around a dozen tins, she was beginning to run out of strength and a man from the audience came to her rescue. She, however, had hoped to complete the column on her own, regardless as to whether she or it collapsed. As it happened, because the man didn't understand English, Clare was unable to explain that she didn't want help, so they worked silently together, creating what became a thirty foot high illuminated silver column. I thought it was lovely that the man felt he could help like that.

"To the right of the stage, Dave Williams played the glass game. The pieces had been randomly laid out and Dave's job was to move them around until he was satisfied that their positioning was aesthetically pleasing. The Game is usually played by two or more people, but it wasn't long before a woman from the audience asked whether she could move in. Dave explained the idea of the game and they played it together for the rest of the performance.

"During this time, in front of the curtain with which he had hidden the band, Dave King wove fine string between three four-foot high white poles which earlier that day he had screwed to the floor of the stage. When he'd used up all the string, he suspended a light bulb between the poles and then, at the base of the poles, lit joss sticks and small smoke bombs which in the still air created a single, solid cloud that slowly drifted into the audience and finally disappeared. Following the cloud, Dave then walked through the audience to a flight of stairs to the side. From there he let a large roll of paper run quietly down the stairs and across the floor, almost meeting the stage. Again, something beautiful happened. A Japanese man walked from the audience and sat down cross-legged on the paper, watching the rest of the piece as if meditating. After the show, he thanked us for our performance. A week later he somehow found his way to Dial House. He loved it and we loved him."

As well as all this, New York artist Geoff Hendricks had spent the entire set sat meditating on top of an earth mound in which symbolic artifacts had been buried.

After the Ices festival, Pen & Gee continued Exit on their own, with the accent less on music and more on performance, combining images and theatre with sound. "We did two gigs at Oxford," remembers Gee, "which were arranged by the guy who now runs the Tate Portrait Gallery." They did an outside piece, with Pen wrapped up in bandages (a picture of which can be seen in Gee's art book, *Crass Art And Other Pre-Post Modernist Monsters*). Gee notes: "That was quite a frightening piece because a guy threatened Pen with a knife, and he couldn't see who he was talking to. The guy wanted him to speak but Pen wasn't allowed to speak."

More than a hint of artistic self-discipline there.

Gee & Penny decided they needed a break and travelled through

America for three months. Penny: "My father worked for the World Bank as a civil engineer. He had worked for British Rail – he'd resigned when Beeching was appointed to the job that he was in line for. He was also offered a job managing the new Disneyland in Florida, which would have been a far better job. Rather than being at the World Bank where he got sent to Korea just at the end of the Vietnam War. . ."

So the parents moved to America, Penny visited and "we decided we'd travel across America together. Which is what *The Diamond Signature*[1] is partially about."

While they were there, an Exit performance piece was done in their absence, though it did involve Steve Ignorant. A diary of events that occurred while the pair were absent was kept, and a week before their return, the diary was put into a container and taken to the sea at Southend. The Exit performers walked out with the tide, buried the container and then walked back as the tide came back in.

Penny Rimbaud remembers that on his and Gee's return from the States, he didn't want to continue operating in the same way, which he acknowledges, "was a bit guru-like. I wanted to withdraw from that. There was a sort of philosophical change there."

Pete Sutton: "Jerry (Penny) was always the voice – we used to call him 'guru Jel'. His art was talking – verbalising thoughts."

One thought now caused a reality: Exit had left the building and ceased to exist.

If Exit were no more, the people that broadly made up the outfit were still active. The next creative involvement would come with a series of performance collaborations with Anthony McCall. Following on from the title and concept 'Landscape For Fire' performed for Ices '72, these would involve lighting a series of spectacular fires as darkness fell. Like the Stanford Rivers Quartet musical pieces, each performance would be meticulously scored.

Anthony McCall: "On August 27, 1972, Pen and Gee plus a number of other members of the Exit group (all of whom lived and worked out

[1] Penny's book, published by AK Press

of Dial House), performed 'Landscape for Fire II' with me on a deserted aerodrome on North Weald, a couple of miles from Dial House. After our initial meeting (I had travelled out to North Weald) to discuss locations, Pen and Gee and I hit it off, and somehow, while scouting for likely locations the idea emerged that Pen and Gee and company would help me to realise the piece. I was extremely grateful for their intelligent enthusiasm, for I had already decided that I would make a film of the piece in 16mm without quite considering important questions as to how the whole performance would actually be realised. Although I was unaware of this at the time they had far more experience than I of mounting productions. After 'Landscape for Fire II', we went on working together. Pen and Gee and I did most of my subsequent Fire pieces together (about five over two years). One of them they did independently of me in Colchester, and sent the score, maps and photographs to me in New York, which I still have. They were extraordinarily serious about each undertaking and very disciplined."

In his book *Shibboleth*, Penny Rimbaud describes Exit as "our jealously guarded failure to communicate", and you can't help thinking he's got a point. If you haven't been to art school, or perhaps even if you have, you may have been tempted to think about the tale of the Emperor's New Clothes with regard to the avant garde. Dave King remembers: "All these things could be the Emperors New Clothes. But at the time it was fascinating. You can have a bloke sitting on a pile of sand with a tortoise wandering around the pyramid of sand. It's like, wow, I have seen that before! Ha ha! I mean, what else are you going to do? The pop music was alright if you liked pop music – The Kinks was the soundtrack of our college years, and Cream, The Downliner Sect, John Mayall's Bluesbreakers." You may also be wondering what Anthony McCall was trying to express with these pieces ...

Anthony McCall: "I am not sure that I would have been able to answer the question at the time, although I was quite certain about the structure and shape of each performance. Over a three year period I did a number of these sculptural performances in landscape. Fire was the medium. The performances were based on a square grid defined by 36 small fires (6 × 6). The pieces, which usually took place at dusk, had a systematic, slowly changing, structure. The performances consisted of the creation of changing configurations of these small fires coupled with a sonic element based on the foghorn. The questions that interested me (at any rate, the questions I could articulate) involved the relationship between the duration of the performances and the attention spans of individual members of the audience."

The book *Anthony McCall, The Solid Light Films And Related Works* shows a move, however wrapped up in art, towards the streets. You might even consider it in a lineage that ends up in the present day with graffiti artists such as Banksy: "For the Exit group, one of the most interesting aspects of McCall's performances was its inhabitation of the exterior realm staked out earlier by Krapow's happenings and more contemporary land art practices: 'Anthony's piece appealed greatly to us because although the "happenings" element of his work was one that we too had been developing, the idea of moving out of the confines of galleries and performance venues into open space was something that we hitherto had not really considered.'"

Shortly after this, Anthony McCall moved to New York, but Penny and Gee decided to continue and mutate the idea of fire performance. Rather than dealing with bureaucracy, however (as they had at North Weald Airport), they decided to perform the pieces without authorisation. The first was on a hill by a main road near Colchester, that as well as attracting the attention of the traffic and a small word of mouth audience, attracted the police. With no frame of reference, however, the police simply gave them a warning.

After this it was decided not to continue with the fire pieces due to the emerging conciousness of their environmentally dodgy nature. But the idea of performing on or in "squatted" space would stick around for quite a while. . .

HIPPY HIPPY SHAKE

At this time, Dave King – who would later design the Crass symbol that to this day adorns clothes and tattoos worldwide – moved into Dial House. Dave: "The house drew people who wanted to get out of town – there was a strong rural appreciation. I was still at art school when the house had been started. But I'd go out and visit and spend weekends there for seven or eight years before I moved in."

Dave finally quit his job and moved into Dial House on a permanent basis, where he would stay for the next year. Tired of working in design groups, designing for other people and for not much money, he was attracted by the inexpensive way of life at the house. "As Penny said once, the house was supported by magic," he says. "It seemed like things happened spontaneously. In some ways it seemed effortless . . . I tend to veer towards the mystical, and it's something that's very hard to talk about because in cold print it always sounds absurd or naïve."

Anyone who has visited Dial House – and there have been literally tens of thousands over the years – will attest to its magical qualities. Perhaps an absolute rationalist might describe the atmosphere as 'weird' but whichever angle you come from and however you choose to perceive it, it's hard to deny that Dial House is as different as anywhere you might find in Britain. It can even be vaguely unnerving.

Dave King's take on the place is hard for even the cynic to deny: "What was very interesting to me was the atmosphere of timelessness that seemed to exist around the house. It seemed like the days could last forever. And, being young, you'd maybe also stay up all night. There was a certain benign drift that would happen, that I think is the potential source of mystical experiences. In the mystic traditions of different cultures, one of the things you do is detach yourself from the day-to-day, with the idea that you might experience some kind of enhanced perception. The whole situation encouraged that kind of cutting loose – in that kind of circumstance, it is possible for certain kinds of altered reality to be experienced."

On a more earthly level, Dave also remembers how "early on" when the outer reaches of the London Underground Central Line would still reach out past the house, the tube driver would stop between official stops to let people get off and slide down the embankment. A different kind of magic perhaps, and one it would be very hard to imagine happening today, even if the furthest reaches of the tube line hadn't been closed down by the powers that be. A time before the arteries hardened and clogged innocence in the UK.

Also starting to visit the house by this time was a very young future Crass vocalist Joy De Vivre. "I think it did have magic actually, but it depended on the brew of people being good," she says. "Dial House on its own isn't anything, but there were times when the garden was full of very lively, spirited and incredibly well-meaning people."

Phil Free: "Prior to the band, it was very much a sixties aspiration – if you aspired to dropping out or to having a place in the country, here it is!"

If the contention that magic existed and exists in Dial House is a controversial one, the arrival of Phil Russell, aka Wally Hope, in the story ups the ante considerably. Hope was yet another local kid who had taken to visiting the house. Penny Rimbaud famously describes the first time he encountered Hope, performing a weather miracle, no less: "He was gifted with a strange kind of magic. One day in our garden, it was early summer, he conjured up a snowstorm, huge white flakes falling amongst the daisies on the lawn. Another time he created a multi-rainbowed sky; it was as if he had cut up a rainbow and thrown the pieces into the air where they hung in strange rainbow patterns. Looking back on it now it seems unbelievable but all the same I can remember both occasions vividly."

"So there's a few of them sat in the back shed one day, when they hear the customary war-cry. It was a day very much like today: warm and sultry, with no clouds. May or September, Pen's not too sure. And Wally dances out backwards from behind a bush. He's weaving his fingers in a magical pattern, and there's this strange grin on his face, like some Jester-Fool from a demented Tarot. 'Watch this,' he says, winking, and he dances back out of sight. When he reappeared he was dancing backwards again from the bush, but this time accompanied by a snowstorm. The snow was lashing about in the still, warm air as Wally's arms twisted and jerked. The sight was so incomprehensible it sent their minds reeling. The people in the shed looked on astonished while the snow swirled and span and Wally's arms shifted around amongst it, stirring it up. And then Wally winked again and danced back behind the cover of the bush taking the snow with him. Finally he walked out normally, as if nothing had happened. It was no longer snowing."- Fierce Dancing, CJ Stone*

Wally Hope was born in Cyprus in 1947, to rich and adoring parents. However, when he was 12, his father died suddenly. Relations between him and his mother worsened when she discovered she'd been cut out of the will, and when he was 16, she went back to her native Scandinavia, leaving Hope in the care of guardians. A brief period at art school (like pretty much everyone else in this book) ended when he declared "they were destroying my imagination by demands I should do it their way."

When he was 20, his mother returned home to be told by Hope that he'd been having a wonderful time. He also told her of his experiences with drugs, upon which she rang the police. In what was thought of at the time to be a harsh sentence, Wally was subsequently sent to prison in Wormwood Scrubs notorious A block. On his release he travelled in East Africa and visited a number of communes in the USA. Living off an allowance that would keep him going until he received the main part of his inheritance on his until his 30th birthday, Wally spent winters in Ibiza and was considering settling in Cyprus until the Turks invaded. It was in Cyprus that he conceived the idea of an alternative society of sun worshippers based at Stonehenge: an idealistic egalitarian society where everybody was called Wally and nobody had possessions. Imagine that.

To kick start this, he envisaged the Stonehenge Peoples Free Festival.

After he had started turning up at Dial House, the idea was mooted and the old Exit silkscreen/gestetner sheets were brought back to life. The first Stonehenge Festival was to take place around the Summer Solstice in the summer of 1974. Rimbaud & Wally Hope got printing.

"We shared Phil's disgust with 'straight' society, a society that puts more value on property than on people, that respects wealth more than it does wisdom. We supported his vision of a world where the people took back from the state what the state had stolen from the people. Squatting as a political statement has its roots in that way of thought. Why should we have to pay for what is rightfully ours? Whose world is this? Maybe squatting Stonehenge wasn't such a bad idea." –
Penny Rimbaud – Last Of The Hippies

Landscapes for hope. A poster for the first festival reads:

"FREE STONED HENGE OFF ROCKS OFF EVERY SUN DAY FOREVER"

With a picture of the Turin Shroud sitting atop the flyer between pictures by Gee Vaucher of the pyramids and standing stones, there is a clear attempt at inferring a mystical, if not religious, emphasis to the event. "The Turin shroud picture was an icon he carried round with him, like a juju," remembers Penny Rimbaud. A poem lower down the page reads:

"THANK YOU GOD FOR THIS AMAZING DAY
And the leaping greenly spirits of the trees
And a blue dream of sky and for everything
Which is natural, which is yes.

I who have died am alive again today
This is the SUN'S birthday, this is the
Birthday of LIFE and of LOVE and wings
And of the gay great happening
Illimitable earth

How should tasting, touching, seeing
Breathing any lifted from the NO
Of ALL nothing, human merely being
Doubt unimaginable you

Now the ears of my ears are awake
Now the eyes of my eyes are opened"

"On the 20th June 74 off the floor, the laughing Rock'n'Roll Movement spearhead tribal clan entrenched, Home Sweet Dome, to Arthur's banner, The UNION WALLY, Best mates with all, FAR OUT communication, and totally missed by the system class, scandel monger media."

OUR FATHER, THE SUN wants the Lion to lie with the Lamb, seeing the Leopard can't change its spots, Energy Crisis only in the brains and hearts of AHH MEN, so the greatest revolution is by EXAMPLE, RALLY at Salisbury Plain, the Henge.
Or accept Hell confusion of the war."

The whole poster was printed out in 'rainbow print' with different coloured inks running into each other, befitting the fashion on the times. "We found we could 'do acid' on paper," as Penny Rimbaud puts it.

Wally Hope was also respectful (or naïve) enough to write to his new neighbours before the event. In the spring of '74 he sent a letter to the farmer around Stonehenge:

"On the RoAD Home
Sunday

Dear Sir,
with all well meaning respect,
Our Lord God and his son Jesus Christ, have ordained a spiritual Pilgrimage to Stonehenge on 20th June 21st etc, to fulfill the Two COMMANDMENTS
Love God
Love your neighbour.
you are and will be our neighbour we beg for help, Friendship and trust, if the gathering is overflowing big, we will give you any help you need, but you must

respect we are to God's Law, and trying to balance the violence, corruption,
insuing 3rd world war, oily energy crisis, to Manual communal Farming Love
Peace and Freedom
Your Best mate WALLY
HELP For the Kids X"

Aside from the leaflets, which were handed out mainly in the densely
hippiefied Notting Hill area, the only other promotion for the festival
was from the pirate radio station Radio Caroline.

"The Department of the Environment said they were looking after
Stonehenge for the people. We said, we are the people, we'll help look
after it," a 'Wally' remembers.

Basil Brooks, Zorch: "There was a little police Cortina parked in the
road – that was the police presence! Innocent days."

Not many people turned up for the first festival. Rimbaud describes
it as a 'few hundred' whereas Andy Worthington (in his book *Stonehenge:
Celebration And Subversion*) counts "about 500 people at the most".
Musical entertainment came from a band Worthington describes as 'early
synth pioneers' called Zorch that was in fact a synth duo – the UK's first,
allegedly – who were purported to have a mind blowing lightshow as
well as a psychedelic-synth sound.

The Wallies of Stonehenge ("Everyone's Wally") recall a similar movement 'Jacuerie' from the beginning of the French revolution, in which
everyone called themselves Jacques. In this particular revolution, a group
of 'Wallies' decided to stay on at Stonehenge until December 21.
Technically they were breaking the law and were finally taken to court.
After Hope had lectured the judge on the evils of present society and the
merits of an alternative one, *The Daily Express* chortled 'The Wallies Give
The Judge The Willies'.

As in so many of these situations, the reality didn't quite live up to the
romantic (hippy hippy) hype. In the *Evening Standard* of August 15, 1974,
journalist Robert Strange described a typical day with the Wallies after a
three-day stint living with them:

"12 noon: A few Wallies are starting to get up. And after several
attempts, somebody manages to light a camp fire, around which everyone sits smoking a shared pack of cigarettes.

2pm: In an old oil can, the Wallies start to cook up some porridge, which is left to bubble on the fire with nobody attending it until it eventually burns and becomes completely inedible.

5pm: There is a welcome diversion from the rain and wind sweeping across Salisbury Plain when two policemen arrive at the camp. Although outwardly friendly and chatting about the publicity the Wallies have received, the policemen have a good look in all the tents for drugs."

8pm: The camp fire is built up and as the Wallies sit round discussing the effects of various drugs and their future at Stonehenge, two of them throw unpeeled potatoes, dirty carrots and a few onions into the porridge tin to make a stew.

Midnight: The stew is still cooking but still tastes inedible.

2am: Chris Wally – the cook – finally declares the stew is cooked and in a happier mood from the effects of their drugs, the group tucks in."

A Wally remembers: "We were all so stoned out you couldn't make it to the road half the time. And every day the acid was given out; sometimes in the morning, sometimes early evening. People were always talking about spacemen, God, ley lines, Stonehenge, Glastonbury, pyramids in Egypt and Central America, triangles, love, dope and where they came from. After a while, the fuzz sussed that we were doing a hell of a lot of dealing and two of our cars were hot."

After finally leaving Stonehenge, due mainly to the cold weather, about 30 Wallies moved into some disused army huts near Amesbury.

Free Festival veteran Roger Hutchinson remembers: "The man behind Stonehenge (whose real name I have forgotten but better known as Wally) was also a visitor to our fire. My new passion of festivals met his spiritual passion to establish a conceptually and spiritually more pure event at Stonehenge and we talked the night away – me calmly tripped out and he having never come down from a particularly heavy acid trip in Cyprus a year previous. He was an exceptionally good man who was done down by the dropouts (the Wallies)."

Having considered the first Stonehenge Festival a success, Wally Hope embarked on planning the second, for the same time next year.

"Wally spent much of the first two months of '75 handing out leaflets in and around London. Dressed in his 'combat uniform', a bizarre mixture of middle-

*eastern army gear and Scottish tartans and driving his rainbow striped car com-
plete with a full sized Indian tepee, a large multicoloured tent, strapped to the
roof, he was a noticeable and colourful sight, a sight that those greyer than himself,
in appearance and thought, would certainly not have missed. In May, he left our
house for Cornwall; we had done all that we could to prepare for the festival and
Wally wanted to rest up in his tepee until it began. The day of his departure was
brilliantly hot; we sat in the garden drinking tea as Wally, glorifying the golden
sun, serenaded us, and it, with a wild performance on his tribal drums. He was
healthy, happy and confident that this time round he'd win again."* – Penny
Rimbaud – *Last Of The Hippies*

Having spent the winter in Ibiza (which must have been a bit nicer than
Amesbury, where the poorer Wallies had been meantime), Wally Hope
revisited his friends. Weeks before the second festival was due to take
place, however, police arrested Hope at the Wallies Amesbury squat for
possession of acid. He was immediately taken to Winchester Prison and
then sectioned for refusing to wear prison uniform, saying it brought
him out in a rash. This was taken as a sign of madness and he was taken
to the prison doctor, who diagnosed schizophrenia. Visitors reported
him complaining bitterly about the quantity of drugs he and other
inmates were being forced to take.

Wally was then moved to the Old Manor mental home in Salisbury.
As only close relatives were allowed to visit him in the mental home,
various Dial House people went posing as relatives.

Mick Duffield remembers himself & Penny Rimbaud going down to
visit. "We talked about getting him out but we decided he was in too
much of a state for it to be a good idea. Then he was released and the
drugs he'd been given, being like a chemical cosh, disabled him and he
ended up choking on his own vomit. He was reduced from being one of
the most energetic, intense people I'd ever met to someone who was disabled by the drugs he'd been given in so-called hospital – they thought
he was mad."

Gee Vaucher: "I found it shocking to see someone transformed so radically . . . he was really unusual in the amount of energy he had. He could
come round and literally talk non-stop for eight hours. I'd never seen
anyone who could do that before."

With Wally Hope still incarcerated, the second Stonehenge Festival went on regardless, and was a much bigger affair: two stages, thousands of people and a substantial and well received collection for the farmer whose land was being squatted for the event. Amongst the performers were the Here And Now, Hawkwind, Zorch, Trucker (Dozy, Beaky, Mick & Titch without former singer Dave Dee) and The 101ers, featuring future Clash frontman Joe Strummer.

Eve Libertine: "I went on holiday with Nemo to Cornwall – I had a little van and we put windows in the back. On the way down, we stopped and stayed the night at Stonehenge."

If egalitarian utopia was the plan, there is surely a generation of people who remember that hippies were quick to establish alternative status symbols, thus putting off the have-nots in droves. It was a superiority complex that Crass, to their credit, would carefully avoid, even when the temptations of band popularity rose their heads.

Eve Libertine remembers: "I've never really enjoyed festivals – I thought there was rather a hierarchy of the wealthy hippie tipi people – they were very beautiful. I remember beautiful, attractive bare-breasted women with things in their hair and men doing the whole native American thing. I found it quite cliquey. Then there were all the ... other people! I never particularly liked the music. The generator never seemed to have arrived. And it was quite cold and uncomfortable."

It was equally uncomfortable for Penny Rimbaud, who was accused from the stage of being a plain-clothed policeman – a Stonehenge Festival experience shared some years later by yours truly.

Two days after the festival site had cleared, Wally Hope was declared cured and released. He took two days to drive the 150 miles from Salisbury to Epping, stopping every twenty minutes to sleep. Some cure.

He arrived at Dial House clearly in a dreadful state: pale, bloated, shuffling. His face was pale and puffy with no signs of expression. Gee fed him a diet including ginseng and other curative herbs but it was soon clear this was nowhere near enough.

Despite the protestations of Gee and Penny, Hope decided to leave them in order to go to the Watchfield Festival – a free festival that bizarrely had Government co-operation.

Penny describes the moment he last saw Wally Hope: "If he was shamanistic, which he was, his greatest power was with the weather. Some shamans have animals, some have plants; his natural force was the weather. As he stepped out of the back door, this massive fork of lightning struck down into the vegetable patch, ten yards from us. There was a massive clap of thunder and a devastating downpour, and that was what he drove away in. You sort of knew it was the end."

Wally Hope died shortly after the festival. The official verdict was suicide, but Penny Rimbaud suspected he'd been murdered and began a year long investigation into his death. He came across harrowing information, which he used to write a book about Wally Hope called *Homage To Catatonia*.

"We found evidence of murder cover-ups, of police and gangland tie-ups, of wrongful arrest and imprisonment on trumped up charges and false evidence. We learnt of the horrific abuse, both physical and mental, of prisoners in jails and mental hospitals, doctors who knowingly prescribed what amounted to poison, who were unable to see the bruises inflicted, by courtesy of Her Majesty's officials, on an inmate's body – wardens and interrogating police are requested to punch below the head, where the bruises won't be seen by visiting relatives. We learnt of wardens who, to while the day away, set inmates against each other and did 'good turns' in return for material, and sexual favours. We learnt of nurses in mental hospitals who deliberately administered the wrong drugs to patients 'just to see what happened'; who, for kicks, tied patients to their beds and then tormented them. The official line, that the purpose of prisons is 'reform' and of mental hospitals is 'cure', is total deception – the purpose is 'punishment'; crude, cruel and simple – punishment.

"Beyond the world of police, courts, jails and asylums, we were faced with the perhaps even more sickening outside world. Within this world, respectable people, smart and secure, work, day in, day out, to maintain the lie. They know about the abuse and cruelty, they know about the dishonesty and corruption, they know about the complete falsity of the reality in which they live, but they daren't turn against it because, having invested so much of their lives in it, they would be turning against themselves, so they remain silent – the silent, violent, majority.

"Beneath the glossy surfaces of neatly combed hair and straightened nylons, of polished cars and sponged-down cookers, of pub on Friday and occasional church on Sunday, of well planned family and better planned future, of wealth and

security, of power and glory, are the 'real' fascists. They know, but they remain silent. 'First they came for the Jews and I did not speak out – because I was not a Jew. Then they came for the communists and I did not speak out – because I was not a communist. Then they came for the trade unionists and I did not speak out – because I was not a trade unionist. Then they came for me – and there was no one left to speak out for me,' wrote Pastor Niemoeller, victim of the Nazis." – Penny Rimbaud – *Last Of The Hippies*

These days, Rimbaud seems ambiguous as to whether he thinks Hope was murdered: "Sometimes I do and sometimes I don't. When I first wrote *Last Of The Hippies* I didn't take that line at all. When I first wrote *Homage To Catatonia*, I certainly thought he'd been done in. I felt I had conclusive documented proof. Most of that got burned."

It got burned because Penny feared for his life. "It changed my life in that respect. Prior to that I was very relaxed about everything. I used to sleep in the garden. We never locked our doors, but I started feeling I wanted to lock them.

"When I was investigating Wally's death, the police turned up. Police I didn't know – we were quite used to the local bobby coming down and looking through the herb rack etc. Basically they'd come to say 'fucking lay off'. There was a sense of discomfort and ill-ease. That's when I burnt the evidence – all except that which was owned by other people, which was what I then used to write *Shibboleth*.

"Ultimately, as I said in Shibboleth, it doesn't matter a fuck whether he was deliberately murdered or not, he was murdered. He was existentially murdered – he certainly died as a result of his treatment, no question of that. Call it what you like – that's doing someone in, isn't it?

"When I was writing *Homage To Catatonia*, I went through all the evidence and all the dates and times to do with when Wally's body was being shifted around, didn't add up. I used to go through it all every day and then all of a sudden I saw it – it was like a jigsaw. I went through the roof – I knew I'd got them, I'd solved it. It categorically showed he'd been murdered."

If so, he wasn't the only Wally from Stonehenge to meet his fate in such a way.

Penny Rimbaud: "That was an area that almost lead to my death.

Another Wally – Wally (surname censored – we'll call him NoName) was found in Epping Forest tied to a tree with a joint in his hand. I can't remember the time sequences but it was when I was working on Wally's death. I got a letter from some 'Wallies' in Brighton saying 'look into this'. So I started looking into that & it turned out that there it was a sort of connection between Brighton gangland and the Essex police, and that Wally NoName was a small-time dealer who'd probably been working on someone else's patch and had subsequently been fixed up. Certainly all the evidence suggested that he couldn't have committed suicide. I got some fairly substantial evidence. Then I started thinking 'fucking hell, what are you supposed to do with this?'"

Then one day a taxi pulled up outside Penny's house. Out-stepped Mrs. NoName – Wally's mum – and Rimbaud got an immediate instinct that "something seriously wrong was going to happen". Penny asked somebody else to go down to the door. "She put her bag on the side and put her hand into it and . . . I just knew . . . she said later that she'd come to do me in. Not only had she lost her son, she'd then been given false hopes through my looking into all this stuff. I hadn't got back to her when I said I would, because I was trying to muddle through all this crap. Net result, I was going to get it." In the end, she was pacified and left happily.

"So all that stuff happened with Mrs. NoName and I just freaked – I couldn't deal with it. I was living here on my own and I just felt frightened. Frightened on every level – I felt lonely, scared of what I was doing, so I just went into the garden and burnt it. In this book (*Shibboleth*), I thought I'd try and set the record straight."

It was decided that it would be fitting to spread the ashes of Wally Hope over Stonehenge during the third festival.

Penny Rimbaud: "There was a guy called Chris who was the King of Tipi Valley – he was the guy who actually purchased a lot of the land, the leader of the whole Tipi movement.

"I made this little box in which they were contained – it was very artistic – I used to do art boxes, which were little wooden boxes – inside them would be shells and bells and bits of grass – those sorts of things. A bit Zen in a way – magical boxes. You couldn't get in them, they were sealed. I did a similar ritualistic box for Phil's ashes.

"I got the ashes from his guardians, then Chris came to pick them up to take them to Stonehenge. He was confronted with massive storms on the way there – a tree fell down narrowly missing his van, preventing him from going any further. Again, there was a heavy weather involvement.

"By the time I got down to Stonehenge, Sid Rawle was doing his whole hippy priest bit – he'd got the ashes in my box. I can't remember the detail of what it was he was doing, but I found it offensive. I felt very excluded – I'd done two Stonehenge festivals with Wally, done all that stuff in the courts, trying to clear his name. I'd done all of that work, and Sid just took over. I felt very lonely, very isolated when I went down to that festival. I felt that Sid was using Wally. I felt the manner in which he was doing the ceremony was disrespectful.

"Wally wanted a festival which was for the people, that was his only interest. Stonehenge was *absolutely not* politically motivated. At the time, there wasn't any fence at Stonehenge, it was just a load of rocks in the middle of a field. He knew that a lot of it was M.O.D. land, but his idea was just that we could bundle off to Stonehenge and have a nice time, away from the hassle that he knew kids were being set up with at Windsor[1]. The idea was just that it was something nice. The fact it became a major political battle would have upset him immeasurably. The Windsor politicos resented the fact that he wasn't taking on a political agenda. And he didn't get much support for them, in fact quite the reverse – by and large he was criticised."

In the autumn of 1995, underground newspaper *Squall* printed an article 'Wally Hope, Victim Of Ignorance' telling essentially the same story that Penny Rimbaud had in *Last Of The Hippies* (though assuming Penny was a woman!).

---

[1] The Windsor Free Festival was held annually between 1972 and 1974, in Windsor Park. Being situated on Crown land, it was a more confrontational idea than Stonehenge and the last festival finished in violence as police attacked festival goers. Even the right-wing press responded indignantly to the police actions, and the resulting bad publicity for the Government led to an unofficial policy of tolerating free festivals until Margaret Thatcher decided differently in 1985 when new age traveller families on their way to Stonehenge were savagely attacked by the police in what became known as the Battle Of The Beanfield.

It provoked one Nigel Ayers into writing: "I knew Phil Russell aka Wally Hope and was present at many of the events described in the article ... He was a classic rich kid acid casualty who would ramble on for hours about Jesus being reincarnated in Cyprus in 1960. The people who made a hero of him once he was dead couldn't stand him when he was alive." Penny Rimbaud replied in the same issue, acknowledging Hope as, "tiresome at times, particularly when he was on his Jesus of Cyrpus soap box, but he was also a poet and a visionary... When he was alive I loved him, when he was dead I missed him."

Up till now, Penny's has been the only voice we've heard regarding Wally Hope. Indeed, some members of Crass feel his story to be barely relevant to the contents of this book. But as a part of the counter-culture, his story can't be ignored, particularly seeing as he has risen to almost mythical status in some free-festival-goer and anarchist circles. Penny Rimbaud also strongly feels that without Wally Hope, Crass would not have taken the line they did.

"He didn't come across as mad," reflects Zorch's Basil Brooks, "but in those days we were all a bit 'out there'. He certainly didn't come across as a casualty. He was approachable, infectious, very enthusiastic ... he wasn't autocratic like some of the other underground figures."

Steve Ignorant remembers: "Nice bloke with a beard – he'd always look you directly in the eyes. I remember liking him a lot."

Pete Wright, on the other hand says, "I'm afraid that I'm rather unaffected by Mr Hope. I know that Penny feels that the man was somehow pivotal, especially since Penny himself was very much involved with Wally's activities and fate, and so would feel deeply affected. And since principles are only really engaged when the effect is somehow to your own disadvantage, asserting your own principles or reality is a risky business."

Joy DeVivre: "He was just one of those extrovert, excitable people. He could spurt amazing ideas and visions. I'm sure some people just thought he was completely mad, but he was a very loving, hopeful, Blake-ian kind of person."

Mick Duffield doesn't buy into the idea of Wally as shamanic magician. "I didn't, no" he replies, when asked about Wally's supposed weather miracles. He pauses for an age, searching for the diplomatic words. "I thought they were . . . coincidences. . . Wally was one of a series of involvements that I wouldn't say was particularly involved in Crass' story."

Despite burning most of the book, sections of *Homage To Catatonia* survive. In those, we can see the emerging visual styles that would reappear on *Feeding Of The Five Thousand* and subsequent record sleeves. The constant writing/with dashes/rather/than punctuation in trademark typewriter font is present, as are Gee Vaucher's stunning and overtly political collages.

It was at this time that Gee's style really came into its own, confronting the viewer with stark and sometimes harsh reality in a style that, as much as anyone of the era, could be recognised as 'punk art'.

Gee explains: "I found it a very useful tool to get people to look at a subject that wasn't very nice to look at usually. That they would be drawn in, not realising that they were looking at a rotting corpse. I found that quite interesting – as they drew back they'd realise, but it was too late. I used to work with everything in here," adds Gee, gesturing to her head, "and then I would illustrate everything I had in here very precisely."

Against this, Gee can also be surprisingly light about her heavy subject matter and artistic styles. On collage, for instance: "I was just throwing some bits of paper around, and if one of them happened to settle on top of another one, then I thought – whoo!"

Whoo indeed!

The scenes in these early works from Gee put one immediately in mind of the 1956 Richard Hamilton collage 'Just What Is It That Makes Todays Dream Homes So Different, So Appealing'.

Illustrating a gulf between UK post-war austerity and US prosperity, Hamilton's collage is credited as kick-starting the UK Pop Art movement, helpfully featuring a bodybuilder clutching an outsized lollipop with 'POP' emblazoned upon it. The bodybuilder is stood in a room, surrounded by the consumer items of the age – a pin up models a lampshade as a hat while a dutiful housewife vacuums the stairs. Through the window, an outside view shows a theatre, atopped by a billboard advertising an Al Jolson type singer on bended knee. A poster advertises Young Romance on the wall, next to a portrait of Abraham Lincoln.

It would have been startlingly confrontational at the time, appearing to take pot shots at the consumer society during the supposed post-war golden age of giving life meaning by owning 'things'. In other words, materialism. You can look at the piece and find meaning and questioning without the slightest hint of pretension, even in this day and age. In the fifties, it was little short of revolutionary.

Like Vaucher, Hamilton was born into a working class London background – Pimlico in this instance – and left school with no qualifications, only to find himself and his vocation at art school (St. Martins College of Art). He would later teach at the Royal College of Art, promoting David Hockney and Peter Blake, amongst others, and teaching future Roxy Music singer Bryan Ferry in a separate job[1]. A prominent light in CND, Richard Hamilton would go on to befriend Paul McCartney and design the collage for the inside of *The Beatles* double LP, or 'White Album'.

Hamilton also co-founded the Independent Group – a collective based at London's ICA which proclaimed that 'art should be mass-produced, sexy, transient, big business', not a million miles away from Andy Warhol in that respect.

In other words, Richard Hamilton represents many key words later to be associated with Crass: anti-materialist / revolutionary / CND / independent. But the collage itself makes the connection most loudly of all.

"There's no condition called schizophrenia; it's a term of personal and social invalidation" – J. Berke

"Without exception the experience and behaviour that gets labeled schizophrenic is a special strategy that a person invents in order to live in an unlivable situation." – R.D. Laing

"Since the beginning of time, mental illness has been a powerful political weapon against those seeking, or operating, social change. A lot of the definitions of

---

[1] Ferry would later write the immortal 'In Every Dream Home A Heartache', perhaps not coincidentally.

'madness' are bogus inventions by which those in authority are able to dismiss those who dare to question their reality. Terms like schizophrenia, neurotic and paranoid, mean little more than what any particular, or not so particular, individual chooses them to mean. There are no physical proofs for any of these 'conditions'; the definitions vary from psychiatrist to psychiatrist and depending on which is considered undesirable or subversive, are totally different from one country to another. Because of these different standards, the chances of being diagnosed schizophrenic in America are far higher than they are in Britain and this led one psychiatrist to-suggest that the best cure for many American mental patients would be to catch a flight to Britain. The label of 'mental illness' is a method of dealing with individuals, from unwanted relatives to social critics, who, through not accepting the conditions that are imposed upon them by outsiders, are seen as 'nuisances' and 'trouble makers'.

"The works of psychologists, notably Freud, Jung, and the school of perverts who follow their teachings, have, by isolating 'states of mind' and defining some of them as 'states of madness', excluded all sorts of possible developments in the way in which we see, or could see, our reality. By allowing people to learn from the experience of their so called 'madness', rather than punishing them for it, new radical ways of thought could be realised, new perspectives created and new horizons reached. How else has the human mind grown and developed? Nearly all the major advances in society have been made by people who are criticised, ridiculed, and often punished in their own time, only to be celebrated as 'great thinkers' years after their deaths. As mental and physical health becomes increasingly controllable with drugs and surgery, we come even closer to a world of hacked about and chemically processed Mr. and Mrs. Normals whose only purpose in life will be to mindlessly serve the system; progress will cease and the mind-fuckers will have won their battle against the human spirit.

"Once labelled 'mad', a patient may be subjected to a whole range of hideous tortures politely referred to by The Notional Health Service as 'cures'. They are bound up in belts and harnesses, strait jackets, so that their bodies become bruised and their spirits beaten. They are locked up in silent padded cells so that the sound of their own heartbeat and the smell of their own shit breaks them down into passive animals. They are forced to take drugs that make them into robot-like zombies. One common side effect of long term treatment with these drugs is severe swelling of the tongue; the only effective cure is surgical — the tongue is cut out — what better way to silence the prophet? They are given electric shocks in the head that cause disorientation and loss of memory. ECT, electro- convulsive therapy, is an idea adopted from the slaughterhouse where, before having their throats cut open, pigs are stunned with an identical form of treatment; ECT is a primitive form of punishment that owes more to the traditions of the witch hunters than it does to the tradition of science. The ultimate 'cure', tour de force of the psychiatric profession, is lobotomy. Victims of this obscene practical joke have knives stuck into their heads that are randomly waggled about so that part of the brain is reduced to mince-meat.

"Surgeons performing this operation have no precise idea what they are doing; the brain is an incredibly delicate object about which very little is known, yet these butchers feel qualified to poke knives into people's heads in the belief that they are performing 'scientific services'. Patients who are given this treatment frequently die from it; those who don't can never hope to recover from the state of mindlessness that has been deliberately imposed upon them.

Disgusting experiments are daily performed on both animals and humans in the name of 'medical advance'; there is no way of telling what horrific new forms of treatment are at this moment being devised for us in the thousands of laboratories throughout the country. In Nazi Germany, the inmates of the death camps were used by drug companies as 'guinea-pigs' for new products. Nowadays the companies, some of which are the very same ones, use prisoners in jails and hospitals for the same purposes.

"Mental patients are constantly subjected to the ignorance of both the state and the general public and, as such, are perhaps the most oppressed people in the world. In every society there are thousands upon thousands of people locked away in asylums for doing nothing more than question imposed values; dissidents dismissed by the label of madness and silenced, often for ever, by the cure." – Penny Rimbaud.

When Penny Rimbaud was growing up, he lived near a big mental hospital. He would stand at the railings looking in at the patients, wondering how human beings ended up looking like that. You can detect the influence of R.D. Laing throughout the seventies anti-psychiatry movement, questioning conventional psychiatric methods, and Rimbaud was an avid reader. The Wally Hope experience only served to exacerbate things, of course.

Penny is sticking to his contention, previously expressed in both the

Last Of The Hippies piece that accompanied *Christ — The Album* and his autobiography *Shibboleth*, that he witnessed Wally Hope perform weather miracles. "I don't know if it's a matter of sticking to them — if you've seen them, you've seen them. Likewise, other times in my life, when... I've never made it an issue in the sense that I think it's too much to ask people to accept. Like the times when I first lived here (Dial House) — there was an enormous amount of psychic energy in this place, and some of it was rather negative. It manifested in all sorts of ways — visual, sound etc. It actually stopped overnight at the time I opened the house to everyone, got rid of all of the junk and painted the whole place white. Until that point, the energies here were ludicrous and very uncomfortable.

"In journeys in Africa, I've experienced things that make Wally's magic pale in comparison: disappearing people, flying people, all sorts..."

Penny says this with an intense seriousness that essentially dares you to ridicule him, and wins. "When I left Northern Kenya, I'd been staying in a mission up in Pokot land, right at the top of the Rift Valley. They're a very untouched people, still a nomadic people living the life that they must have done for hundreds if not thousands of years. They spent much of the day standing round on one leg, leaning on a spear watching the world go by.

"When I left, I was accompanied, until I was out of their territory, by flying tribesman. I was in a landrover going across this really rough terrain, and there was a platoon of them flying in formation about 150 feet up, until we got out of Pokot territory and then they disappeared. It sounds ridiculous to be saying it, but I saw them — there's no question, I saw them. They were there, unmistakeable — it wasn't a few ducks or something. It's an area of my life that I've never really publicly gone into, but it's been as much a parallel in my life as anything else. There's a big world out there."

Back in the little world, Penny Rimbaud split up with Gee Vaucher, and Gee went to live in New York.

Penny Rimbaud: "She'd seen a lot of possibilities in the States. So — we were never married, but we decided we'd divorce."

So Gee went to live in New York, and Penny was once again on his own at Dial House. Some are of the opinion that this split hurt Penny considerably more than he lets on, which may add an extra dimension to the pain he felt when Wally Hope died. The crowded house from the Exit days had slowly dwindled.

Rimbaud: "It was the time I started on the Wally Hope book, so I was getting darker and darker, and bleaker, and I don't think people particularly wanted to be around me, quite understandably."

After the demise of Exit, a new band started taking shape in the Dial House rehearsal room. Ceres Confusion[1] were an exceedingly experimental traditional outfit, owing far more to avant-garde traditions than rock'n'roll. Indeed, listening to their tape 'Doses Of Neuroses', they owe nothing whatsoever to rock'n'roll.

This time around, however, there was a concession to normality in that there was at least a stable line-up which consisted of Peter LeBeau on guitars, Bernhardt Rebours on keyboards and Penny Rimbaud on 'percussion', though the percussion was a far cry from the drums and bongos most people would associate with the word.

"Peter Le Beau had played with Exit, and his brother – Dick Le Beau – was one of the founder members of Dial House," says Penny. "We described the music as psycho-rock. We took the Exit style and added jazz-rock fusion into it so it was more rocky and driving. And out of that grew that *urgency*, which is something I think we introduced to punk. Whilst the Pistols played pretty fast, they didn't play *urgently*. Ceres Confusion carried on a lot of the freeform experimental approaches that Exit had but on a more funky level."

Penny sees them operating in the same musical area as John McLaughlin's Mahavishnu Orchestra, on the jazzy side and Jimi Hendrix in the rock corner. "There was a lot of feathery avant-garde sound, but also a rocky beat."

Bernhardt Rebours remembers his introduction to the Dial House scene: "A guy who I was at school with came up to Dial House with me

[1] Pronounced See-rees Confusion, hence a play on words.

one day and ended up living there. He moved to Canada and got married."

The guy was Richard Le Beau and his brother Peter played the guitar. Bernhardt Rebours recalls: "Peter and I had got into a little band called Firebird that rehearsed at Dial House – that didn't go anywhere. We did one gig at a college in Canterbury, but it didn't really work. It was all so . . . lame.

"I'd really liked the way Penny worked with me at college. This is at the time when things like Steve Reich and Terry Riley and that minimalist sequential music was coming out from America. It was a big influence for me. It was something I really liked working through, almost into a meditative state.

"It was at the time when the Mahavisnhu Orchestra was really making an impression. Peter wanted to be John McLaughlin, he had the SG double-neck and all the rest of it. I was into piano at the time, and Pen had made a percussion kit from bicycle wheels and bits and pieces. He had a strange foot-pedal operated radio that tuned the radio into different noise between the stations. There were contact mics on bicycle spokes, tin cans – it was incredible. I had a cheesy electric piano, and my big investment of the time was a monophonic synthesizer."

Ceres Confusion would play every Friday night in the music room at Dial House, taping their results onto cassette, one of which was the above-mentioned 'Doses Of Neuroses'. Bernhardt remembers: "We'd start about 8.30, play for a couple of hours, have a break then get back into it until maybe about midnight or one o'clock, totally exhausted. . . It was an environment where we could really learn to be instinctive, intuitive, about the direction the music was going."

The closest the band came to unveiling their sound live to the public was at the Stonehenge Festival. Bernhardt: "I think it was the last festival they had which was right up against the Stones, not on the other side of the road. We'd heard that Van Der Graff Generator were playing there. It just didn't feel right – it felt really decadent, it didn't feel a good environment to play in. We'd brought all our gear down, but we just couldn't face it. So, no, we didn't do any gigs – I don't know if anybody would have stayed for very long! Because it was so intense, it was like Mahavisnhu Orchestra meets punk. It was so extreme – some of it was incredibly beautiful and delicate. Some of it worked, some of it didn't.

"It was like World War Three in music, it was so total. And yet you could hear within that a quiet centre that was beautiful. It was complete nonsense as a band to listen to, because it was so intense it was almost unlistenable. The playing was 'wrong' from beginning to end, but it was absolutely perfect for the people that were playing. Some real unexpected beauty crept out.

"It was so earthy, the way Penny was wrecking his percussion kit. He was forever replacing Ovalteen cans because they were just getting mashed into these incredible sculptures. Salvador Dali-esque cans — absolutely thrashed to destruction."

In just a few years, Gee would mention to Bernhardt that a band had just moved into Epping and were in need of a bass player. Bernhardt got hold of a bass guitar from one of his old Firebird band, and went off to join Poison Girls. A week later they were in the studio recording 'Piano Lessons', their first single.

As Ceres Confusion "stopped bothering", in the words of Penny Rimbaud, Bernard and Penny started talking about putting a more theatrical outfit together. One woman who expressed an interest in contributing to this new project was Sue Lothian, who would surface almost thirty years later as the woman who bought Dial House for its residents when it was put up for auction. The idea was to feature Penny Rimbaud and as yet unknown women on vocals, and to be "more flamboyant" as Rimbaud puts it. "This would have been at the same time as the Bromley Contingent — in '75/76 — it was very much a mirror of that."

Names were bandied about: Les Bohemes, Malade Imaginaire, but before anything came to fruition, a young punk rocker would return to Dial House and change all the plans. . .

CH-CH-CH-CH-CHANGES

In 1975 Patti Smith released her seminal debut album 'Horses', featuring the first song 'Gloria', with its memorable opening line 'Jesus died for somebody's sins but not mine', taken, along with the next five lines of the song, from her 1972 poem Oath. It was a line which Crass would paraphrase (to: 'Jesus died for his own sins, not mine') not only in the 'Reality Asylum' song/poem, but as a phrase surrounding their symbol on official badges and snide t-shirts ever since.

Although Patti Smith had done something wonderful and new with her music, she was also a definite link to the past – connections with Blue Oyster Cult and Rolling Stones fixations hardly marked her out as the sort of Year Zero punk that had just come straight out of nowhere and left the past behind.

"I didn't like it," says Steve Ignorant of Patti Smith. "I found it depressing and dark and a bit creepy. A bit decadent and a bit too considered. I just couldn't relate to it. It's weird, cos I can relate to *West Side Story*, but not things like Richard Hell or The New York Dolls. And Patti Smith – I thought *Horses* was one of the best albums ever – I'll give her that – but the rest of it was just too avant-gardey for me."

Nevertheless, the lineage from freaks to punks was strengthening. Alistair Livingstone, who would achieve prominence in the London punk scene as Kill Your Pet Puppy correspondent and Gerard Malanga/Bez–style dancer with The Mob remembers: "Between four and six every Wednesday for three years from 1979 to 1981 I used to hang out in Small Wonder record shop in Walthamstow. I had to go to evening classes in engineering at Waltham Forest College. Small Wonder was a warm place to waste some time before college. Since I was such a regular customer (I didn't have a record player, but bought records anyway), I got to know the owner Pete Stennet quite well. We would chat away and he would play whatever new records had come in.

"Although the mainstay of the shop was punk, Pete was not a punk. Nor, although he had long hair, was he a hippie. He could get quite irate on the subject. 'We never called ourselves hippies. We were freaks.'

"Hippies, as far as I could work out, never really existed. It was a lazy journalistic label given to members of the late sixties/early seventies radical generation. But they never called themselves hippies, they called themselves freaks."

It's a moot point as to whether 'freaks' were a different grouping to 'hippies' or merely a newer way of describing the same people, but either way, things had changed irrevocably from the sixties. The post-war economic boom was over and the more delicate and naïve of the hippy dreams had died with it. Of course, there were still plenty of political and social radicals – not to mention plain good old rock-'n'rollers – squeezing into the political and social spaces the alternative society had created, but the atmosphere was different, more confrontational and angrier.

What had undeniably changed in a more substantial way than mere haircuts and trouser width was the British Economy of course. And with this, the counter culture had been slowly but surely reacting to the changes. In his memoir *Harmony In My Head*, Buzzcocks guitarist Steve Diggle remembers: "Fucking hell. Yes were huge then, think about that. It's weird but you've only got to see the newsreels from back then and you can see that England looked like it had literally had the colour washed out of it. You look at the clips of hippies walking down the Kings Road in 1973 and compare them to the hippies going into the Apple Shop in 1967. Or walking down Carnaby Street. You can see the difference and the seventies had the advantage of better film didn't it? It sounds stupid, but there's a definite difference between sixties colour and early seventies colour. It was brutal and heavy in the seventies and it showed just how styleless England had become. Moustaches and beards had even been cool in the sixties, but by 1973, they looked shit! People had taken it a beard too far and they were lost."

Gee Vaucher remembers "hippies" in a wider chronological context and with a far more colourful palette: "I think peoples' concept of the hippie culture is really off the mark – people think of it as what it was at the end, and that's not how it began at all. I think the hippie culture was about finding a voice. I don't think any young person could conceive that young people did not have a voice, full stop. At fifteen, you were still wearing ankle socks – kids took a long time to grow up then. The top twenty was people like Eddie Fisher and Mario Lanza – it really was! Then suddenly. . . I remember vividly my brother bringing in a Bill Haley EP. Then of course Elvis hit and I don't think anyone could realise quite how outrageous this was – he was so *sexual*! The tight jeans and the pelvis thing!

"Before that it was still locked into 'after the war'. Vera Lynne was still singing, Bill Cotton was still playing – that was your top 20! Then CND started and really gave people a group voice. Because information came out that those nuclear power stations had not been built for energy. That wasn't known then. But it was a lie that had been sold to the people. People were beginning to realise they had been told lie upon lie about all sorts of things. I remember asking my mum whether she knew about the bomb in Hiroshima and she said she didn't – she just thought it was an ordinary bomb but ten times bigger. *Nobody* knew about the fallout. She's not stupid, my mum, but she really didn't know what it was until much later.

"What I personally gained from the hippy thing was questioning, and that my health was my responsibility – that was one of the really big things. People started to get back into herbal medicine, into dancing with the spirits. . . OK it was all naivety and the world isn't a great place and it's not going to be done by you jumping up and down and saying, 'I'm invisible', but you did have the seeds of people turning back and regaining their own authority. I started to look at what I was eating . . . as a kid you just jam it in don't you, you don't worry about it, do you. But as you get older you think, 'what is this? Where does it come from?' Why suddenly can't I get a local cabbage, or a home-made loaf? Why has the bakers closed? Why do I have to get a cabbage from South Africa, why can't I get one from down the road?

"The hippy thing hasn't stopped – the organic thing, of trying to create local produce, the ideas of farmers markets – it all comes from that. The punk thing, as far as I'm concerned, comes from that. Why should we say yes when we can say no – it comes out in different forms."

Dave King: "There was a lot of frustration that it didn't stick. There'd been a lot of talk in the media of a classless society. That it was possible in the sixties for a lot of people who'd never had any opportunity before, particularly in the arts, to be accepted for their talent and not their education. There was this hope amongst a lot of people that it would just keep going, that things would get *more* enlightened and *more* liberal, more radical. Then there was the slow dawning horror that this wasn't going to happen. Things started to sink again, to move further to the right. That was felt at Dial House."

The same thing was felt more and more elsewhere on the alternative scene in the UK as well. From the harassment of underground magazines like *OZ* to the the break up of the Windsor Free Festival, through general harassment of squatters and the like, the 'freaks' that made up the 'underground' were getting pissed off with their lot.

Certainly the 'freaks' knew that love and peace was a fading dream. You can be reasonably confident that a certain John Lydon had felt the anger, and the romancing of anger, in songs like Hawkwind's 'Urban Guerilla': "Don't talk to me about love and flowers / and things that don't explode."

"Society, the state and the system, hadn't fucked off, they'd not only stayed right where they were, they'd grown stronger.

"Slowly, as people woke up to the fact that 'turning on' was turning off, and 'dropping out' was copping out, the horrific reality of the nuclear world forced its way back through the escapist blur of those 'psychedelic dreams'. The acid revolution had been fun, but that's just about where it had ended. Beneath the new space, the new time, the new dimensions and the new colours, the same old grey reality had ground relentlessly onwards – the dream was over.

"The dream had been that if you created your own life, independent of the system, the system would leave you to it. Looking back on it now it seems pathetically naive, but for maybe fifteen years, it had sustained the lives of thousands of people. The ultimate failure of hippy was exactly that ostrich-like approach to life;

a hippy utopia surrounded by a world of hate and war was like 'snow before the summer's sun'. Eventually those who weren't too permanently stoned to guarantee pipedreams to infinity, pulled their heads from the sands to confront a society that had got on very well without them, thank you, for far too long. The hippy movement was finding a truly militant front for itself." – Penny Rimbaud, *Last Of The Hippies*

Eve Libertine: "There was a lot of discussion through the sixties. Sexual freedom was a big thing: changing the way that it had always been. After the sixties, it was called 'conciousness-raising'. There were a lot of conciousness-raising groups; then the womens' movement – that was quite angry ... very angry, bits of it. Trying to make change happen. Yes, there was anger there."

Joy De Vivre: "I used to go to Dial House then, but I was a young kid. I wouldn't have known disaffection if it had stamped on my foot. I just remember an awful lot of conversations that I kind of keyed into but also flew over my head. There was a lot of narky debate and clever clever ramblings. It was quite an austere place, and when you went in it was up to you where to go – the door was open, but nobody would come up to you and greet you. It was up to you to go and put the kettle on, or just sit there because you didn't know if you should put the kettle on. On one level, it's confronting and interesting, and on another level it's ... (laughs) I don't know! But it was all part of it being interesting and different – a very challenging place, not altogether comfortable."

Phil Free: "There was a sense of being outside the norm and not being involved in the regular things."

Eve Libertine: "I think the punk thing definitely came out of the hippie thing. Musically, a lot of what happened with the hippie thing was big bands, lots of money and a lot of disappointment, I guess. It was a few people making a lot of money out of it, thank you very much – Richard Branson etc. People had become hippie capitalists, and in the music business, very much so; there was glam and rock and all that stuff."

Other ex-hippies had gone off in a completely different direction. Luminaries such as Marc Bolan and David Bowie had left muddy fields and earth mothers behind, swapping them for make-up, gaudy crazy-outrageous clothing and a general celebration of the weird and wonderful. Glam rock had arrived and was filling the charts with stardust, glitter and the confrontations of openly confused and confusing sexuality.

Bowie in particular had caught the imagination of the nation's sharp youth, but Penny Rimbaud looks back on it with disdain, considering him to have used the counter culture and then not given anything back: "I think people like Jagger and Bowie stole our hopes and turned them into money. Their castles are built on our money – the movement's money. People believed in that sort of stuff. Bowie could have done something but he didn't do anything."

Steve Ignorant, on the other hand, was a confirmed member of the Bowie generation: "I was enormously into him. I used to buy every record I could." It was an interest that lasted until the Thin White Duke released *Young Americans*.

"Living in Dagenham," Steve adds, "the appeal was that if you dyed your hair or had a little bit of make-up or wore a bangle, you'd get the piss taken out of you, but because it was David Bowie, you didn't. You could dress up like that and because everyone was into his music. It was so obvious that girls liked it – thank you David Bowie! And good music to shag to, I have to say!"

Alternative culture would produce some books with lasting appeal in the seventies, notably Nicholas Sanders *Alternative London* – a guide to just about every aspect of living an alternative life with hardly any money in the capital. It was an invaluable source of information that effortlessly traversed subcultures and when punk happened it became the bible a second time around for the new generation of squatters, layabouts and ne'er do wells.

Where stuff of real value to diverse living cropped up, it was often found to have a hippie/freak past that didn't quite fit in with the blanket condemnation of hippies by Malcolm McLaren and other punk figures. Steve Ignorant: "It was hippies that set up Release and did soup kitchens, the *Little Red School Book* of course ... hippie people did do good things as well!"

Gee Vaucher, meanwhile, was now firmly ensconced in New York. "I thought it would just be a couple of months but it turned into a couple of years." She went to stay with a friend: "I had twenty quid in my pocket and a plastic bag full of old stuff." She hit the ground running: "I was lucky – I hit New York at the right time. I walked into the *New York Times* and I just got a job straight away." In no time at all, Gee Vaucher had made a name for herself. "I had the front cover of *New York* magazine and everything. I was seen as a political artist so the things that I got were great – just fantastic subjects, from the mafia to nazism to Watergate."

'Punk' in its initial American form was just getting off the ground in New York, particularly at a club called CBGBs. "I lived round the corner," says Gee, "so I was down there every night. Patti Smith would be there, and the Ramones, Debbie Harry – all those bands. So I used to go all the time. I had a great way of getting in for nowt and nicking beers for nowt!" Gee chuckles. "It was a really great place then."

She also remembers bumping into a Sex Pistol during her time in the big apple. "I can remember picking up Johnny Rotten outside one night – he was absolutely paralytic. He was a total wreck, on his own, outside CBGBs. There were these girls trying to come on to him, it was just awful." So Gee hoisted him up and helped him back to the address he was staying at on Houston (Avenue). "These girls kept in toe and I thought, this guy is just gonna be walked on for what he is. He looked so vulnerable and tiny. So I took him back to where he was staying, took him upstairs and laid him on the bed. And the girls were still trying to get off with him." So Gee decided to sit guard until they left. "Then I wrote a little note and stuck it in his jacket saying if he ever needed any help, just to ring this number. I never heard from him – he probably thought I was just another fucking wanker."

Back in England, Penny Rimbaud had taken to heavy drinking and rants about the power of Christianity. It's eminently possible that this was not entirely unconnected to the death of Wally Hope, who had spent half his life talking animatedly about Jesus. "He was fixated on Jesus the prophet, but he wasn't a Christian. The Sun was his God. Certainly he was very bound to Christian ideology and morality, but he changed the roles of all the figures and myths of Christianity and rewrote them in his own words."

CRASS

"It made me very angry indeed that just as in the myth of Christ – Christ *could*, while sitting in the garden of Gethsemane and seeing his executioners appear over the hill, have done a runner. Likewise Wally could. He made of himself a martyr. He did have the option, all the way down the line from when he was first arrested to when he was killed ... he could have got out of it. But he didn't. He went on that auto-destruct path that Christ chose to do."

"I've never been happy with Christianity since I was a kid. But that certainly could have brought it to a head – in Wally's behaviour I recognised the same stupidity that I interpreted in the Christ story."

While The Sex Pistols were causing minor explosions on the Central London music scene, and the music press was waking up to the need for something new, on the Epping outskirts, Penny Rimbaud started work on his *Reality Asylum* pamphlet.

One day he was in the kitchen with Dave King, still living there at the time, on one of his frequent large drinking bouts and he got into a rant about the way that Christianity was so intrinsically wrapped into everything he was taught to believe. "I was getting more and more into it – diving around and screaming and yelling, like a real catharsis. When I calmed down again, Dave said 'You ought to write that, you know,' so that's what I did."

Christ's Reality Asylum took Pen about two weeks, writing it "pissed out of my head" in the mornings and printing the days work in the evening. "I never edited it, it was just exactly as it was. I did 100 copies and they were sold by Pooles bookshop in Charing Cross Rd. I sold them all."

Although Penny recalls this period with less than total affection, Dave King – the only other communard by this point – reflects more positively: "It was good – we had this great meal we used to make – a big bowl of rice and cheese and thyme and garlic. It was so simple – every day, it was like, 'Shall we have the meal? Yeah, let's have the meal!' It gave you more time to think about other things ... or think about nothing!"

There was a down side to those times as well, however. "It was a bleak time in some ways," he says. "The house had been set up with the idea of being fairly expansive, of being able to incorporate a lot of different people and ideas. It dwindled down – that was the most reductive point. But I think that's often what happens . . . before something big happens, nothing has to happen. Everything slows down and stops and then things start to expand again – for me, it's a fairly natural process. You could say it was a low point."

Once Penny had completed *Reality Asylum*, he printed it using an old gestetner machine that had been bought in the Exit days, inspired by old hippy broadsheets, themselves inspired by similar ventures on the West Coast of America. "Eventually I abandoned the gestetner and just used the gestetner sheets on the silk screen because it gave a nicer effect." Hence, the cutely named Exitstencil Press was born. The room where the printing took place is to this day known as 'the print room'.

Eve Libertine: "I could relate to it in terms of the feminist angle. I'd read *The Diamond Signature* before that and absolutely loved it. I didn't understand it particularly, but I loved it. I loved the way it flowed. Again, I related to it on a feminist level, though I was very wary and wouldn't call myself a feminist, like I wouldn't call myself an anarchist."

Christ's Reality Asylum And Les Pommes De Printemps, to give it its full name, is a twenty-page barrage of philosophical prose (or is it poetry?) that seems to meander between a dialogue with Jesus, a dialogue with self and a dialogue with the reader. It's, er, extremely difficult to understand: *"Life is empirical/concept/matter/matterofconcept/ intellectual idea/no inherent integrity/exists beyond idea/outside life/life is destroyed within seconds of birth/my parents NEED ME/they die after ME/I was made a physical, intellectual and spiritual materialist, given a stolen universe and made to pay. THE REAL NEVER NEVER. WAS IT EVER?"*

And so on.

The booklet was originally planned to contain a set of poems by Eve Libertine, but she didn't get round to writing them.

Despite the shocking antichrist tone, leading one agent to ask Penny if he was deliberately trying to tempt prosecution, there were precedents for such outspoken attacks on the personality of Christ, which as an art student (and later teacher), Rimbaud would doubtless have been aware[1].

Aside from the militant anti-religious stance of *Christ's Reality Asylum*, the longstanding echo would be felt from the symbol devised to accompany it. When Pen had finished the book, he asked Dave King to design "a little frontis piece. I'd printed them up on this rough grey paper and it had a militaristic, communistic feel about it. I thought it'd be nice to have a little insignia on it."

So Dave set to work on a design incorporating the subject matter of the book – family, state, church – all the power structures. As Rimbaud remembers, he started with the Greek symbol, The Star of Life, which features a snaked climbing a pole in the middle of a six pointed star and can be seen today on many British ambulances as a symbol of health. Having gone through a number of different designs, he came up with what would become known worldwide as the Crass symbol. A striking black and white mish-mash of ancient and modern symbols, it could mean most things to most people: try and you might see within it the Christian cross, the Union Jack, the Swastika and two snakes devouring each others' tails. It looks for all its worth like the sort of symbol you might find in an Egyptian pyramid or an ancient book of spells.

"We were one of the first outside the big boys like Ford, to use a corporate logo so effectively," notes Penny Rimbaud.

Dave King remembers: "He said he wanted something that would crystallize the title. It started out as a Christian Cross with a snake. But a medical symbol? I didn't think so much of that symbol ... all these symbols are in the air, they're archetypes..."

---

[1] Among the most notable was by Johannes Baader who was born in Germany in 1875. Baader was in Berlin by the age of 20, starting his own 'World Temple' religion, which incorporated the idea of a building which would unify all humanity. He published a treatise on Monoism called *14 Letters Of Christ* in 1914 and was certified insane in 1917. He used this new-found status to stage outrageous public performances, having been given a "hunting license" (to quote one of his colleagues) that meant no comeback on what he said or did. So it came to pass that Baader went into Berlin Cathedral and denounced Christ in no uncertain terms to all present. In 1917, Baader founded Christus GmbH – Christ Ltd (echoes of *Christ – The Album*) – which appealed to the pacifists during the Great War, offering them the identity of Christ, thereby exempting them from the call up.

King, unlike Rimbaud, remembers the first sketch as a cross with a snake zig-zagging across it. Between the two of them, it mutated and developed through several prototypes into the symbol that decorates the cover of this book, most of their records and many a punk rock jacket

Given the Christian cross on the Crass symbol, there have been suggestions that the snake represents the devil. But Dave King is ambiguous to the idea: "It was a reflection of Pen's anger at what he felt were these destructive aspects of Christianity. So in that sense the snake was just against . . . it wasn't really Adam & Eve's serpent, it was just something in counterpoint.

"There was a book at Dial House of Japanese family crests, and the majority of them were designed in a circle – it's something that represents the clan and that appears below the neck at the top of a kimono. So the serpent and the cross were conformed into a circle, it just seemed to come to form that way, there were two heads. The third thing that completed the design was the idea that it could be a stencil. The idea of a stencil had been something in the air for a while. It almost pre-dated the idea of a graffiti campaign. There was a guy called Robert Indiana (aka Robert Clark) who did these paintings: he used stencil lettering and a lot of his paintings were circular. He did this image of the word 'love' with the letters 'lo' above 've'; his work was an influence. Then there was a book that everyone was interested in called *Herbert Stencil*, he was called a quick change artist. So, for a while I was Herbert Stencil at art school. I've always been interested in trying to reduce something to its essentials. To make it as solid as possible – you can't really break it. It has an irreducible quality to it – the solidity helps create that sense of resonance. I had a pretty good idea it was a strong piece.

"Also, because the pamphlet that Penny was making was being mimeographed on an early Xerox, and he wanted to do a certain amount of copies. At that time, there was no money or access to printing, so it was like what's the simplest, easiest way – apart from potato cut! – to reproduce, and a stencil was perfect for that. The other thing was the Union Jack. I remember being in junior school and they taught us how to draw the Union Jack, which is notoriously difficult to draw because of the way the crosses of the three kingdoms overlap, there's an asymmetry to it. I wasn't consciously thinking of the swastika though. The biggest single influence was the Japanese family crests."

Steve Ignorant saw the symbol for the first time when it was suggested it would be taken up by Crass. "I thought it looked good – really smart. The only aspect I didn't like was that there was something about it that looked like a swastika." Steve recalls a more recent incident that illustrates the ambiguity of the symbol: "I was standing at the bar and I was wearing my green bomber jacket. I had a little enamel Crass symbol and a barn owl just on top of that. There was a black guy standing at the bar and he kept looking over ... of course, from a distance it looked like a German Gestapo symbol – you had this barn owl that looked a bit like an eagle and then the Crass symbol which looked a bit like a swastika – I soon took that off."

Little could Dave King have known that the sign he designed for a home-published pamphlet with a print run of 100 would still be all around today. It is worn as a tattoo by punks, layabouts and young soul rebels everywhere. "I still see the symbol today in California, on a jacket or a tattoo," says Dave. "I'm tempted to go up to them and say 'do you know that I designed that?' It'd be like, 'piss off granddad!' They wouldn't believe me anyway!"

721984

Thus far our tale has centred around Dial House, where a spirit of free thought was boosted by the optimism of the hippy times and the generally accepted alternative cultures. Many of the facets of the enigma that would become Crass were in place and ready to turn from the green hippy caterpillar into the fully-fledged black-winged punk.

Despite all this, Crass as we know them wouldn't have existed without punk. Whatever the merits and failings of Exit and Ceres Confusion, their "jealously guarded failure to communicate" was never going to have anything like the impact that Crass would have. This was because – much like the Pistols before them – Crass was only really effective once all the ingredients had been added to the mix.

By 1977 punk was everywhere, a veritable youthquake, and the Dial House social circles were inspired. One of the big influences on the band seems to have been some of the Dial House mob going to see The Clash at The Chancellor Hall in Chelmsford on May 29, 1977, the penultimate date of the White Riot tour.

Pete Wright remembers: "We came back from seeing The Clash really enthused. It was an all embracing thing with no prescription. The message was to go out and do it for yourself. It was a really powerful message. We got into it and the buzz became what you made of it. We drew on our experiences and used the existing machinery. That meant, however, that we became all the things we were complaining about. We weren't lead by music. We quoted Ghandi and didn't really appreciate it fully. We were exposed, individually, but protected as well. We all got mental scars from touring, pretty minor stuff compared to some people. We were charlatans. You have to take an educated look at what was happening."

Penny Rimbaud took something different away from the gig. And, surprisingly, not much from The Clash themselves: "There were very few punk bands I enjoyed listening to. I went to see The Clash and The Slits in Chelmsford. I thought The Clash were very exciting, but when I started looking at what they were doing, I couldn't continue my interest. It was another piece of pantomime. I thought they were taking the piss. I found The Slits more inspiring because The Clash were actually a very talented rock'n'roll band. But The Slits were bloody awful! I though, well if they can do it ... so we did."

Dave King: "We drove off down the country lanes to this gig. Penny, Phil, Pete and myself. I thought it was one of the most energetic gigs I'd ever seen. The hall was surrounded by gangs of Teds – Joe Strummer was saying 'go home in gangs' – there was this strange sense: how was one cultural element going to relate to a new version of itself? The answer was with violence. Another ridiculous fashion war, like the mods and the rockers. You have to fight a guy if his jacket is different."

Of course, this was a situation that would resonate at many Crass gigs over their career, with Teds replaced by skinheads as the icons of fear.

Despite the new excitement, Dave King was fed up; if not of life at Dial House, then of the singular nature of his existence there. "I was beginning to feel the isolation. I wanted a girlfriend!" he recalls. "I remember one very attractive woman riding by on a horse once – I chased after her and asked her out. She just looked from a great height and kept on riding. That was your dating opportunities right there!"

In August 1977, Dave King went to visit Gee Vaucher for a couple of weeks in New York and fell in love with the place. He ended up staying till December, then coming home for Christmas. "I packed a few things and moved back, in some ways never to look back." Dave King now lives in San Francisco, where he designs gardens. "The dream of being self-employed continues!"

As Dave exits stage left, Steve Ignorant returns to Dial House and, following the punk exaltations to 'do it yourself', Crass was born.

Steve Williams – or Steve Ignorant as he'll be known for the purposes of this story – had been visiting Dial House on and off for a few years, courtesy of his big brother Dave Williams (who played the glass game onstage at Ices '72 with Exit).

"He seemed very young," remembers Eve of Steve's early visits. He was indeed, as he recalls: "I was an ex-skinhead who went into the suedehead/glam rock thing. Then there was my brother who was always a rebel, but a more typical black sheep of the family type rebel – he was more of a hippie. And my sister, who was a greaser." Pete Sutton recalls: "Steve first showed up about '74. He was a kid into FS1E mopeds."

Steve Ignorant: "I'd always looked up to my brother, and he'd introduced me to Zen Buddhism – the Sound Of One Hand clapping and that kind of thing, It was all really interesting. And to poetry – Walt Whitman, in fact, which I started reading. Then he told me there was this house you could go to where you could go into any room except the private bedrooms. And if you wanted to cook a meal, you could cook a meal; if you wanted to talk, you could just talk; if you wanted to do a drawing you could do a drawing. So I was really intrigued. He said he was living there – in fact he wasn't, he was just bumming a bed for a couple of nights. So he took me to visit."

Steve's initial visit was a serious jolt of culture shock: "When I first went there, I thought they were all fucking nuts. They talked with sort of 16 plums in their mouths, using words I couldn't understand. They had stones inside the house and not in the garden, there was blokes doing flower arranging and all that sort of stuff! All long hair, didn't eat meat, and no telly. I thought, 'What the fucks happening here?!'

"I used to go back to my mates in Dagenham and try and explain it. Of course, I didn't stand a chance because I didn't know what was going on anyway. They'd say 'they sound like a bunch of wankers – what are they doing with fucking bricks in their living room? What are they doing? Why don't you take us over there then? Sod that!'

"But at Dial House, they talked to me as if I was an equal, as though I understood what was going on, and that really made an impression on me. And you were basically able to do whatever you wanted. I played truant a lot from school, and every weekend I'd be up there. Penny and Gee encouraged me to read poetry. At that time there was a wide range of people visiting. You'd have people like Phil – Wally Hope – and Mick

Duffield would show films he'd made. I'd never seen that sort of cinema before. Or he'd bring down an 8mm film by some obscure French director. And there were books I'd never seen or heard of before – so it was a real eye-opener."

In this respect – kids bunking off school and having a place to hang out to receive an alternative education of sorts – you could compare Dial House to Malcom McLaren's Sex emporium over on the other side of London. Both had spent the seventies entertaining lost youth and both would make an enormous cultural impact come punk.

During his visits, Steve Ignorant learnt more about Penny Rimbaud's concept behind the place: "Pens idea of Dial House was that he'd seen a movie called *The Inn Of The Sixth Happiness*, set in Japan, and they had these houses where you could travel from one to the next and if you were a poet you earned your bed for the night by reciting poetry or if you were a cook you cooked a meal. I think the original ideology was to have places like Dial House dotted all over England, Wales & Scotland."

It was a dream destined not to come true – not yet anyway. It's remarkably difficult to pinpoint why Dial House succeeds in avoiding the pitfalls so often succumbed to in shared houses and squats up and down the country – the secret of its survival where so many perished by the wayside remains just that, a secret, for the time being. Steve reflects: "Dial House is a one-off unique thing. Which is a shame. Other places you either don't have to wash up, so there's a sink full of dirty plates; or there's a rota."

Steve Ignorant was born in Stoke on Trent. His parents divorced when he was two, after which he went to live with his grandparents in Dagenham, where he would stay till he was 17. At the age of 17, Steve moved to Dial House for about two months but didn't stay.

At school, Steve was naturally drawn to a spiritual yearning for goodness and even Godliness. "I even started Christian Union meetings in break time at my secondary school," he remembers, noting the irony. Indeed, Steve had wanted to be a priest for a time at school, and was an enthusiastic scholar of the Bible in his meetings. "We'd get together and discuss aspects of the Bible. We were trying to work out the language –

the Kings James version is so difficult: when you go back to the Old Testament, what the hell is this on about? Trying to work it out. Remember, in those days, I didn't even know what an olive tree was – I'd never seen an olive. It wasn't until Pizza Hut opened up in Barking and I got these horrible things on my pizza! And 'pouring oil on their heads' – I thought it was Duckhams Q2, because we used lard in the frying pan."

During Steve's religious phase, a new version of the Bible was issued called *Good News For The Modern Man*, putting the stories into a modern context, which helped considerably with Steve's understanding. But it was a Religious Education teacher – and a Christian – that proved the catalyst in Steve's turning away from the faith. During a lesson, the teacher was explaining that Gautama Buddha was said to have lived for nine years on a grain of rice a day. The teacher vented his opinion that he found this very hard to believe, at which point Steve suggested that if he found that story far-fetched, then what about the story of Jesus Christ raising Lazarus from the dead. Instead of discussing the paradox, the teacher simply told Steve to shut up and sit down. "End of me being in the Christian Union," notes Steve, of the pivotal moment.

On leaving school, Steve, didn't know what he wanted to do. "At one point I was thinking of joining the Air Force," he remembers. "That was after I'd wanted to be a priest, of course. But that was way back. So when I went to Dial House and at that time, to make money, they were doing book covers for White Lion publishers and I thought, 'What a great way to live: they send you the title of the book ,you draw or paint it and they give you the money!' But you had to go to art school, and I needed money, and I was going through a hating my parents stage and I just wanted out. So when my mum and dad insisted I left school anyway, I wasn't that bothered. I thought I'd get a job which was at least something to do with artwork, so I got a job in a printers in Shepherds Market (near Piccadilly in London), paying £14 a week or something. I just couldn't survive on that. I was paying rent to my mum and dad and I'd taken up smoking to be flash, so there was no money left for clothes etc. So I left that and went to work in the supermarket. Suddenly I was earning the princely sum of £26 a week, which was fantastic! Plus I could get promotion when I was 30," he adds, wryly.

After a year (1975/76) back in Dagenham working in the supermarket, Steve went to Bristol for the next eight months ... "to try my luck again. I worked in a hospital down there, and that's where I saw an advert for The Clash at the Colston Hall. I'd heard about punk rock – I'd seen the Janet Street Porter interview with The Sex Pistols. So I went along to see what it was about and I was knocked off my feet."

Steve was also heavily impressed by the Pistols, particularly John Lydon ... "just the laryness of the guy! I thought 'I want some of that'. And he looked great, he just looked mad! I remember asking my – *radical hippy* – brother, who I lived with at the time, what he'd do if I came home looking like that, and he said he'd throw me out and tell me to have a bath! So that was reason number one.

"Reason number two: I'm working in the hospital and this girl turns up, wearing men's trousers with plastic sandals ... 'Fancy meeting up later?' 'Yeah, don't mind if I do!' – aha! Reason number two!"

Steve smiles and lets out a nostalgic sigh: "So the Sex Pistols for the look. But for the sound, and just to blow me away, it's gotta be the Clash. They were just fantastic. I was 18/19 and all of a sudden I felt old. I was still wearing my flares with little turn ups and Salatio shoes. I still had, not a mullet, but a Rod Stewart/David Bowie hairdo – I changed that as quickly as possible!

"The only threatening bands around before punk was David Bowie (but that's threatening in a different way), Slade (but they weren't braces and Doctor Martens anymore) ... you had to go back to Steppenwolf or something like that."

"I remember getting a lump in my throat at the Clash gig, thinking, 'This is it – this is my time now – I've GOT to be a part of it.' And Paul Simenon ... I will say it ... as a bloke, I just found him so sexy ... not that I wanted to fuck him or anything! I just looked at him and thought 'I want to be like him'.

"At the end of the gig, there were a couple of people shouting insults at the band and Joe Strummer told them that if they could do better to get their own band together. It was like a battle cry. I came away from that gig vowing I was going to start a band. I didn't know how I was going to do it, but *I wanted in*. That got me back to London."

So Steve returned from Bristol to London with the idea of starting a band, and ended up back at Dial House. "I wanted to start a punk band, but I didn't have a clue who was going to be in it. I knew my old mates from Dagenham wouldn't be interested. So I went to see Pen, who was living on his own at Dial House at this point. He'd got into punk rock, but more the Patti Smith, Television side of things, and he was writing *Christ's Reality Asylum*. He asked what I was doing, I said 'I'm thinking of starting a band', he said 'I'll be your drummer' and literally it was like that. He asked me to stick around – I think it was so I could feed the goats while he was round Eve Libertine's place. So out came the pinking shears, off went the hair, rips in the clothes, safety pins, old school tie, a pair of plastic sandals from Epping Market, brilliant!

"I didn't look like a punk because at that time I was working in the hospital, and I was enjoying that; putting plaster of Paris on peoples' arms & legs and I was thinking it could be quite a good career to take on. I was thinking maybe I could be an ambulance driver or something. But then I saw The Clash and it blew it out of the window. They brought back all the excitement of being on the terraces – just being different. Being different from being David Bowie and wearing a bit of make-up, which was sort of acceptable now. I'd actually been beaten up by a couple of blokes with Ziggy Stardust make-up on down West Ham once. . ."

The return of the prodigal Ignorant and the absence of Gee, over in NYC, coincided with the short dope-growing phase at Dial House. "Phew! Some fucking stuff that was!" reminisces Steve. "There were lots of contacts – there was Mick Duffield, who was living at Charing Cross Rd at that time." Mick said he'd film Crass and show his films at the same time. "People could come over and stay the night, and we could make as much noise as we wanted to – have wild parties and nobody would be bothered by it."

So, the germ of Crass started as a two-piece, with Steve shouting and ranting whilst Penny Rimbaud played along on drums. The end result, while undeniably amateur and more than rough around the edges, sounds uncannily like a precursor of the rap music that would grow on the other side of the pond a decade later. They weren't called Crass though. . .

Eve Libertine: "What was it they were called? Stormtrooper. Yeah, that was pretty grim! I didn't think it was going to go far!. . .I think there was an element of seriousness in it (at the start). I think Steve was working in a job he didn't like. There was an element where it was time for something different."

Steve was relieved that Penny Rimbaud's suggestion for the band name was never taken up: "At least we weren't called Les Enfants Terrible! Imagine that!" he laughs, "playing to a load of blokes in Barnsley – we're 'Les Enfants Terrible'! All wearing berets and stripey tops! Organic garlic!"

As with so many similar alternative social situations, Crass had a ready-made network of contacts simply through the house and those who were aware of the place. In the spirit of the times, no definite lines were drawn and as people drifted in and out of Dial House, news of a new punk band starting there travelled hastily down the underground grapevine, attracting band members through the wind. The grapevine was fuelled by the fact that bands were using the Dial House music room as rehearsal space, so a network of musicians had been established as well.

Steve takes up the story: "Originally it was just going to be me & Pen. Then a guy called Martin Lee turned up who was a friend of someone, he was a long-haired hippie living in a squat in Huntley Street in Central London. We said we'd got a band together and he told us he had a free festival coming up if we wanted a gig, in a courtyard behind their squat.

"We had about six weeks till this gig. The next week, Steve Herman arrived. He was something to do with Wally Hope, and he'd come out to see Pen. He was a funny balding little guy with a beard, nothing like a punk rocker. But it turned out he could play guitar..." Steve Herman was aboard.

Penny Rimbaud recalls that he first met Steve Herman at Wally Hope's inquest, where Herman appeared as a witness. "His organisational skills were excellent," Rimbaud recalls in *Shibboleth*, "and certainly made up for our complete lack of them."

Hailing from the west country near Bath, Andy Palmer had met Joy De Vivre when they were both students at Colchester Arts School, where they began a relationship. Joy already knew Dial House courtesy of a brief relationship with Dave Williams (Steve's elder brother), and brought Andy along.

Steve Ignorant: "He heard about the band, decided he wanted to join so he went off and borrowed a guitar. I was sitting in Dial House one day, just after Steve Herman and Pete Wright had joined, when Andy turned up. I thought he was a complete tosser when I met him cos he said 'hello squire, how are you?' in a posh voice. Fucking 'squire' you knob! But then I actually liked him after that."

Having Andy Palmer on the scene opened up another new world for Steve: "When Andy first joined, me and him used to knock around together – he had a car at the time and he was living in a flat in Holland Park. He was at Chelsea School of Art – I was always knocking round with him cos he had access to drugs and things. I was meeting people like Simon Stockton (who would later perform occasionally at Crass gigs, doing his own enigmatic brand of poetry) and other artists. The first time Andy took me into Chelsea School of Art, there was an exhibition on. There was a woman standing there and she walked over to me and asked if I was a punk rocker..." Steve recalls some extremely brief foreplay before a quick knee-trembler in the corridor. "I just thought 'this is brilliant!'" Steve recounts with glee.

Penny Rimbaud: "Andy Palmer had a small background in the existing alternative culture, being vaguely involved with *International Times* and Heathcote Williams, and pilfering his guitar from the *IT* offices."

Which just left a vacancy for a bassist: enter Pete Wright.

Steve Ignorant: "Pete Wright would come to Dial House every weekend to rehearse with a folk band he was in. One day he was sitting there saying he couldn't do it much longer. I said, 'You ought to join our band' and he said, 'I think I will'. So by the time of the gig we were a five-piece. We got switched off after the third song by some irate neighbour."

In 1982, Andy Palmer told Radio Tees: "Initially we started out because the energy was 'go out and do it yourself – anybody can do it'. I felt that a lot of the early bands became like preaching – Jimmy Sham, for example, saw himself as a reincarnation of a political leader. We *have* got something to say but that is for people to think about what they're doing – is the life that they lead actually what they want? And to prove through what we're doing that if you don't want to live your life the way you're told that you should lead it, you can live it in a different way which will possibly be a lot more fulfilling. Specific things come into that – our interest in the peace movement, our interest in the feminist movement."

Eve Libertine can lay a justified claim to being the band's first fan, even back in the days of gross musical incompetence: "I thought it was great. I always really really liked the first Crass stuff – I thought it was amazing. There was an energy that somehow tapped into me, that I found inspiring. It came across as anger, but it felt like justifiable anger, which I found inspiring."

Pete Wright remembers: "It was always functional. There was always a theory that we were dangerous and we were constantly being closed down. We'd play with a disco outfit who were always trying to drown us out with reggae, so we took over the PA to convince them that they might want to put us back on. After that it became more of a celebration. We were pushing back that which had been pushed away by the media."

The Huntly Street gig was a success of a kind, with the band playing a few numbers before somebody pulled the plug, much like the first Sex Pistols gig a short while earlier just up the road at St Martins College Of Art. "I didn't have any songs written," says Steve. "The first songs I wrote were dreadful. There was one called 'I Can't Stand It', and 'Song for Tony Blackburn' and 'Demolition'." Two of these songs would end up on the 'live' disc of *Christ – The Album*, but 'Demolition' would appear to be lost forever.

Contrary to popular belief, Steve wasn't directly inspired by reading Rimbauds *Christ's Reality Asylum* epic, though it wasn't for the want of trying: "I did read a bit of *Christ's Reality Asylum* but I didn't understand a fucking word of it. And the way it was written, with all the obliques ... like when people kept telling me to read *On The Road* by Jack Kerouac ... where's the fucking punctuation? I was out of breath reading it. It was the same with *Christ's Reality Asylum* – it actually put me off reading it."

Then came the first of the songs that Steve is remembered for to this day:

"'Owe Us A Living' came about when I went to the shops in North

Weald and on the way back I was carrying two bags of shopping and I was marching – 1-2-3-4 – fuck the politically minded / here's something I want to say. . . .' By the time I got to the top of the hill, I'd got the first verse, so I rushed in and wrote it down. That's was about the fourth or fifth song that I'd written."

'Do they owe us a living?', with the question being answered at the end of each chorus '. . . of course they fucking do!' was a rallying cry for those whose disillusionment led them towards an interest in crossing accepted lines. Steve had taken the phrase from a poem by earlier Dial House resident Richard Le Beau ("Dicky Beau I used to call him," grins Steve) called 'The Window'.

"He was living at Dial House when I first arrived there," says Steve. "He'd written this small booklet – it was all a bit of a dark, semi-depressive type poem, hinted at suicide and all this business."

Crucially for our story, however, it also contained the lines: 'Do they owe the chicken whose neck they chopped for dinner a living? Do they owe me a living? Of course they do.

"So I just took that and put the 'fucking' in," smiles Steve. "'So What' came around because I'd heard 'Light My Fire' by The Doors. And I had this line 'they ask me why I'm hateful, why I'm bad'."[1]

Courtesy of the organisational skills of Steve Herman, the first line-up of Crass managed to get into the studio to record their first demo in a basement studio near Rathbone Place, off Oxford Street in London's West End. They recorded 'Do They Owe Us A Living?', 'Major General Despair' and 'Angela Rippon' and, according to Rimbaud, "partly through lack of experience, partly through sheer irresponsibility, we managed to wreck the studio.

"It was Andy more than anyone – he just lost it. He started falling about . . . I don't think he was pissed but he might have been a bit stoned. I think he just got cross. I got into quite a bit of conflict, particularly with Andy and slightly with Steve, because I thought they

---

[1] Which Steve crammed into the melody for the 'Light My Fire' line 'You know that it would be untrue'.

were behaving aggressively. They were using a punk front to frighten people and I really didn't like it. I remember Andy frightening some old lady at a bus stop and I was very upset – that old lady could have been your mum or my mum, and didn't deserve being upset even if she was a 'bourgeois bastard.'"

As time went on, so did Steve Herman, who got his marching orders from the band. The demo, some of which made it onto the second disc of *Christ – The Album*, indicates that Steve Herman was wanting to push the band into a more melodic, bouncy sound, which contributed to his fall. Having a beard could hardly have helped the cause either.

"It was a bit like the Pete Best thing," says Steve Ignorant. "The more gigs we were doing, the more confident we got. And it was Steve Herman's style of playing – a bit like Burt Weedon meets The Sex Pistols – he was a nice bloke but he didn't look right and didn't fit in. Phil was hanging round anyway and Phil looked like he fitted, plus he could play guitar."

Crass told Steve Herman he was out. Shortly afterwards, he turned up to a Crass gig at Actionspace and started hurling abuse. "So I tried to clump him," says Steve. "His missus pulled me off him. Then he wouldn't return a guitar he'd borrowed. Just playground stuff really, with hindsight."

Steve was replaced in the band by long-term Dial House acquaintance Phil Free, the brother of ex-Exit man Jim Clancey. "I only met him once," says Phil Free of Steve Herman. "He came to a gig, wearing a rainbow t-shirt, with long frizzy hair and a beard. Not a clever ploy!"

Compared to the rest of the band – Pete Wright excepted – Phil was an accomplished muso, having befriended *The Beatles Compleat*, the bible for all aspiring guitarists of the time, and even had previous gig experience, albeit only on the school stage. "My old man made me a ukelele out of a cigar box," Phil remembers with more than a little affection and pride. It's an affection and pride shared in the talents of "extraordinarily gifted" Pete Wright's basslines: "All I ever did was follow the bassline, which is an unusual take for most bands. And his basslines were somewhere else."

Phil Free: "How I got to know Pen was that my brother was at public school with him – the public school my father had gone to, which is a very second rate public school (Brentwood). He got a scholarship and got in. I didn't, so I went to a technical school."

From here, Phil took the usual sixties route to art college – "I wandered in really late because I'd failed all my A-levels" – and he had also been part of the Hornsey Art College Sit-In, where he shared a platform with an interesting array of people. The leaders of the sit-in included future MP Kim Howells and future performance artist Stuart Brisley, whose challenging work would often include faeces. The protest essentially revolved around a restructuring of entry requirements, as Phil Free remembers: "They tried to give it a validity, a status, in terms of a degree course. You had to have qualifications to get in, you had to write a thesis – before, you just showed them your portfolio."

Like many people of the time, Phil was getting by doing odd jobs. One of these happened to be with Penny Rimbaud, when they were both making some money as painters, decorating a house together. It was hardly the kind of audition that most successful bands employ. "While we're decorating, Pen said, 'You play guitar don't you, do you want to be in the band?' Curiously, my brother was moving house and clearing out some stuff and threw out an old electric guitar. I'd never had anything like the money for an electric guitar, but suddenly I'd got this guitar and the notional concept of a band. So I went over to a rehearsal at Dial House after the house was painted, to see if it would work. I was absolutely petrified, because it was playing in public and I hadn't done that since school. I smoked a joint, so I had absolutely no idea what was happening."

"I remember Pete asking me why I wanted to be in this band and I said it seems like it's the only thing you can do," says Phil Free. "Either you start throwing bombs or you make a statement – you *must* make a statement. I suppose I'd been out of it bringing up the kids for some years and I suppose it's something one could do that wouldn't get you into trouble. A chance to scream abuse at somebody. But I was very stoned at the time! And I think they must have been drunk or stoned as well because they didn't register the fact that I was playing a different song to them!"

Anyone who's ever been in a band will also appreciate two other attributes that Phil brought to the equation, which never hurt anybody's chances of getting the job. "I was on social security at the time so I had all the time in the world. And I had a van!"

In London, punk rock had its very own club in the shape of the Roxy at 41–43 Neal Street, Covent Garden. It had originally been a gay/trans-vestite club called Chaguaramas, a sometime hangout of the Bromley Contingent and other early punks. Then, towards the end of 1976, the place went into receivership and the owner, René Albert, let it out to Andy Czezowski, who reinvented the place as a punk club and gave birth to a legend.

Andy Czezowski remembers the early energy that centred on the club was way more than the fashion scene that had given birth to the early punks. Speaking to 3ammagazine.com, in reply to the suggestion that the place was populated by the initially naïve concept of 'weekend punks', he said, "The Roxy wasn't about that, you had people there in office gear after work, shop girls, that kind of thing. There was no snob-bery involved, or at least there shouldn't have been. They were all just punters at the end of the day, there to see bands."

Which could be seen as both great and tragic at the same time. The lack of snobbery brought about by the 'anyone can do it' propaganda lib-erated many a mind (despite its obvious untruth – clearly not anybody could do it). But 'they were all just punters' sticks in the punk rock throat a bit.

Czezowski gave up on the place after 100 nights, explaining to 3ammagazine.com: "Basically what happened was the Roxy became a victim of its own success. The two old queens that owned it saw it making money for the first time in ages and cashed in by selling it. So they sold it and the first I knew was when the new owners, some dodgy East End villain types, told me to get out. They booked bands like the Boomtown Rats and the place collapsed. They didn't have a clue or any love for the music, they were just trying to buy into something they saw as successful. So no, I wasn't involved, they just got someone to put it together as a cynical cash-in kind of thing."

Despite the cynical nature of the Roxy management in its second phase, it remained a top punk hangout, and one of *the* places to play to get yourself noticed.

Steve Ignorant remembers the Roxy as "a seedy little shithole that just fitted that whole scene perfect. A real dump – it fucking stank in there, the sound was awful. You went downstairs and there was a little square room and a tiny little bar, a tiny little stage and a DJ booth."

In contrast, Penny Rimbaud remembers the Roxy with fond affection: "I used to go down the Roxy a lot as well, because I really liked the atmosphere. I liked the live vibe of it, but as to the idea of listening to that on a record... I remember the first time I went to the Roxy, with Eve. We were both pissed put of our brains and she was running along the street with a rose hanging out of her mouth which she'd picked up off the street. I was 33 or 34 then. I remember the youthfulness and the charm and the gorgeousness of it. Rushing down into the Roxy and getting more pissed. There was a band called The Bears on. They were absolutely awful, but it didn't matter. Then we went home and fucked like hyenas. It was all wild."

Eve Libertine, too, remembers the Roxy with affection, including a gig by The Nipple Erectors, fronted by future Pogue and lovable rogue Shane McGowan: "The audiences always seemed very young and male. It reminded me of lion cubs, all this young male energy. Not many women. But once I realised what was happening, I was incredibly fired by the enthusiasm and the energy – the energy was amazing. Pogoing and the actual warmth of people – it was so unlike what it looked like it was. There was an incredible communication and comradeship. I thought it was so passionate about stuff that mattered. I really loved it. The Roxy was like nothing I'd ever encountered – all these people really packed in and pogoing – the feeling of togetherness I'd never really experienced."

Crass themselves played the Roxy twice, with wildly different results. Steve recalls: "The first one was alright. I remember I went up to a girl and said, 'Can I sleep with you tonight?' and she said yes. I thought I'd try it, you know, punk rock an' all that. I went back to Deptford, where she lived, in Speedwell Street, and met a bunch of people there from Goldsmiths (Art College, New Cross). One bloke called Charlie was in a band called This Heat."

Then the band secured a gig at Covent Garden – not the throbbing metropolis that it is now, but then a derelict ex-market space about to be pulled down. Somehow they got on the bill, but Penny couldn't do it, so Charlie from This Heat stood in on drums. The whole set was videoed – by someone, somewhere. Next up was Chelsea Art College courtesy of Andy Palmer, who was studying there. It was, in Steve's words "a really fucking violent night – the students really didn't like a load of punk rockers coming in. Odd, horrible."

"I was the only person left in the audience," remembers Eve Libertine, "pogoing up and down on my own. Virtually everyone had gone! But I thought they were brilliant. I can only say that it touched something in me very strongly... I don't attach to things very much, I tend to go through life in my own sort of space. But I was very touched by what they were doing. I can only think it was because there was something very genuine there."

The members of Crass saw gigs as a time for drunken celebration as much as anything else, a party which swiftly subsided the second time they played the Roxy Club. With their set being even more chaotic than usual – due in no small part to Penny, Andy and Steve having imbibed various substances – the band were turned off half way through their set. They responded by refusing to leave the stage. Their threatening behaviour resulted in the sound being turned back on, after which by all accounts the evening turned into a glorious celebration of independence from band and audience alike.

At least that's how Penny Rimbaud remembers it. He wrote famously and beautifully about the gig and his reaction to it in the first edition of the Gee Vaucher/Crass newpaper *International Anthem* ('A Nihilist Newspaper For The Living'). The article – unpleasantly, nay nastily, subtitled 'articulating he falls on the skinned dog' – was one of Rimbaud's most heartfelt and powerful pieces of writing, somehow managing to use the gig as an analogy for the ills of the world, and the band's reaction as a noble stance. As a piece of anarchist invective, it has rarely been surpassed.

Back Britain? Fuck Britain.
Too many times have the working population of Britain been asked to make an effort on behalf of their country. Their country? What is that country of theirs? Effectively it is the sum total of years of ineffective government, a cock up, a hypocritical, complacent and dangerous lie. Government kills; right?

Union Crass logo. *(Dial House Collection)*

Wally Hope at the first Stonehenge festival in 1974. *(Basil Brooks)*

A flyer for the first Stonehenge festival. *(Dial House Collection)*

The first Crass gig, Huntley Street, 1977; above, left to right: Andy Palmer, Penny Rimbaud, Steve Ignorant and Steve Herman; below: Penny Rimbaud and Steve Ignorant. *(Mick Duffield)*

Live at the Dublin Castle pub in Camden, 1977; left to right, Pete Wright,
Steve Ignorant, Andy Palmer and Phil Free. *(Dial House Collection)*

On stage at Actionspace, 1978; left to right: Steve Ignorant,
Andy Palmer and Pete Wright. *(Dial House Collection)*

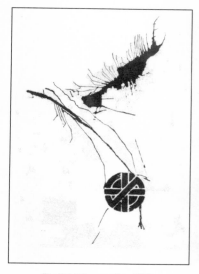

The *Eklektik* magazine, 1978.
(Dial House Collection)

The Crass live, 1978. *(Mick Duffield)*

**Soundchecking, 1978: left to right: Andy Palmer, Steve Ignorant, Pete Wright,
Joy De Vivre, Penny Rimbaud and Eve Libertine.** *(Dial House Collection)*

Crass live in 1978; left to right: Penny Rimbaud, Phil Free, Pete Wright and Steve Ignorant. *(Dial House Collection)*

Steve Ignorant and Andy Palmer, on the road, 1979. *(Dial House Collection)*

Crass graffiti at Bond Street tube station, 1979. *(Dial House Collection)*

'How a teen mag's bullshit detector let them down': **NME** relays the story of Crass' infamous hoax on *Loving* magazine. Rimbaud explained their intent was 'to expose all this absolute shit they're shovelling out. I mean, they actually put out *Our Wedding*, which is totally over the top. I don't see how anyone could have taken it seriously. We were amazed when they agreed to put it out.' *(NME)*

Steve Ignorant, live, 1980. *(Dial House Collection)*

Ireland. Right?
Vietnam. Right?
Democracy is a lie. Two party totalitarianism. The realities stay the same. Democracy is a many headed feudal warlord, his horse is the head of the prick that blocks my throat. A gag.
Tomorrow we eat better; today we always wait. The begging bowl is a crucifix. Who ate my dinner? Who's hanging where?
It doesn't matter, we're fighting. It doesn't matter. Who the fuck cares if they can't hear us? They can see us can't they? Can't they? It doesn't matter a shit if the sounds aren't right because right now we're in a battlefield and that's never too tasteful. I start screaming and screaming, searching out faces in the audience that might understand what it is we are trying to do. This is our fucking music, our fucking time and no grease arse manager is going to start cutting it about.
At last, the man on the street is finding a voice...

Steve Ignorant remembers the gig with a little less romance: "At this time we were into drinking – J&B was the chosen tipple. Then there was the famous Roxy gig: looking back on it, it wasn't really worse than any of the others. Maybe if we'd have had some proper set lists or if we'd done a bit more rehearsing, it wouldn't have been a problem. But of course, Pen wrote about it...

"We were switched off cos we were shit – big fucking deal. We had quite a few songs by then – 'End Result', 'Reject Of Society', 'General Bacardi'. That was the point where we decided right no going onstage pissed – if we're going to be serious about it, let's be serious, cos of the stuff we were writing. Pen wrote 'Punk Is Dead' about that night ... everybody in the place that night was really pissed. I remember the floor being beer-soaked and getting thrown around it a lot. Nobody could stand up straight."

Phil Free: "The Roxy was absolutely terrifying, Christ knows what we playing! I was just trying to get through the two or three chords that each song required. We didn't rehearse a great deal, but it was simple stuff so it didn't require huge rehearsals. I can remember going from a job I was doing somewhere – driving over and getting changed from my carpeting clothes into my punk clothes..."

"It was incredibly loose – I remember dressing in a white shirt with the tails hanging out: it felt so dangerous, because nobody wore a shirt not tucked in. It was quite extraordinary – it felt very scary to me."

"After that night," Steve remembers, "Penny ended up sleeping underneath a bench on Tottenham Court Road station. He was found by the station staff, and all he could remember was Mick Duffield, who lived in Cambridge Circus. Mick got him a taxi home to Dial House from central London.

"Then we did the Acklam Hall, Actionspace a couple of times, but nothing really moving until Small Wonder took us on – that's when the exposure started."

Over the winter of '77/'78, Crass played regularly with the UK Subs at the White Lion pub in Putney and Actionspace in Central London. The two bands had met when they played a Rock Against Racism gig together – the only gig Crass would play for the movement as they were offended by an offer of payment from the organisers.

Nicky Garratt, guitarist with the UK Subs, wrote in his book *UK Subs, The Early Years*: "At the White Lion show, Crass had an argument with Charlie over a Subs song 'All I Wanna Know (Is Does She Suck)' during the set, claiming it was sexist. Some members of Crass pulled Charlie from the stage. But later, after going through the lyrics with them and explaining the context in which the song was written, things were resolved and we decided to do a double headline show way out in a residential area of Northeast London. We advertised it in the music press, yet for some reason still unknown to me, only two people showed up. We watched Crass and Crass watched us. Both bands turned in great sets and it was, for me, one of the best shows from that period. That is until we split the £1 taken at the door."

Steve Ignorant opines that the 'Does She Suck' incident was "jokey, laughy – nobody could get the arsehole about the UK Subs ... it was one of those things that happened that has turned into a bit of a myth."

UK Subs vocalist Charlie Harper concurs: "The Crass girls pulled me offstage and beat me up! I was just laughing the whole way through ... these girls trying to beat me up." Charlie retains an obvious affection for Crass: "You just get a band you fall in love with, and they were one of those bands. By then The Clash were almost like pop stars. Every other band was like *pretending* to be a punk band. Then they came along with their big anarchy stance, and their uniform – it was absolutely brilliant, we just loved 'em. The musicians do everything really simple, the guitarist who played with his thumb, a great front man – they seemed a little more . . . educated than most."

Steve Ignorant remembers the UK Subs gigs – and the Subs themselves – with fondness: "It turned into quite a healthy little gig that did. I loved it – excellent. Charlie played the harmonica at that time. He was so un-punk looking – a hair dresser! Brilliant band and a great bunch of people – just getting pissed and taking the piss out of each other, it was a good cosy little thing."

As a cute counterpoint to dingy pubs in Putney, and much to Steve Ignorant's delight, Gee set Crass up with four gigs in New York. The big time – the big apple.

It was the first time Steve had ever left the UK. "I hadn't even been to the Isle Of Wight before! I thought it was fantastic – I just went loopy. You could get amyl nitrate on the street corner, smoke grass in peoples' houses! There were these places called transvestite bars, where women were actually men but looked like women! The beer was cheap, the food was great, no-one thought you were weird if you were vegetarian. And I found it less threatening than Tottenham or Dagenham on a Saturday night at chucking out time."

Gee: "I avoided booking the obvious. I said I'm not going to book CBGBs or Max's (Kansas City). I booked the Puerto Rican Club and the Polish Club. We did the Puerto Rican Club with James Chance & The Contortions. One of the people concerned with the Contortions lived in the same building as me, so I knew all that lot."

Steve Ignorant: "James Chance had been demanding all night – a typical American shithead who's idea of punk rock was to wear a suit with a little square patch cut out of the knee. His thing was to rush into the audience, grab people and wrestle them to the floor. He did it a bit too close to Andy . . . what do you expect him to do? The boot went in . . . so that gig got stopped"

Gee Vaucher: "I thought they were great – I knew it'd be great because Pen doesn't concern himself with anything that's not!"

The first time they came across racism was one of the New York gigs, where they were playing with a reggae band. "You had to get in a lift to access the stage upstairs, but the man running the lifts made the reggae band walk up, refused to let them in, at which point we just said, 'Fuck you, they're coming in the lift with us.'"

Of the gigs, Eve remembers that "the audiences were more arty than England. It was more of an 'art' thing. Being there didn't feel the same as it did here, there was a warmth here … in my vague memory I'd say it was cold there and it was *warm* here."

On a more literal level, the weather was scorching, and dressing all in black didn't help. Eve: "It was bloody hot, we were all sweltering!"

Gee Vaucher: "I remember us all walking down the Avenue of the Americas and we were all wearing black. A police car drew up alongside and said, 'What army are you?' 'We're the English army!' we told them."

Artist Anthony Maccall remembers seeing Crass "in Manhattan – in SoHo somewhere, I think. I was bowled over by the velocity of the music and the no-kidding seriousness of their stage persona. They lined up across the front of the stage, in black uniforms with Crass armbands and the Crass logo banner behind them and you were hit by this angry, sonic blitzkrieg which continued for the duration of the performance without a break. I'd seen punk bands in New York at CBGBs, The Mudd Club and Tier 3, but their visual persona and music was utterly unique."

Pete Wright: "We realised, even at the time, that our presence in Manhattan was pretty much irrelevant."

After the mini tour, Gee decided to come back to the London to work with the band. "My time was up – I was getting very political and I was asked to alter something: I was asked to do something on President Carter's brother, who was a complete wanker. So I did something that was a bit tongue-in-cheek and they asked me to take a bit out. So I did," Gee adds, incredulous at her own behaviour, "and I felt so bad about it, I though 'never again', next time they ask me, I'm not going to do it.

"And it did happen. There was a really horrible attack on gays in Central Park by these 15-year old Catholic middle-class kids. They went in with baseball bats, cracking skulls. I was asked to illustrate that, so I did this collage, which wasn't about cracked skulls, it was the ambience and the peace in Central Park, with two guys kissing. The editor of New York magazine at the time, who was actually a closet gay, went ballistic.

"I thought, mmmm, ok, time to work with my mates again. I'd proved my point in New York – I'd found a lot out about myself that I didn't know I had, and I'd come back a very different person. I was a lot more confident with people."

Phil Free remembers the New York gigs as a landmark in terms of the band getting serious: "You come back and you think we played New York and we didn't take it by storm. We'd approached The Ramones' manager to see if they wanted to play with us, but they fought shy of the opportunity! Thank Christ we didn't when you hear the, er, terrible goings-on. When we came back, it was either we've done the pinnacle or we're going to be a band."

NIGHT OF THE LONG KNIVES

"Read no more odes my son, read timetables:
they're to the point. And roll the sea charts out
before it's too late. Be watchful, do not sing,
for once again the day is clearly coming
when they will brand refusers on the chest
and nail up lists of names on people's doors.
Learn how to go unknown, learn more than me:
To change your face, your documents, your country.
Become adept at every petty treason,
The sly escape each day and any season.
For lighting fires encyclicals are good:
And the defenceless can always put to use,
As butter wrappers, party manifestos,
Anger and persistence will be required
To blow into the lungs of power the dust
Choking, insidious, ground out by those who,
Storing experience, stay scrupulous: by you."
– Hans Magnus Enzenburger

"Art is not a mirror to reflect reality, but a hammer with which to shape it."
– Bertolt Brecht

One of the great spaces the punk explosion left in its wake was the ability to reinvent yourself. As John Lydon became Johnny Rotten, and John Beverley became Sid Vicious, so a million punks across the globe destroyed their past in order to create their future. Steve Williams became Steve Ignorant and Phil Clancey became Phil Free. All bets were off – for a brief moment, you were free.

After months of drinking and having fun, Penny Rimbaud perceptively spotted the moment was there for the seizing. It was reinvention time – the fun was over and the work had begun.

As has now been written into Crass folklore, Penny Rimbaud gave the rest of the band an ultimatum: either they stopped messing about and get serious or he wasn't interested anymore. The band famously responded by kicking him out of the band, albeit only for one night.

Rimbaud: "People were beginning to take us seriously. Initially, we used to literally empty places. We completely emptied Chelsea Art School – there were a lot of people at that one ... to a person, the place emptied. Then suddenly it seemed to change and there were people listening. It seemed that for our own health, we either started to take it seriously or we just didn't bother to do it. So I set an ultimatum, and basically I was expelled because the ultimatum wasn't acceptable."

Penny is of the opinion that he only set the ultimatum because he knew any expulsion wouldn't last. "It was obvious we could make something of it. We had got a tool and it could be used. But were we going to be serious about it? I've got better things to do than just fuck about. I'd have lost interest if it had been as it was for the first few months – a bunch of lads just doing our songs and coming home. It would have had a limited time span.

"Basically I said I'm bored with this – either we're going to get this together or I'm not going to have anything to do with it. That's when the Splinter was formed, and I left the band for 24 hours. To my mind, it wasn't that it wasn't going anywhere, it was going where all rock'n'roll goes, straight up its own arse. I thought we've got find something which makes this artistically and creatively worthwhile. Then it doesn't matter whether you sell records or not – the satisfaction of it is judged in creative terms, not financial terms. And that's how throughout, we were able to judge the value of what we did."

Eve Libertine, though not yet a part of the band, remembers concurring with Penny's view. "If you're going to do it, do it properly," she said. "So, yes, I was a part of that." Together with Joy and Gee, she set up a band too – going by the name of Splinter.

"They outdid the Slits at being appalling," says Penny Rimbaud, looking as though he's been drinking vinegar without the Taoist disclaimer.

Eve Libertine: "It was just a bit of, 'Let's try and see what we can come up with'. There was Joy on drums, Gee on bass and I was on guitar and probably singing. None of us could play. We did a track called 'Savage Tribe', sort of a bit of a chant, pretty basic! I think we had one rehearsal. We had a short life!"

Joy De Vivre: "I have a funny feeling about that day because I think it was Pen's way of trying to deal with having women in the band, and what we were going to do, whether we ought to be doing something on our own. Vi from Poison Girls said that the women should be doing something on their own too – though why she said that when she was working with a bunch of men, I don't know. It was just a few hours of toying around with having our own splinter group."

Steve Ignorant doesn't remember Splinter at all, but evidently feels he got off lightly: "What a crap band that would have been – fucking hell! How could that last more than 15 minutes? Those three in the same room? Jesus!"

Back in Crassland, Steve recalls the mood of the time: "Pete had started to write songs, and I'd started to write more songs, like 'So What'. It was obviously getting a bit more serious. It wasn't like Pen said 'either we do this or I leave'. It was like we had to come to a decision – either we believe in what we're doing or we're just taking the piss. Which Pen didn't want to be a part of – 'That's fine but find another drummer'. First it was, 'Don't smoke (dope) before we go onstage, just drink', then, 'Actually, perhaps we should cut down on drink as well.' Because all of us were just getting really out of it. Well, everybody except Pete."

Eve Libertine: "Around the same time, Penny wrote 'Punk Is Dead' about the night at the Roxy. I remember him saying we've got to sort ourselves out, and I remember thinking he was right. Andy Palmer really took exception to 'Punk Is Dead'."

Phil Free: "I don't remember people sitting around the table one day and saying we're going to get serious. But you begin to think, well, I don't want to turn up completely legless next week." He recalls a gradual tightening up of the Crass act, starting at the most basic of basics, from buying a job lot of strings so the guitar had a full set, then moving up through being in tune and "all starting at the same time even if we didn't finish together".

Part of the new improved Crass came about as the women took a more active role in affairs. Eve had also started a relationship with Penny Rimbaud, and though she didn't make it into the *Reality Asylum* pamphlet, she did make it into the band.

Steve Ignorant wasn't completely sold initially on the idea of women joining them: "I wasn't sure that I like it at first, cos I could see the laddy, Clashy, Sex Pistoly thing slipping away. But at that time it was a new thing and no-one else was doing it and I thought, 'No actually, this feels good, this feels right', and I don't want all that stuff anyway.

"At first it was really difficult for me to just stand there while they were doing their bits with the audience just wanting 'Owe Us A Living' and shouting 'get your tits out'. I'd just be cringing, hoping they didn't think we were wankers. What really changed it was when we brought out *Penis Envy*. Because musically that was the most listenable, and Eve's voice wasn't that bad, as it goes! Pretty good album. After that there was a minority of women that came to gigs to talk to Eve, Gee and Joy. Up until that time, you'd only had women in bands who were copies of Siouxsie & The Banshees. But after that it seemed there were more girls starting their own band, or you'd start having bands like The Slits where the girls outnumbered the boys."

Steve Ignorant: "We got Eve involved because she was doing *Christ's Reality Asylum* onstage – the Patti Smith type thing. The first time she ever did it was when we were playing in Holland, at the Paradiso in Amsterdam. Because the place used to be a church, it was decided that it would be a really good idea that Eve would do *Asylum*."

Up till this point, Eve Libertine hadn't been taking much notice of the punk rock explosion sweeping the land. "I was really busy with children at the time", she remembers. "I was doing the school run four times a day; keeping the house, making the food, baking the bread – life was quite full actually: there were four children, and enjoying being in the countryside, growing vegetables in the garden, just living my life really. That was what was important to me at the time.

"I knew something was going on. I remember seeing The Sex Pistols on *Top Of The Pops* cos we always used to watch *Top Of The Pops* with the kids. I remember thinking what appalling rhyming. It was 'anarch-khyst' and antichrist."

Eve Libertine was born Bronwen Lloyd Jones in Liverpool in 1949, though her parents moved to Dulwich in south east London when she was two. "My parents were quite unusual. My father was a conscientious objector in the Second World War and my mother was fully supportive of that. My mother was fired for refusing to take dictation for enlisting young men to fight. So they were very very moral people. I think that probably had an effect one me. I became a vegetarian when I was fourteen – that was quite unusual in those days. When I told my parents, my mother said, 'Right, we'll all stop then.' So we all stopped.

"I remember when I was very little, my mother chatting to what I then thought was an odd old lady selling *Sanity* magazine. I think things like that infiltrate you, those sort of slightly different things. I've thought for myself for as long as I can remember."

After a brief and seemingly happy stint at a comprehensive school in Dulwich, Eve's parents moved to Loughton, Essex, where she attended a girls school and rued the time: "My education was complete and utter crap – I didn't learn a thing. I left school the day before I was sixteen." Eve left school with three 'O' levels, in art, English Literature and English Language. "It was a waste of time as far as I was concerned. I enjoyed writing essays and I enjoyed the art classes – and that was it really."

Loughton College of Further Education was the logical next stop for someone who "didn't really have any idea of what I wanted to do. I had been going to classes when I was fourteen, at a Polish club. There was an artist there that my parents knew who did art classes on a Saturday morning. He was quite a well known artist. He always said, 'Whatever you do, don't go to art school.' He thought I had something, and he thought that art schools ruined people."

Penny Rimbaud was teaching in the art department of Loughton College of Further Education. "He was lively, full of ideas. The teachers at that place were amazingly young – 23, 24, up to their early thirties, and they were very enthusiastic. Most of them were working artists. They were very good, most of them. But I didn't really have much to do with Penny at college." Later on, however, she visited Dial House over a long period of time. "Then I became involved with Pen," she says.

"When I very first went to Dial House, it was quite heavily Victorian – I remember lots of lacey things and lots of clocks – lots of interesting things. Then all that went and it became much more empty, and painted white. It had a very different feel after the change."

Also joining the fold was Joy de Vivre.

Steve Ignorant: "Andy had been to America to bring back Joy de Vivre from a broken marriage crap thing. He went all the way over to Phoenix and brought her back. She came to live at Dial House with Andy. We knew Joy from years ago because she used to live in Ongar, just up the road. She liked what we were doing so she got involved and wrote 'Women'."

Joy De Vivre: "I've always felt the band was a unity of an accidental group of people who just happened to nurture that integrity in each other . . . a particular ferment."

Joy first encountered Dial House as a local teenager living in Ongar, about two miles from the house. She'd heard about the place via schoolfriends who'd visited previously. "The house was notorious locally," she remembers. "It was 'oh, that weird bunch' – weirdos and hippies. 'Art students' was the usual thing they were called. It was middle-class kids who were drawn to it, because it was art-based – Dial House was experimental art and all sorts of weird stuff going on. If it had been a druggy, hippy community then we would have probably got more of a social mix."

At the time, Penny Rimbaud was working as a coalman, back when coal was still delivered in lorries. One day, Dave Williams took over his round for the day, met Joy and the two began a brief relationship, which inevitably introduced her to Dial House.

Joy's first impression of Dial House was romantic: "The whole commune thing I found a very attractive idea – I'd always wanted to go to Summerhill and the whole thing appealed to me. It was fascinating. And the avant-garde scene: that's what was happening at Dial House and that's what I found most intriguing."

She was a very shy young woman when she first encountered Dial House. "I was quite intimidated and overawed. I did lots of sitting and watching I think really. I desperately wanted to be a part of it but I felt like an observer."

Joy had previously flunked out of Art School to go to America for what turned out to be a failed marriage – "I was very interested in all the political side of Art School, but by the time I had got here, it had all dulled-down" – and the American sojourn meant she missed out on punk. "My best friend had died and I was very lost and did all sorts of things which were sad and difficult. Not in any big dramatic way. But I didn't really connect with punk that well. When I got back, the band was operating out of Dial House and I went to live there because it felt like some kind of refuge. It just felt natural to fall into it."

Joy De Vivre made her debut performance with Crass at a gig at the Acklam Hall in West London, screaming the lyrics to 'Women', and "trying to make myself heard above this racket".

One of the first noticeable changes on having women in the band was the banning of the word 'cunt' from the lyrics, which explains why 'runt' crops up a lot in many early songs.

Penny Rimbaud had taken to wearing all black clothes – not unlike beatniks – a couple of years previously, and now the rest of the band began to adopt the same look. It soon became the Crass uniform: clothes, guitars, amplifiers all became black.

Steve Ignorant: "I just used to wear old Oxfam trousers with stripy socks and see-through plastic sandals with any old jumper or shirt that was going. I had dyed red henna hair. I used to like wearing denim – Levis. Pen always looked really smart cos he had his Seditionaries and his black shirt with his chains. At that time he'd dyed his hair very blonde, so he looked very striking. Andy Palmer was wearing black a lot. Pete Wright tended to wear sandals and look a bit old-studenty.

"It must have looked a bit weird – I think we must have looked like one of those bands who were on the Stiff label – under the punk umber-alla, but not really punk. All deciding to wear black gelled it all together and made it look striking and probably a bit frightening.

"The true story is that we used to have this really old washing machine. Someone fucked up the washing so that all the clothes – including my white socks – came out this grey mushy colour. It was a pain – doing eight peoples' washing – so we just thought let's dye it all black – it'll look smart and won't be such a hassle on wash day."

Eve: "I wore it for a long time afterwards as well. Weird isn't it? A whole house full of people in black – poor children!"[1]

Joy De Vivre: "It was just so that there was a kind of solidity between people and because there was a real drive against picking it out a per-sonality. Even though Steve was a really strong personality and was bound to be the front man. I thought it was fine because I didn't want anything to detract with what we had to say."

Eve: "It looked good – it seemed like a nice colour to wear. Also, we didn't really have very much money. Quite a lot of stuff got dyed – we didn't go out buying clothes, it just wasn't like that."

Onstage, the wearing of black doubled up with what appeared to be a crypto-fascist banner and produced an image of the band that was open to misinterpretation to say the least. The beatniks may have worn all black but so did the Gestapo, and as Crass tended to wear trousers tucked into black bovver boots, it was tempting to see them in this light.

Steve Ignorant: "We played the Triad at Bishops Stortford and a bunch of people (who were at that time The Epileptics – later to become Flux Of Pink Indians) thought we were Nazi bastards, and were throwing ice cubes at us. Ooooh! Ice cubes! We confronted them afterwards and became friends ... We never wore swastikas or anything like that, although because of the nature of the (Crass) symbol, which is slightly swastika-y, Union Jacky and wearing black."

Joy De Vivre: "We were playing around with contradictions. It would

[1] At the time, there were four children living at Dial House: Phil Free's three children and Nemo, Eve's son who had been born there. They didn't wear black, for those who were wondering.

be silly not to realise that it could be read in many different ways. It was a way of making people question stuff rather than just taking it in."

Andy Palmer later commented: "What we're saying is too urgent to be able to say with an acoustic guitar and a joint in your mouth on the stage – flower power is out of the window now. What we present *is* austere and it *is* confronting and we spend a lot of time to make it like that. We mean what we've got to say and we take it very seriously. You can't just chant 'all we are saying is give peace a chance' anymore because it doesn't have any effect, and we *are* trying to have an effect."

The austere and confronting nature of this particular avenue of dress sense is recalled by Steve Ignorant: "I remember Andy, myself and Joy De Vivre being in Epping on a Saturday morning. Andy was wearing black trousers, black Doc Martens, a khaki shirt and black braces. His hair wasn't spikey – I had spikey hair. We went in a pub called the George and Dragon and a bloke came from behind the bar and said, 'And you can get out for a start!' I started wondering why and he said, 'Not you!' and he points at Andy Palmer. He thought he was a brownshirt. He said, 'I'm not having fascists in my pub'. I think this bloke had been in the Second World War. . ."

Around this time Crass introduced an additional aspect to their lives shows, the screening of movies, usually in conjunction with the live show. To this end, old Exit cohort Mick Duffield re-entered the fray.

Mick Duffield was born in East London, and his father was the publican of the Blind Beggar pub on Whitechapel Road, which would achieve notoriety for the incident therein where infamous London gangster Ronnie Kray shot and killed fellow villain George Cornell.

The family later moved out to Ongar in Essex when Mick's father took up new employment as a salesman. After primary school, Mick attended the local grammar school then went to art school in Thurrock on a foundation course that led him to Chelsea School Of Art. "I spent one day there," Mick chuckles in an echo of Gee Vaucher's London art college experience. "That was enough! I just decided it wasn't for me. I didn't want to be in an institution at that time. There were too many other interesting things going on."

Being a "sort of" hippie, Mick had been travelling, but not for him the hippie trail to India: "I went to the Arctic Circle and Morocco. That's as far as I got. I had a train ticket that enabled me to travel anywhere in Europe, so I went as far North and as far South as I could."

Of hippies, Mick says, "To be involved with it at the time felt like it was something really new that was going to have a dramatic effect. In reality, it obviously wasn't in the same league as civil war or a mass political revolution like communism. It was more like a mish-mash of loosely thought-out ideas that made you think as a young person that you were involved in something more radical than it was. In reality, I don't think it can be claimed that it very perceptibly slowed the momentum of the military, industrial, technological, individualist, consumer mania."

Mick moved into Dial House after spending the best part of a year living in Blake Hall on his own, in a rented outbuilding. "I was working in London, trying to get into the film business. In those days, to get into the film business you had to have a union card and one of the ways to get one was to go and work at the film lab. So I was commuting into London, processing film, and probably taking too many drugs for my own good. I managed to keep that together for several months and then decided that keeping it up for (the required) two years was boring. It was more interesting to have a more direct involvement with the interesting things happening at Dial House. So I moved in there – it was open-ended. There was enough space and it was remarkably generous of those already there to maintain an ethic of being that flexible. It was very unusual."

After nine months or so, Mick began to find Dial House somewhat oppressive. "It had a very definite aesthetic and a code that was largely determined by Penny and Gee. It obviously gives you strong foundations if you establish a place initially. They'd done all the work making it habitable. You *could* contribute but you could never be part of that founding experience and feel as grounded. In that sense it was *their place*."

This was the early seventies and Mick soon moved on from stills to buying a Standard-8 movie camera. He moved to London and was living in various squats, one of the more long lasting of which was on Charing Cross Road, a block of flats occupied by a disparate bunch including Steve Herman, briefly a member of Crass, and a young Shane McGowan. Here on Charing Cross Road Mick began work on the film

Autopsy, later to be shown at Crass gigs before the band played, and this multimedia dimension soon expanded to include film loops, back projection and various experimental films and video.

Mick Duffield: "Film is largely used to reproduce experience of events, whether drama or documentary – seeing/experiencing by proxy – chaotic reflected light is collected and made coherent in an image by a lens then 'fixed' in a time controllable medium which in turn is made to shape light which again is 'seen' (collected and shaped by another lens – in the eye) for the brain to interpret. Film developed out of a fascination with being able to extend eyesight – seeing a convincing representation of events without having to be there. I was interested in using film as direct experience itself as well as for its representational power, so deconstructing the image and the illusion. So I might bake the film in an oven before/after or not using it in a camera, scratch, colour, paint, reverse, mirror, burn, refilm, stamp on, twist, stretch, and mess with the natural progression of time."

Though this loosely coincided with punk's attempt to deconstruct and stamp on illusions, there was no overtly political thread in Mick's early work. "Only in the sense that an artist might often struggle with their own ingrained patterns of seeing and thinking," he says. However as a result of the times – Thatcher, the Cold War, the disillusionment with sixties counterculture and its nebulous dreams, etc. – Mick's *Autopsy* and later *Choosing Death* did incorporate anger, disgust and sardonic humour to become more overtly political.

He first moved to Islington, to a house with no electricity, which he shared with people who were involved with a group called Actionspace, in Cheney Street off Tottenham Court Road, which would be one of the first places Crass played. Filmed by Mick, footage of this gig is in *Autopsy*, which would in turn be shown at Crass performances. "I was working on a couple of things in the Charing Cross Road squat that were more performance art related. Then I started making *Autopsy*, with a much stronger political intent before and as Crass became a band. . ."

The times were angry and so was Mick: "Thanks very much for the education. So there's been two world wars this century, mass orgies of death and destruction, and now we're limbering up for a third which will outstrip the other two. Eh! Thanks but no thanks."

Steve Ignorant remembers filming with Mick: "I remember him saying to me that he'd like to take me out and film me doing odd things, like buy a newspaper and rip it up in front of the bloke who's selling it.... I was thinking what the fuck would I do that for? I want to see how the football's doing! I didn't know then what Mick wanted. I do now, but back then, Mick Duffield's friends were talking in such syllables that I just couldn't understand it."

Although the discussions escaped the final cut, Steve *can* be seen in Mick's film *Autopsy*, sauntering round the Elgin Marbles in the British Museum watched by an obviously worried and animated security guard.

Also present at the Charing Cross Road squat was Steve Herman. "He was captain video – he had one of the early portable video recorders and cameras. I think he was doing community video."

Mick started working with Crass live, effectively turning their shows from normal rock'n'roll performances to multi-media events, which was trailblazing at the time. "It developed as time went on. It started out as a single screen with one film and quickly developed into several screens and specialised loop projectors, back-projecting and front-projecting."

It's a shame that, with all his film equipment, Mick didn't really film Crass' live performances: "They were very difficult to film, because with Super-8 film you needed far more light than was available at a Crass gig – all you'd get was shadows, and black – that would be about it. So it was a bit pointless filming the gigs. I did try and remember asking somewhat desperately for maybe 60 watt bulbs instead of 40 but there was no deal."

Perhaps unbeknown to the members of Crass, their deliberate policy of anonymity, mixed with tales of their remote farmhouse in the country, lent them a certain mystique in punk circles. Everyone wants to know the answer to a secret, as any stage magician or amateur-psychologist will testify. Eve Libertine rebuffs the perceived secrecy: "I don't think it matters who the person is, it's what they put out. If somebody has written or painted something that I find inspiring, that is enough for me – that is what they wanted to give me and the world. It's none of anyone's business, and if they want know, then sorry, that's a shame, but I'm not interested in that.

"There *was* a conscious decision not to put anybody forward," she says, "which was a bit hard because Steve was always the singer, doing more of the personality thing. Because the voice is a personality, so if you're singing, your personality has to come through your voice. We were saying that what was important wasn't our own personal feelings. No-one could be made into a hero."

When Johnny Rotten is cited as an example wherein attitude can be at least as inspiring as, ahem, product, Eve remarks: "The house was open. I don't suppose any band has had so many visitors – they could see us all there. We were anonymous onstage, but the house was open … what could someone get from Steve or me spot-lit? Only that we were stars. But they come to the house, they can see us doing what we're doing. And anyone could come to the house – *anyone*. And people came. They camped in the garden, they lived there or they came with their fanzines … a day taken up with people we would never see again, talking about *anything*. There has never been, and probably never will be, such an open band, and yet so anonymous onstage. The stage was a *set*, a platform for what we wanted to say – it wasn't about who we were as individuals. That makes complete and utter sense to me. And afterwards, we were there in the audience – we didn't go to a dressing room afterwards and then get taken away to a hotel – we jumped off the stage and anyone could talk to us.

"There'd be a lot of talking. And that's what would come of it – of discussion and arguments – what we would end up with is what we would perform. So we were all in there.

"But it's not the place for personal differences. It was a piece – a theatre piece – we were performing. I think there are a lot of elements in it that make it more of a theatre piece than rock'n'roll, but saying something that we really meant and believed in. Not a theatre piece where we were acting."

"Writing graffiti is about the most honest way you can be an artist. It takes no money to do it, you don't need an education to understand it and there's no admission fee." – Banksy

Another thread of Crass' multimedia assault on conformity came in the form of the stencil graffiti campaign.

Penny Rimbaud: "Eve and myself went out to Paris in 1977. We saw this stencil graffiti – actually quite Banksy-like, a lot of portraiture. I think it was Turks doing it. (It was political.) When we got back, we decided we'd start a campaign. So we dedicated every Saturday to it and we used to travel between Liverpool Street and Notting Hill Gate. We'd travel with a set of up to six different statements which were destined for appropriate posters. Within about three months of us doing this, a group of Christian Fundamentalists started doing something similar, making Christian statements. Because there was a moral aspect of what we were saying, we didn't want to get confused."

Up until this point, the statements had been kept polite – *Fight War Not Wars* – and the like. The initial campaign was planned to avoid all possible charges of vandalism. "We decided we'd always be very neat and clean about it – we'd always put it on the appropriate poster, we wouldn't spray on property. The initial ones had no reference at all to the source – it didn't carry the symbol."

They decided some clear blue (or even red and black) water was needed between Crass and the Christians: "It was almost like the Christians were appropriating what we were doing – you could have seen it as being all one programme. So that was the point at which we started putting the Crass symbol on it, and slightly beefing up what we were saying." They were still careful, however, to avoid use of any language that the average commuter might find offensive. "We didn't want to offend," reasons Penny. "We just wanted to help people think, to reconsider. . ."

The campaign was kept going solidly for 18 months, until band commitments made it impossible to continue.

Mick Duffield: "It was quite challenging. It was like a military operation – we'd divide up the mechanics of doing it: one person would be responsible for the stencils, one for the spray paint, another person masking what we were doing. We'd emerge out of a tube station and spray something, as fast as we could and disappear again. We did the Cenotaph, which was quite exciting, cos there's a good chance you could get arrested for that. Of course it was the early days of surveillance cameras – nowadays you'd get picked up in 20 seconds . . . unless you were even more organised than we were. . ."

"It was hard work, being in the stuffy underground, surreptitiously coughing while you sprayed the can, the smell of the paint filling the station and then nipping on the next train. But it was very satisfying – it used to stay there for quite a while."

Steve Ignorant: "I didn't like doing it. It was Penny and Eve that instigated it, then it became sort of band policy. It was brilliant the way they did it: they made the stencils and got paper bags, then put the stencil in the bottom, so it's the bottom the bag. So when it came to doing the spray painting, you just held the paper bag up against the wall and sprayed inside."

The stencil graffiti craze became a minor revolution in the UK for a while as people the length and breadth of the country followed Crass' lead and took up political sloganeering, subverting adverts ('subvertising') and society throughout the land. All too quickly, however, this would be eclipsed by the influx of American 'tag' graffiti. In some cases, this would involve beautiful, talented and colourful art; in most, something that more resembled a coloured snail-trail. Either way, the short-lived political anarcho-graffiti ideas had been usurped by a culture that said little more than 'I woz ere'. Stencil graffiti is now on the rise again, however and being more accepted as art all over the world.

Crass, drawing on both the wide artistic and cultural experience of their members and the spirit of the times, had metamorphosed from a bunch of lads out on the glorified piss to a serious multi-age, multi-gender, multi-media assault on conformity and narrow minds. They were ready to take on the world.

621984

As the group began to take themselves seriously, so did those who were observing them. The great leap forward in this regard was the release of their first record.

Crass had approached old Exit soundman and close friend John Loder and recorded a new demo reflecting the harsher sound and the serious intent. Loder had built a studio in his garage in North London called Southern where he was busy recording jingles.

The songs on the demo pretty much mirror the versions that would turn up on vinyl. If you were searching for differences, you could say that both Ignorant's vocals are a touch more Rotten-esque and Wright's a touch more rock'n'roll. Tracks laid down were 'End Result', 'G's Song', 'General Bacaradi', 'Securicor', 'Angela Rippon', 'Major General Despair', 'Owe Us A Living', 'Punk Is Dead' and 'Tired'. 'Tired' has some great effects on it and is better than the released version – why on earth they left it off *The Feeding Of the 5000* is anyone's guess. Both 'End Result' and 'Punk Is Dead' have extra lyrics. Though they're largely indecipherable, 'Punk Is Dead' contains the lines 'Punk was just a way of bemoaning the fact / a whole generation was afraid to act' as well as appearing to contain the line 'I'm sobering up' which may be a nod towards the previous chapter, though Penny Rimbaud can't remember. Perhaps if you can remember the early Crass gigs, you weren't really there. The demo marked a far heavier sound, much more hardcore, mean and lean than the Steve Herman inspired first demo.

Steve Ignorant: "A friend of the band by the name of Tony Lowe counted among his various jobs doing displays in record shop windows. He gave a copy of the Crass demo cassette to Pete Stennet at Small Wonder Records. Pete phoned the band expressing an interest in meeting up and putting out a single. By this time we'd actually established the set. I think it was Pen who came up with the idea of doing a 12″ single with the whole set."

In another break from rock'n'roll traditions, the whole thing was recorded in one day, perhaps one of the advantages of having a rehearsal room in the same house you live in. A preview tape of the first Crass release, *The Feeding Of The 5000*, gave the band their first coverage in the music press, courtesy of *Sounds* journalist Garry Bushell, who would prove to be something of a nemesis over the next few years.

"The spirit of '76 is alive and well and living in Ongar (in a commune)," began the piece, continuing, "Such is the strength of their beliefs that they hide themselves away in a cottage commune in Ongar where they pick potatoes for subsistence wages. Hippy punks, d'ya think?" The picture of the band – the same out of focus pic as on the record insert – caption declared that the band made The Clash sound like Child. Which, given the zeitgeist, must have made thousands of spikey ears prick up.

Describing Crass as "pretty unforthcoming about their backgrounds. They're mostly disillusioned middle-class, aged up to Rimbaud's 40 years," Bushell is largely forgiving, however, describing the record as, "thirty minutes of invigorating energy".

Penny Rimbaud's wildly disproportionate response was to write Bushell a letter, listing the inaccuracies in the piece: growing your own food is hardly the same as picking potatoes for subsistence wages, and besides, Dial House was macrobiotic at the time so potatoes were out of the question anyway. Given that the general nature of Bushell's piece was benign and positive, and the political atmosphere of the times, it's tempting to wonder if class wasn't something of an Achilles heel in the Crass camp.

Penny Rimbaud: "I wrote a very rude letter to him saying if you're going to bother writing about us, at least get in touch. I know where he got the information from – Pete from Small Wonder – that was Pete's little idea of how we were. He (Bushell) took offence at that, probably quite rightly. . ."

Shortly afterwards, *Feeding Of The 5000* hit the shops, and it was a revelation in all sorts of ways: the price was revolutionary – 12 tracks for £1.99, at a time when the average album would set you back £3.99. At a time when many punk records were sold via mail order, and advertised by the specialist shops in columns in the back of the music press, this kind of a deal leapt out at you. It suggested, above all else, an integrity that many had been searching for but few, if any, had been offering.

Penny Rimbaud: "We wanted to do stuff as cheaply as we could because we knew people couldn't afford to be buying records all the time. What I was always trying to do was to share whatever gains we had with as many people as possible. And that's how the house has operated. Wherever we became advantaged, we used that to help as broad a part of the radical community of which we were a part, to expand it. The 'pay no more than' was because we knew well that if we sold stuff cheaply, places like HMV would sell them at their regular price."

Penny rejects any idea that this handily doubled up as good marketing technique: "Absolutely not. It was all designed to ensure that the purchaser got the best deal that they possibly could. We wanted to give people real value, and part of the reason we could do that was because we lived here – we grew our own food, we didn't pay much rent or develop expensive drug habits or want swimming pools. So we were effectively passing on the advantages of us living cheaply. It's the complete opposite to how most marketing is done."

Steve Ignorant: "I didn't care what fucking price it went out at – all I was interested in was getting a record out. But it was 'keep it cheap, then people can afford it and still have enough for a packet of fags and a pint of beer' type of thing. It was also because Dial House always tried to run itself self-sufficiently and so we didn't really need any money from it. I can't stress it enough – there was no idea of us making loads. We called it *Feeding Of The 5000* because we didn't think it would sell that many – we thought Pete was taking a big risk. But it turned out he wasn't. . ."

Pete Wright: "If we'd sold our records at full price, they wouldn't have sold."

The first thing that stood out about the record was how much swearing it contained – certainly enough to make sure that this disc would receive no airplay anywhere, ever. And the anger in the vocals – raw, unprecedented, primal and very genuine anger – was quite frightening. Then there was the blasphemy on tracks like 'So What'. Then, paradoxically it seemed at the time, there was overt peace campaigning of 'They've Got A Bomb', complete with CND symbol on the lyric sheet, and the feminist message of 'Women' screamed out over an out of tune radio.

The songs themselves were astonishingly confrontational in both content and presentation. The very first phrase on the vinyl leapt out at you and screamed – really screamed – 'fuck the politically minded', setting the Tourettian tone for the rest of the record. This again piled on the credibility. There was absolutely no chance of these little ditties appearing on *TOTP* or being heard on Radio 1. *Feeding* was a record that clearly wanted to take punk way back underground, to reclaim some of the privacy lost to the tabloid sensationalists from the reaction to the Pistols Grundy interview onwards.

The sheer intensity of the singing and the noise that underpinned them was also unprecedented. Steve Ignorant's vocals were the angriest ever, until Pete Wright took over, sounding for all the world like he was going to have a heart attack in the studio. Joy De Vivre just screamed. There was precious little concession to conventional rock'n'roll to be found anywhere. And then there was the lyrical content, all squeezed into and typed out on a double album sized insert.

The very first track, entitled 'The Sound Of Free Speech' was simply silence. The ghost of John Cage, a cover version even. The lyric book of the second pressing explained why: "Once again the violent majority assert their bigoted reality through the silencing of others. 'ASYLUM', an antichrist/feminist statement has been erased because no company would press the record if the track was left intact. With the first 5,000 pressings we decided to forward cassette copies to people requesting them. Since then we have tried to get 'ASYLUM' pressed ourselves plus 'SHAVED WOMEN', both with Eve Libertine on vocals. We will market it as soon and as cheaply as possible, hopefully around cost price. Sorry it's all such a fuck up – CRASS.'

Steve Ignorant: "Pete Stennet phoned up and said that because the pressing plant was in Ireland, the people there had read the lyrics and were offended by them and refused to do it. He wanted to shorten it. But Pen said no, we'll call it 'The Sound Of Free Speech' and just have silence."

Of the first 5,000, several hundred punk rockers took them up on the offer and received the cassette of the track.

Later versions of the album, when re-released, reinstated the original track (a more basic spoken word track than the subsequent single without the backing noise). They also came with the – by then – standard fold out sleeve bearing the legendary Gee Vaucher poster of a severed hand hanging on the old barbed wire above the phrase 'Your Country Needs You'.

In the absence of 'Asylum', 'Do They Owe Us A Living?' kicked off the record with perhaps the nearest thing the band had to an anthem. 'End Result' was another prime cut of deep dissatisfaction with life. Again written by Steve, he explains, "That was written about growing up with my parents and grandparents in Dagenham. All of that way of life that I didn't want any more – it was just a two fingers up to that really."

Reviewers seemed to take particular offence at the song's line: "They all live for that big blue sign that says / it says FORD". As well they might – while a hundred lefty bands bleated about the right to work[1] here was a song subliminally and sublimely suggesting there might be more to life than donating upwards of forty hours a week to capitalism. The theme was backed up by the first line of 'Reject Of Society' – "Not for me, the factory floor."

Steve Ignorant: "I think Tony Parsons had a go at Penny Rimbaud because of that, because his dad grew up in Ilford or something – the working class thing. In those days, when you'd drive into Dagenham along the A13, there was a huge big sign that said Ford. All of Dagenham was built to cater for Fords. When I was at school, the two options I had was work in a supermarket or work at Fords. That's what that song was all about. And my dad calling David Bowie a poof – that sort of thing."

---

[1] Musicians! Work! As if!

With 'They've Got A Bomb', and the CND symbol in the background on the lyric sheet, Crass initiated their part in reviving the fortunes and influence of the Campaign For Nuclear Disarmament and the wider peace campaign in the UK. It was a cause they would continue to promote throughout their career, though it was about as fashionable as the flares (along with sandals and duffel coats) many thought accompanied it at the time. The awkward gap in the song, where a silence splits the song down the middle was accompanied at gigs by a sudden darkness in the room and film of an atomic bomb exploding. The length of the silence, stretching any comfort of sense of rhythm out of the window, was far more unsettling than, say, the Pistols ' I Wanna Be Me', and again betrays the artistic roots of the band and their willingness to try new ideas.

Elsewhere, both 'Punk Is Dead' and 'Banned From The Roxy' are superficially reactions to the Crass gig and subsequent banning from the Roxy punk club in London's Covent Garden. Two more anthems, the drum and vocals dominance of 'Roxy' call to mind a prototype rap music, while 'Punk Is Dead' railed against the new punk stars as a new social elite, and it clicked.

'Banned From The Roxy' wasn't overly concerned with being banned from the Roxy at all. It simply used the experience as a metaphor to release anger: first, a personal anger trying (and largely succeeding) to find justification for itself; then externalising the anger "against what I feel is wrong with this land". Belfast, Mai Lai, Hiroshima: "The shit they get'...'defence? Shit! It's nothing less than war, and no-one but the government knows what the fuck its for". I enjoyed that bit too, Tony.

The intro and the song itself seem almost funky in the present day and age – you could do the hand-jive to the beat. But at the time, it was part of the spikey, film-noir, hirror-horror collage that deliberately shocked the listener out of a complacency that even the earlier punk bands hadn't prepared the listener for.

The noise-collage behind the needlessly cynical 'Women' reflected the lack of direction in the song, though it also marked an important challenge to the average male listener on another level – traditional feminism had entered the punk fray, with the vocals symbolically fighting to be heard above the male instruments. It had hung around on the fringes with The Raincoats and The Au Pairs, but Crass was later to take it much further. As were the Greenham Women, of course.

Joy De Vivre: "It was a woman's voice saying something fairly difficult about men and women. It's also a picture of how women's voices get drowned out," she adds, pointing out that this was deliberately reflected in the way the background noise (none dare call it music) constantly threatened to overwhelm the voice. "What was going on was a platform where you could actually say something and challenge the normal picture of women being the victims and to actually address men as victims – it was kind of important to me. When I was younger I'd been to a few feminist meetings with much older women and I'd often felt dismayed by the man-hating stuff, but I also understood that it was nec-essary and inevitable. Not that I'm an apologist – I suppose it was just that whole thing that was going on between the political and the per-sonal."

'General Bacardi' criticised the hippy generation's failings, while simultaneously suggesting that members of the band had been involved with that. The hippy tag was something Crass would never really shake off, despite having left it behind – not a problem that would afflict Joe Strummer and his pub rock/ Stonehenge days.

'Fight War Not Wars' confused even further – the song simply consisting of that phrase repeated over and over again. Clearly not rock'n'roll.

During one of the weaker songs, 'Angels', Crass use the old Exit tech-nique of sampling random radio, complete with John Cage's between-channels racket to great artistic ability, but appalling political judgement, particularly with hindsight: "I think perhaps Jim Callaghan is the more dangerous of the two, because he is more successful." Callaghan was the Labour leader of the time – the more dangerous of the two. The less dan-gerous? Margaret Thatcher.

The nearest thing to rock'n'roll was 'Securicor', featuring Pete Wright on vocals. 'Securicor' is feasibly the best track – Pete Wright's vocals are astounding, as is the notion that Securicor functions as capitalism's private army. Equally 'Sucks' and 'You Pay' featured Pete attacking belief systems and praising anarchy with a vaguely eccentric vocabulary. To hear him screaming 'It's fucking stupid' was disconcertingly fucked up, like spying on a nervous breakdown.

Apart from a rerun through 'Do They Owe Us A Living?', the final track was 'So What', a more punky and less arty run through the blasphemy theme that would later see a young punk in court for singing it at a priest. If 'Asylum' was the arty Patti Smith antichrist statement, Steve Ignorant wasn't holding back or dressing it up. "So what if Jesus died on the cross / So what about the fucker, I don't give a toss," he raged, in what at the time was a seriously extreme way of tackling a hitherto taboo subject.

Looking back on his writing of the song, Steve recalls "My attack in 'So What' was daring God – where's this thunderbolt of lightning? I read this book *Brighton Rock*, written by Graham Greene. He became a Catholic because his wife was one and, as is often the case in these situations, he became more Catholic than she was. All of his books were dealing with that thing, and in *Brighton Rock*, there's a character called Pinky. He's asked by his girlfriend if he's a Catholic and he says, these atheists don't know nothing. Of course there's hell, torments and agonies. And I thought, yeah, he's right, because it's far easier to believe in all that down there than it is up there. So I wrote 'So What' against all of that thinking that maybe there is something in it, being a pistol at the back of my head that if I'm not good, I'm going to be in purgatory. And that's bullshit – you shouldn't have to live your life like that. I think I'm a pretty good geezer in the things I've done."

For the average punter, however, the biggest shock was the viciousness of the attack on religion.

Steve Ignorant: "When I was at school, I'd always had this idea of being a nice bloke, I wanted to be a missionary. I'd met this teacher, who was a Christian, and he introduced me to a book called *The Cross And The Switchblade*, which is about a priest who gets a calling from Jesus to go into New York and help the gangs stop killing each other. Even as a non-Christian, it's still really interesting to read about his life. He actually converted a couple of gang members, one of whom was called Mickey Cruise, who became huge in the Christian movement over there. That book really turned me on to it.

"In a funny way, I wrote 'So What' to see if there'd be a bolt of lightning if I wrote 'So what about the fucker, I don't give a toss'... and there wasn't, and there never has been. So in a funny way, it was daring."

The attacks on Christianity and the person of Christ were extraordinary and must have made most listeners feel that they'd led lives more sheltered than they'd ever imagined. "It was articulate," says Pete Wright. "Penny's take on Christianity and culture was very articulate."

As well as being the artist responsible for Current 93 and an old friend of the band, David Tibet is a Catholic: "I always considered such attacks as an attack on the Imperium of Christendom, rather than on Christ Himself. It has a profound and marvellous heritage, most primarily in recent times in, of course, Tolstoy.

"But I do feel that their occasional attacks on the person of Christ were misconceived and impotent. It never disturbed me, but I felt that when they got on that track (passionately though they no doubt felt about it), it lessened the completeness and complexity of what they had done. 'Reality Asylum' was an amazing work, but I felt that the anger was misdirected and infantile. I don't think Jesus died alone in any of the fears that Pen surmised he did; but I guess we won't know that this side of the Second Coming. When Igs sang the lines of 'So What' I felt disappointed at such pointless venom.

"The biggest problem I had with their recorded output was what I felt to be the excessive use of profanities, which made their work easy to overlook or dismiss as merely foul-mouthed outrage for its own sake. They had something amazing and liberating to say; the message would have been clearer still without the swearing, and it put a lot of people off them who would have been remarkably moved by the clarity and beauty of Crass' vision if they had not been put off by the obscenities."

Feeding Of The Five Thousand came out at a very fortuitous time, swearing-wise. The Jam had just changed the lyrics of 'The Modern World', replacing 'two fucks' from 'I don't give two fucks about your review' to 'a damn'. Whatever reasons this was done for, it smelt like a bad case of sanitisation. Generally, the move towards more acceptable 'New Wave' and even 'Power Pop' bands could easily be seen as industry-led attempts to replace punk with a kind of 'punk-lite' that retained the more crass elements of the style (if you'll forgive the pun) whilst neutering all the content that made punk so special in the first place. Of course, even much of this middle-of-the-road music was enormous fun, but it left a gaping hole for somebody like Crass to come along with a record so extreme – particularly in the swearing department – that the load was clearly too wide to perform a U-turn in the direction of *Top Of The Pops* or *Multicoloured Swap Shop*. The band, then, were not for turning, but were all the F-words an effing tactical mistake?

Penny Rimbaud took the anti-bourgeois line to defend the tactic in 1984: "If the rationality, compassion and reason in our work is lost in a few 'fucks' then the people it's lost upon shouldn't fucking listen to it in the first place cos they're not worth bothering with. Cos they're never going to change their position if common language is going to get in the way of them and positive thinking. So I absolutely support the use of fucks. The person who believes in something doesn't care how it's expressed – it's of no concern at all.

"The primary thing people have to overcome is their social bigotry. Most working class people don't care too much about fucks being in the song. Most middle-class people are going to care quite a bit about it. Fuck is a class issue."

Only someone middle-class could say that.

"I always tried to find ways of not swearing," says Steve of the songs he wrote, which leads to the obvious conclusion that he failed quite spectacularly. Perhaps Steve sums it up best: "I dunno, it's just swear words. When I write a song now, I deliberately don't put them in, because it's too easy."

If there was a dada-esque intention to confuse with the record, then it certainly succeeded. Was this a product of rural hippies who like so many others had run to the countryside in the sixties to drop out? This was certainly the feeling you got from a ploughed field on the sleeve and a CND symbol on the lyric sheet. Or was it a product of urban punks, as suggested by the inner-city collage on the other side of the sleeve, and tourettian vocals that took anger to an unprecedented level? Confusion. Contradiction. Dada.

Up until this point, the early punk bands and pioneers had always made you feel inadequate. It wasn't much fun to be told, while at the peak of your youth and ready to take on the world, that punk had died by the end of 1977. It nagged at the back of your mind that you'd missed the boat, that you were some kind of imposter, that these people were right and all you had was a history you'd missed out on by the narrowest of margins. A 'second generation' of punks was inevitably going to form a second generation of bands, if only for how ungracious and ungenerous the first wavers had been about them.

Tony D: "Pete of Small Wonder gave me this cassette and a copy of *Christ's Reality Asylum* and a copy of *International Anthem*. I thought the writing was great but the cassette was shit. Great literature, crap sound. But then I played it more and more and realised what they were singing about and I changed my mind, I thought the music was great."

"Open the door to the lovers of outage / Let them try something new"
Penetration, Lovers Of Outrage

Outrage was punk's calling card. It was as if the outrageous clothes – for which Vivienne Westwood & Malcolm McLaren must be given credit – sanctioned all manner of other outrageous behaviour. Whilst most people used the space this created to have a bloody good laugh, Crass saw the opportunity for something more tangible.

Joy De Vivre: "[With the advent of punk and Crass] Dial House did become a very communal and outreaching space. Maybe that wouldn't have happened if there hadn't been this incredible intensity before. It's easy to dismiss it as pretentious crap but I don't think it was. There was always an intensity and passion about it. Like the way none of us wanted to be stars – we didn't want to be terribly impressive and avant-garde – it's just the mode of operation."

Phil Free: "There were deep and lengthy discussions about what constitutes 'avant-garde' and 'outrageous'. . ."

Joy De Vivre: "I don't think it was particularly outrageous. . ."

Phil Free: "At the time it *was*. I think it was outrageous to us as individuals and as a group to be doing stuff like that."

Joy De Vivre: "Because it was pushing boundaries. . ."

Phil Free: " It's not that you thought 'we must push boundaries', but you were going somewhere where. . ."

Joy De Vivre: "Yes, you don't so much go out thinking that, but you end up doing it because that's what you're interested in doing."

Phil Free hints at another source of the schism between Crass-viewed reality and the rest of the world: "You think about something and maybe you rehearse something, but when you go outside in the harsh light of day or in the village hall or wherever you're doing it, it suddenly takes on a different colour, a different perception. So you try and brass your way through it."

Released the same week as the Fall album *Live At The Witch Trials*, the record was received badly by the music press. Underneath the title 'Obscene oaths do not a revolution make', *Sounds* journalist Garry Bushell began: "It's so hard to take Crass seriously... They flirt with fascistic uniforms – how risqué – but they claim to be anarchists and hide behind CND badges – how relevant. They write lyrics a/lot/like/this and sometimes LIKE/THIS and being middle class they think class doesn't matter... Crass lyrics are a reiteration of Teach yourself Anarchy (learnt in half an hour, guaranteed ineffective) punctuated with lots of fucks for street cred (bet they went to Univesity) ... you're full of shit, spirited shit maybe, but let's face it, Crass? Precisely."

In *NME*, Tony Parsons took a similar view: "... very good value, very angry, very trite and very boring. The Clash and TRB's politics are facile but inoffensive, whereas Crass are facile and offensive, directing their self-righteous superiority, vehement cluck-clucking and anachronistic three-chord thrashing at such disgusting rubber duckies as security guards (you wanna cosh the driver, cut a record with Ronnie?), factory workers (you gonna support the dead sheep if they quit and move into your Epping commune?) and, of course, them, one system, society (rage and rant but keep it non-specific spread the guile, make it painless, make it product.) ... this is a nasty worthless little record..."

Nasty it might have been, but it would prove to be far from worthless. Crass responded to these two reviews by printing them in full on the next pressing of *Feeding*, under the headline 'Reputations In Jeopardy'. The review as part of the product.

Bushell's abrupt U-turn can be attributed partly to Rimbaud's rude letter, of course, but maybe also the press release booklet that accompanied the album to reviewers, *Life Amongst The Little People.* This was a Penny Rimbaud rant about a failed attempt by Crass to play at a failed attempt to revive Windsor Free Festival and a meeting at NYC airport with a macho American GI.

It began: "Pete of Small Wonder asked for a press release to accompany our record, *The Feeding Of The Five Thousand*, we're not interested in the colour of hair or ages, or how many teeth we've lost or how many strings there are on a guitar, or why this or why that. This release gives some impression of where and how we work."

The introduction homed in on sartorial decisions: "We wear black / a reflection of values / your values / a reflection of values / our values / all values / contained on the meat-rack / the corpses in the butchers cart / you pile them up / we wear black / we are hidden by your prejudice."

As you read through the diatribe, it's easy to see how Messrs Bushell and Parsons could find the whole package ungenerous and disagreeable. The booklet ends: "We seek a future that is our OWN, away from the oppression history and tradition. We seek some reality that is OURS, yet all around are the LITTLE PEOPLE."

Another challenging aspect of the Crass image was that they were largely of a different generation to the punks championed by the music press. The fact that two of the guitarists were bald seemed only to add to the generation gap. In normal circumstances, this would count heavily against a rock'n'roll band – you couldn't have imagined it with any of the first wave of punks, much less with most other 'pop' music – but given the subject matters they dealt with, and the extreme methods of delivery, it lent Crass a certain gravitas.

Fellow, er, older person Charlie Harper, the omnipresent UK Subs main man opines: "We were much more politically aware, we were teaching the younger ones what was going on. How they were being cheated, how they were being put through school like a factory: they were being brought up to be factory fodder. And if they weren't factory fodder, they were cannon fodder. We were trying to preach that kind of gospel. We thought no-one was listening to us, but it kinda spread. We saw it almost as a political duty. Punk wasn't meant to last – no-one really wanted it to last. I saw it more as an art form than anything else."

"[Punk] was never exclusively a teenage movement," says Pete

Wright. "That's what it became. Things were missed about punk because people look at 1977/78 and it seems prejudiced about age and background. We ran an open house policy, and if there were any prejudices, you weren't welcome. We were more about a meeting of minds than a society. It depends where you think punk came from. It's difficult to transport it out of London. In the winter of '77, it was a great thing that involved a few thousand people. Couldn't really find a way of upping the ante. What do you do with attitude? The problems that existed for us then exist now. We didn't really have an overview of ourselves, but we knew that creatively, we could do damage. We were a generation older. If the thinking was linear, then we should take responsibility for that. When I think about how naive I was at 15, 20 or 25, the pressure we were putting on kids (as a band) were enormous."

Of course, there was always a danger that the Crass gravitas could turn into something less healthy altogether, which Pete acknowledges: "We became leaders in that area. We were all aware of our guru status. We appeared not to promote ourselves. Although some people got damaged, we did a lot of good. It came from people's ability to be articulate. You find bands that are successful in their context and behaviour is the expression. Intellectual arguments come from intellectual backgrounds."

Steve Ignorant: "The release of *Feeding* saw a quantum leap in the bands' popularity – it was what a significant portion of the great punk public had been waiting for. The 'real' punks had been waiting for a 'real' punk band to come along and Crass was in the right time at the right place, saying the right things."

Crass stepped into a void: the old capitalist cliché of having a unique selling point (their obvious sincerity) and a gap in the market (the wake of the good ship punk, looking back at the ship breaking up willingly).

Steve Ignorant: "I remember the first time we played the Acklam Hall and quite a few people tuned up. We were used to playing three-quarters-empty echoing places with the sound of pool games going on. Then suddenly all these people turned up with Crass written on the back of their jackets. And we were filling places like the Acklam Hall & Actionspace."

When places filled up, they filled up very specifically with punks – seas of leather jackets, bondage strides and crazy coloured hair, all wanting to see a punk band that wasn't, for the most part, punks.

Joy De Vivre: "For me, it's not so much punk as that punk allowed that platform and that anti-war voice. We used the punk stage, but I don't know how punk we really were in some ways."

Joy rejects, however, any thoughts that Crass was jumping on a band-wagon, preferring to think of the Crass-stance as a band who operated in the enormous free speech crater that the punk bomb benignly left in its explosive wake.

Phil Free: "The theory was that anyone can do it. You can have your say. And of course, we were actually crap: the singing was just shouting with a random chord sequence."

"I didn't want to be a glamorous presence," says Joy. "I just wanted to get up there and yell my piece."

When Crass yelled their peace, they also yelled their anarchy. What proved to be one of the most contentious parts of the Crass image was that of being anarchists. Proper ones. Maybe.

In a radio interview Penny Rimbaud was asked if the band were anarchists: "We talk about this a lot and we always end up saying we're people first. We would agree with most anarchist theory; equally well, we would agree with most pacifist or feminist theory as well. What we want to put across as people is that the world's a mess. It's a cruel and barbaric earth to live on, and we want to say, 'Well, we're saying no … we don't agree with what's happening to the world – we won't be ruled, we won't be governed, we won't be told what to do – it's our life, we've only got one of them. It's our planet, we've only got one of them. And we want to reclaim it, we want to say it's ours. And the more people who individually say that, the more individual people can live. It doesn't matter at all about the government, they can get on with their rules and regulations. We've got to learn to step outside of that and form our own rules, for ourselves, for each individual. And if that comes at odds with the status quo, then we must oppose the status quo, which is what we do on a lot of levels."

While Steve Ignorant had no qualms about describing himself as an anarchist back then, he's more reticent now. "I've realised now that I don't know what to call it, where my political thing comes from. My 'anarchism' – or whatever it was – didn't come from an anarchist background. I tried to read *Malatesta* once and I just got bogged down in it. And I've never read Kropotkin and Bakunin or any of those people, it just didn't appeal to me. It didn't make sense to me. I know that for reference if I need to look at those books I can, and I know they're making important points, but I know that for me, where I was coming from was the black and white sixties movies like *A Taste Of Honey*, John Osbourne and a film called *To Sir With Love*.

"One day we were all talking about books around the table," continues Steve. "Pen was talking about Tolstoy and I chipped in with *To Sir With Love*, and was met roars of laughter, it was quite a joke. When there was the yearly clear-out of books, out it went. But the Maigrets stayed. That book *To Sir With Love* is about one of the first black men to go into the East End of London and teach unruly white kids how to respect themselves and other people as human beings. Which *I* thought was the basis of anarchism, wasn't it?

"So maybe I *was* anarchist. I grew up with David Bowie and that turned my head, what he had to say. And I've got far more time for what he's got to say than bleedin' John Lennon! Or even Elvis Presley – I'm sure in his time he was a bit of a rebel, but for me it was David Bowie. And I was interested in what The Sex Pistols and The Clash had to say. If you to ask me I am an anarchist. I suppose it's the closest thing to what I believe, but I'm not going to loads of bloody rallies or meetings to sit in a semi-circle and chunder on about the miners' strike in Poland in 1918 or whatever."

Penny Rimbaud: "In all honesty, I wasn't aware of anarchism until about one year into Crass. I knew what it meant in the loose term of the word before, but in terms of a label, it was more by default. We'd got a peace banner to tell people we weren't interested in kicking shit, and we put up the 'A' banner as something to get the left and the right off our backs. It was then that we started getting asked what we meant by that. I realise that outside of my own libertarian stance, I didn't know what the fuck it was about. It was then I started looking at what it actually meant in terms of its history. I hadn't actually had that much interest in it and I can't say I have now to be honest. When I was at school, I had

extensively read about the anarchist involvement in the Spanish revolution – I really studied it, not as part of the curriculum, but because it
interested me."

"Look at me – I can set you free"
– Carry No Banners, Menace

As time went on, Crass put up more and more banners until the stage
finally resembled some kind of anarchist Nuremburg rally. As years went
on, the 'Crass bands' would ape this with obligatory slogans on old bed
sheets. Originally, however, the motive was a little more simple.

In 1984, Andy Palmer told Radio Free France: "There were both left
wing and right wing influences who were trying to co-opt what we
were saying, which was largely why we adopted the anarchy symbol, just
as a fuck off to any politicos. Then we came up against the established
anarchists, and their establishment idea of what anarchy meant, and as far
as we could see, putting anarchy and peace together was a complete contradiction to the idea that they had of what anarchy was, which was
chaos and no government, general violent revolution, which was the
opposite of what we were trying to say. So we put up the peace banner
together with the anarchy banner. And then the peace movement came
along and said that their idea of creating peace was through politics and
political demonstration. So freedom came into it as well – individual
freedom. Since we started using those terms, we've been trying to get
out of the pre-conceived meanings that people will put on them all the
time. Any form of definition like that eventually works against itself."

Penny Rimbaud: "We were increasingly being forced into that and
that alone, that we were forced into withdrawing some degree from
them."

Steve Ignorant: "You'd turn up at places and you'd be playing in front
of something like Maurice's Late Night Bar, which wasn't really fitting.
So we thought we'd cover it up, a bit like theatre, and rather than have
their décor, we'd have our décor."

Steve Ignorant: "We played in a place called Ferryhill. It was during
the Falklands War and a lot of the squaddies were on leave. We didn't
know but at midnight, the place turned into a disco. The people started

coming in while we were still packing away. The women started asking questions about our banners, and asking punks how they did their hair. Then their blokes came in, clocked them being interested and started flexing their muscles. The fact that we had banners up started people asking questions and added to the atmosphere."

Now truly up and running, Crass' artistic backgrounds and vivid imaginations quickly expanded from gigs with banners to a multi-pronged multimedia attack on the status quo and the establishment. The written word was another branch. With a bit of money under her belt, Gee had earlier started her own paper, *International Anthem*, with the strapline 'A nihilist newspaper for the living'. Still in regular contact with Pen back in England, Gee had enlisted his writing services, along with those of Eve, for the first issue. It sold through an independent network and radical bookshops. This was now followed by further issues, with Andy Palmer also producing a magazine *The Eklektik*.

Another sign that the establishment was keeping at least half an eye on the activities around Dial House was the treatment of its inhabitants at airports, as Gee Vaucher recalls: "I was getting stopped a lot at the airport coming into England at the time. They were trying to do me for carrying seditious material – quite pathetic really. So I was taken down below – I insisted on my phone-call. We had a standby lawyer by then, through John (Loder) and he acted very quickly – got the lawyer onto it, and they let me go."

521984

In January 1979, Crass played Manchester's Factory Club, with Ludus, in front a reasonably impressed Paul Morley, reporting for *NME*: "It's sharp music of fiction and friction that requires too much concentration to fully appreciate. Consequently, you'll probably find them drab or distant. Being a pervert, I found them delightful, though certainly not disgusting, as some think, and definitely not as demanding and dramatic as they need to be to succeed."

Also in January, British public sector workers went on strike in response to the government's 5% limit on pay rises. The period became known as "the winter of discontent" and would see uncollected rubbish piled high in the streets, a metaphor for the rising unemployment that forced the ruling Labour government to call a general election that May.

On the punk front, the first months of 1979 had seen a transition from the decline of the first wave to the emergence of a second which was growing apace. The remnants of The Sex Pistols had proved they weren't worthy of the name by releasing the movie *The Great Rock'n'roll Swindle* and The Clash had toddled off on their first US tour, but Stiff Little Fingers had released *Inflammable Material* which was an encouraging nod towards the DIY ethic. The fan could now be the musician. So, as ever, could the art student: Adam & The Ants had built up a massive following, taking out full page adverts for their new 'Zerox' single in *Sounds*. Ironically, despite Malcom McLaren's cynicism, it was his ideas, largely pilfered from sixties libertarian activism, that would colour the punk movement far more than the utterings of The Sex Pistols, Rotten partially excepted.

The mod revival too was in full swing, helped in no small way by the maginificent Who film *Quadrophenia*. In its own way, that too changed punk: young kids looking for the trendy new thing were far more likely to be attracted to the safer, cleaner Mod image. It took a great deal of the 'poseur' element out of punk, which was actually a shame in some ways, and coincided with the advent of the 'real' punk, partially a reaction to the increasingly more 'real' times and partially the simple dumbing down that affects all youth cults as they grow.

Meanwhile, despite the relative lack of success of their previous visit to New York, Crass embarked on another foreign trip, this time to Holland and Germany. The band was accompanied by The Poison Girls, who were regularly touring with Crass by this point. The Poisons (as they were known) had moved from Brighton to Epping, where they'd struck up a close friendship with Crass, sharing libertarian ideas born of their similar generation. Their singer Vi Subversa was a fortysomething housewife with kids who offered a wonderfully erudite anarchist line on domestic situations as well as confronting and confounding stereotypes.

The tour of Holland was set up by one of Gee's New York friends, a Dutch photographer called Henno.

"The house was a frenzy of preparation for weeks," says Pete Wright. "Days were spent in the fumes from the copying machine, from the aerosols and inks of the 'banner production department' – bed sheets vanished – banners appeared, from the soldering of audio, video, and lighting leads. The place stank. The garden was strewn with the custom-made cabinets of the group's equipment, the black silk-emulsion paint drying on the hessian surfaces. Everything matched. The band logo shone silver from the boot-proof Crimpeline of the speaker fronts. Very neat. Very fetching."

By this point, the whole Crass live performance was beginning to veer away from a straightforward rock'n'roll show and towards the more considered theatrical multimedia nature of their later shows. The gig at the Paradiso in Amsterdam – fittingly an old church – saw Eve Libertine's debut performance, starting the set with 'Asylum'.

Pete Wright: "Punk had not really touched Holland at the time, other than the publicity surrounding The Sex Pistols, and other bands on the major labels. Punk bands were expected to be naughty, but in a conventional way. Generally, they were.

"I remember in Holland they used to gob a lot. I think they'd heard that punks behaved like that," recalls Eve. Whatever the plastic ambience of the Amsterdam gig, however, the band playing in Dusseldorf, Germany, was on a different level altogether.

Steve Ignorant: "We were late and all the punks were outside getting cold, in the rain. The police turned up to see what was going on and the punks turned a police car over and set fire to it. So we turned up and there's all this melee going on, and the police wanted to cancel the gig. So in our broken translation, we explained to them that if they stopped the gig now, they were going to have more trouble, so they'd better let us play. Which they did, and the gig went off peacefully."

The events in Dusseldorf led the band to take the highly unusual step of a general refusal to play abroad, which they would mostly keep to for the rest of their days.

Steve Ignorant: "Because that happened, it was decided that we were out of our depth talking about anarchy if we didn't know the laws of other countries – what you can or can't get away with. Is it right for us to be promoting this stuff – fuck the system etc – if we can't inform people how to do that responsibly and be safe while you're doing it? And because of the language barrier we didn't feel we could promote the ideas we were promoting here."

Holland, where the band was still relatively obscure, was an easier ride. Pete Wright watched a support band with Phil, who decided to "give them a taste of the Roxy". They eased into the throng, a head taller than the locals. Phil seized Pete's shirt front and sprung him aloft, a good two or three feet, "like a black Zebedee".

"They went bouncing and whirling in mock violence, thrusting, dragging, hurling, jumping to the music," says Pete. "Andy and Steve appeared nearby with Eve and Joy close on their heels. The little whirlwind spread to become a leaping mass as the Dutch punks took the cue. People fell and tumbled, and were plucked to their feet by nearby hands. The little crowd sweated and leapt in a celebratory melee. The Crass people had missed this wild intimacy. Obscurity has its freedoms."

Back home, Crass finally found a French pressing plant willing to press 'Reality Asylum' and decided to release it on their own label as a single. Backed with an Annie Anxiety composition 'Shaved Women', it remains one of the most radical singles ever released, certainly the most radical to have sold in such numbers to young kids.

If *Feeding* had been shocking in its condemnation of Christ, then 'Reality Asylum' was more so. The poem was akin to a broadsheet equivalent of a tabloid 'So What'. No doubt about it, this single was heavyweight, as exemplified by the prose inside the sleeve:

"NOTES. 28/5/79
I have felt fear, fear of the thunderbolt from His Mighty Hand, exclusion from some heaven, fear of unknown fear.
I was born free, free body, free mind, until I breathed the moral air and became aware that my 'free' body was female, Eve's guilt, and that my 'free' mind was left to strive with others definitions of good and evil.
Now I need to exorcise myself of those things which have bound me in that powerful stranglehold of reverence for so long.
Everyone is born a sinner? The void, the abyss, black-hole, emptiness, fear; we all struggle there.
Father forgive, for we have sinned against Thee; or is it a more worldy power against which we sin, a system within which our objection to being formed, ordered and distorted, is our crime?
The barbed-wire fences between our trees; we all struggle there.
We are held, believer or not, by God Our Father's blessing; which way are the guns firing? God is on our side, for power, for possession, the pain in His Name, again and again, God at our side.
Can I really believe in this God of Masculinity, first in a long line of hideous male structures (the church, the crown, the state, the family), and where do I stand in this order of power?
What choice do I have?
martyr/mother/victim/martyr/whore/victim/martyr/witch/victim.
What choice?
I'll find new names for myself and a new place to stand.
Eve Libertine."

The (re-recorded especially for the single) track starts off with young 'Gem Stone', daughter of Poison Girls vocalist Vi, and future Rubella Ballet bassist, saying a prayer. "I am no feeble Christ, not me," an adult female voice interrupts, starting the spoken word poem – a savage attack, not apparently on Christianity, but on Jesus Christ himself. If *Feeding Of The Five Thousand* had shocked, then 'Reality Asylum' took the tactics to a whole new level. If the Buzzcocks wanted a generation of kids to turn up the volume to annoy their parents, Crass made you turn it down so they couldn't hear the blasphemy.

Eve Libertine: "I felt quite nervous actually. Because I was brought up in quite a religious household. I thought it was probably quite a good thing to do. I guessed trouble was a possibility, because of them refusing to press that track."

Written by Penny Rimbaud, 'Reality Asylum' was an enormously brave single, risking as it did not just worldly prosecution, but eternal damnation too.

Eve Libertine: "I *did* question it. But I think it was relevant, from a feminist angle. Christ was celibate, Mary was celibate, the whole thing of women's sexuality . . . it was quite hard for me because I was brought up thinking Christian. So I certainly had to question it but I saw it from a different angle through the 'Asylum' lyrics. So I was prepared to do it."

One reason for this was the way Eve saw the record: "I do see it as an attack on religion, even though it's seemingly attacking Christ. It's attacking what religion took from this man – and I'm sure there were many of them – wandering the earth saying brilliant things. We probably wouldn't have heard about him if he hadn't been crucified. I'm not interested in all the various teachers, even though a lot of them said some wonderful things. I think Christ said some amazing things. All the basis of all the religions would be coming from the same place, but Christianity has been used so powerfully for putting down women and sexuality. That's how I always saw Asylum – not anything to do with what I would call spirituality."

"There is something beyond all that. It's very likely what Christ was talking about, because he said some amazing things. Straight on the point as far as I can see. As did many other spiritual teachers. So I can easily justify Asylum within myself."

Nevertheless, even a confirmed atheist would have raised an eyebrow at the contention that Jesus Christ dug the pits of Auschwitz?

Eve Libertine: "Because it was Christianity against Judaism – the religion of Christianity caused that to happen."

In its multi-layered attack, the poem also accuses Christ of 'cockfear, cuntfear' and alls him a 'lifefucker'. It's a remarkably aggressive comment on the idea of Christ.

Eve Libertine: "The historical thing of Jesus we don't know. How long after his life were the Gospels written? I mean, how much do we really know about 100 years ago even with all our technology. And this is word of mouth, so ... the language wasn't very pleasant, no! ... Yes, the language was a tactic. But I don't have any problems with it. I probably wouldn't do it now cos, over the years since Crass, I've moved from the anti-this anti-that type thing. I do think it has value, but I think one can be caught up in it. So I stepped away from that and brought the positive in. You can get buried under the negative and the anti-stuff, but at the time I think it served its purpose and I don't regret it. I can still read over it now and still accept it.

"After Asylum, we did have some letters from Christians saying they sort of understood it. I was surprised by that. I can't remember getting any letters that said 'How could you do this?'"

Joy De Vivre: "Even though none of us were Catholics, it probably made all of us feel uncomfortable. It was actually really difficult to speak out in that way."

The thought is inescapable: if mums up and down the land thought Crass had surely booked themselves a season ticket to Hell, what on earth did the bands own parents think?

Joy De Vivre: "My mum had always been fairly radical in her thinking, but it was always that one step ahead of her. So she'd puff along behind and she'd get scared, then she'd get confused about it. . ."

But never completely offended?

Joy: "No, she wasn't like that. She wasn't religious. I didn't find it particularly a problem, except knowing how it would sound 'out there', it would be extremely offensive and misunderstood. But. . . (to Phil Free) you wouldn't have played it to your mum would you?"

Phil: "No! I'd go down to visit my parents on the Kent coast with my kids and for a while we had a van with the logo painted on it – cos that's what you did. Then someone spray-painted the logo on the public toilets down on the beach, and my mum was horrified!"

Joy: "They'll think you've done it!"

Phil: "I used to shave my head for reasons that are fairly apparent [baldness] because there wasn't a great deal I could do. I remember when the old man died, my mum asking me if I could grow my hair for the funeral. So there you are, you've got five days to get your hair going!"

Mick Duffield: "As an atheist, and seeing organised religion as being an integral part of the con trick of the establishment, 'Reality Asylum' was a great challenge to Christian hypocrisy. I thought it was great."

Ironically, in all this, Crass still seem to have an invisible but eminently apparent vein of spirituality running through their output and attitudes. "I think it's just humanitarian," says Eve. "Possibly Jesus was a great guy, a lot of what he preaches about is great, as are virtually all the prophets. Looking beyond the materialistic way of life, being decent to other people. You could say that that's Christian, but it goes beyond that: the sexuality, the crucifixion, sin ... I don't think you have to bring in religion, I think you can just be a human being and relate to other human beings."

'Shaved Women' on the flipside, was an Annie Anxiety poem set to music, the main driving force of which was the sound of trains on a track, meant to signify the cattle trucks on their way to Auschwitz. The opening scream from Eve Libertine on vocals: "Shaved Women collaboratooooooooooors!" was ugly in a never heard, almost beautiful way. You could call that a feminist statement in itself, it was certainly a liberating moment. Eve simply sounded like a bag lady on speed having the mother of all tantrums and hurtling towards the sanatorium. It required a remarkable lack of vanity and artistic honesty, given that women singers usually consider their voices second only to their looks when it comes to vanity.

With its proud instruction 'Pay No More Than 45p' on the sleeve, Crass proved to any doubters that the cap on the pricing of the *Five Thousand* record was no publicity stunt. This time it really was for real. It was also a wonderfully impressive own-goal in the financial department, with each single losing the band money, so the more it sold, the worse it was for Crass on a financial level. Only they and New Order can share this proud artistic boast. And, like New Order, Crass had the most noble of intentions, as Penny Rimbaud explains: "I felt it was an extension of our fortune – we were being fortunate in selling stuff, fortunate in not paying much rent and living very cheaply. It was a way of extending that, sharing it with people. I used to feel we were the prow of a ship cutting through a sea of turd."

As a result of their fiscal incompetence, the band decided to get John Loder more involved with the financial side of affairs as well as recording. Loder effectively became Crass's manager, an arrangement which would last until the end of the band.

'Asylum' was the first Crass Record to feature the stencil lettering on a black circle that would come to represent their brand as surely as Beanz Meanz Heinz. It was a straightforward influence from pop-artist Jasper Johns, the American artist who emerged in the late fifties to influence both Pop Art and Minimalism and who was a notable forerunner in the use of stencil lettering.

Strangely enough, the first example of a Crass cover can be found a few years previous on a children's book called *The Blue Tomato*, which Penny Rimbaud illustrated in the days before Crass. It consisted of a painting of a blue tomato, with the title in a circle around it in stencil lettering. An acquaintance of the band actually bought a copy in a secondhand book store, curious at the resemblance to a Crass cover.

Penny Rimbaud: "The reason we did that single ourselves was because we knew it would create too many problems for Pete [Stennett from Small Wonder]. It quite shook him up, because the police went there first. He'd got his own life and he didn't want police coming round – in those days, dope was still something you could suffer for!"

You could also suffer for making records, as Crass was to discover. In the wake of attempted clampdowns on the newspaper *Gay News* and the play *The Romans In Britain*, serious consideration was given to prosecuting Crass for the 'Reality Asylum' single. To this end, a couple of Scotland Yard's finest were dispatched to Dial House to scout the situation. Like so many punk rockers before and after who visited, the place wasn't quite what they expected

"So they came here and they were completely shocked by what they found," says Penny Rimbaud. "I think they thought they were going to find semi-illiterate morons not knowing what the bloody hell they were doing, living in some decaying squat. From the start they were completely non-plussed and actually very charming. They had to go through the motions, appearing to be pushing for a prosecution, but in the end they dropped it. I think they realised that if they had pulled it off, they would have given us the same sort of platform that the Pistols had got in the mass media. I do think it was probably a very deliberate policy to ignore us at all costs, which is why other people always suffered at our expense. Even to the extent that the police used to park at the bottom of our road and tell stupid stories to young punks who were visiting – they wouldn't come down here and confront us."

"I was a bit nervous, I have to say," laughs Eve, "because it was *my* voice – I was the only identifiable person. The police were chatty and chummy. I think they found it a very easy case compared to what they normally have to do – you think what obscenity they probably had to deal with – some nasty nasty stuff. I would have thought they would have wondered what they were doing here."

Penny: "It wasn't the local police force – we always used to get on very well with the local guy. He always used to come down when there was a big thing on at Greenham cos he always knew the van wouldn't be here, it would be down at Greenham. So he'd always come down just to let us know that he knew. But he was great – he'd normally bring a plant down for the garden ... we got on alright, it was like an uncomfortable alliance – it was more the Epping & Harlow Police that seemed to like driving by."

Eve remembers the relationship with the local policeman as an off-duty one (for both sides): "He just used to come in and glance at the herb rack. Was his daughter having guitar lessons or something? No, I can't believe that's true..." she giggles.

Given their politics and increasing notoriety, the relationship of Crass to the local forces of control was remarkably trouble-free. "[On] only one occasion they stopped us in Epping and they were very aggressive, pulling us out of the car and calling us scum and that sort of thing," says penny. "So I booked in to see the chief – or whatever they're called – at Epping Police Station and said look, your guys are getting a bit out of hand here. He ended up saying, yeah, you know, they're just young roughnecks. . .

"But generally, we were just left alone. Having seen what happened to Phil (Russell, aka Wally Hope) and having spent a lifetime in radical politics, I'm surprised by how comfortably I've survived it. Partly, I think, because I'm polite."

As with *Feeding*, it wasn't only the songs on the 'Asylum' single that stood Crass apart. The single was released initially in a gatefold cardboard sleeve. Subsequent repressings took the weirdness even further, as the sleeve folded out to six times the single size to reveal a poster of a man (not ostensibly Jesus Christ) being crucified.

Penny: "The big foldout poster – you could look back to the sixties, where people used a lot of that sort of tactic. No-one had done it on a record before, but the whole idea of broadsheets was very much a sixties thing."

Actually, the first Public Image single came with a fold-out newspaper sleeve the previous year, but nothing quite so striking had featured on that sleeve. The single was also notable for its line-up notes, which included: "Members of Crass not on this recording: Steve Ignorant. . . Lead Vocalist. Joy De Vivre (Virginia Creeper) . . . voice."

Steve Ignorant: "What I liked about it was that it was a bit David Bowie-ish – the sort of thing he'd do. It'll get people asking questions – the mystery – we'll sell more records, keep the interest going. By that time we knew we had a foot in the door so we could experiment. And if it fucks up, we just won't do it again."

It was certainly an unusual move that once more hinted at a band so far removed from both straight and rock'n'roll conformity that a generation became fascinated. It is also worth noting that Gee Vaucher doesn't yet make it onto the list (or the spelling – she's still G. at this point). The smallest stirrings of a 'scene' were hinted at as well as early cohorts Annie Anxiety, Poison Girls and Fatal Microbes are all namechecked on the sleeve.

On a lighter note, the 'Asylum' sleeve also signalled Joy's move away from being Virginia Creeper ("it was so completely naff!") towards becoming Joy De Vivre.

'Reality Asylum' jumped to the top of *Sounds* new 'Alternative' singles chart, supplied to them by Small Wonder (though in those early days it would feature a different indie shop each week, with wildly differing charts). It would vie with the Ants single 'Zerox' for number one spot, confirming both bands as emerging totems of punk. *Feeding …* would usually be nestling a few places below, keeping it company.

With their new found popularity in tow, Crass went into Southern Studios to record their second album. The religious parody title theme was kept from *Feeding* for *Stations Of The Crass*. This time it was an enormously ambitious double album, three sides of new stuff and a live side from a gig at the Pied Bull (later to become the Powerhaus) in Islington.

The product was all wrapped in the (now trademark) wraparound sleeve and sold for just £3, still less than a normal single album.

Stations of The Crass is, in many ways, the most varied of their albums, not to mention the best selling. It sees the band experimenting with different sounds, not scared to leave space in the music or try influences from different genres. Most of all, it sees them sail defiantly in the opposite direction from rock'n'roll. Which isn't what Penny Rimbaud thinks: "We were being briefly, slightly a rock band."

If the aim had been to shock with 'Asylum' opening up their first album, Crass carried on the tactic with their follow-up. 'Mother Earth' took child-killer Myra Hyndley as its specialist subject, using the hated murder-icon as a weapon to reflect what they saw as the sick society that produced her. Of course, they'd learnt by this stage that a bit of controversy never hurt as well.

Steve Ignorant remembers that the tabloid paper the *Daily Star* had put Myra Hindley and Ian Brady on the cover of their paper, doubtless as a ruse to increase sales. "They asked their readers whether she should be freed, and of course they got all these letters saying she should be left to rot in hell. The Crass song is about using her to sell papers – who's exploiting who here? 'Cos that's a fucking horrible thing to sell your paper on. Of course they're going to say hang her – so would I."

Politically, the album took up where *Feeding …* had left off: The Clash are endlessly harangued for selling out ('White Punks On Hope', 'System'), the left firmly rejected ('White Punks On Hope' again) and religion and the state firmly abused ('Demoncrats', 'I Ain't Thick, It's Just A Trick').

'White Punks On Hope' was a musical revelation – from the spoken word vocal we can presumably still attribute to the Patti Smith influence, the music veers into normal punk before truly going off on an unexpected trajectory. Heavy dub bass and heavily effected guitars; the employment of dropouts – the musical type this time. Crass was attempting a take on reggae! And it worked! Shame about the lyrics then, which chose to harangue the anti-racists rather than the racists. "Black man's got his problems and his way to deal with it / so don't kid yourself you're helping with your white liberal shit".

Penny Rimbaud is animated in his defence of the Crass stance: "The Clash were massively woolly with their psuedo-reggae and their hip 'we're really black white people'. In the same way rock'n'roll always has: Mick 'black' Jagger, Elvis 'black' Presley. Rip it off the blacks, modify it, commodify it and sell it to the whites. That's precisely the history of rock'n'roll, which is a pure piece of racist imperialism. It was the stealing of a cultural heritage from the blacks. There was a television show featuring us and Aswad – it was at the height of that stuff with the Anti Nazi League. We were saying what do we know about black problems? Don't undermine their position with liberalism. Well that's exactly what Aswad were saying too. It confirmed right down the line our stance – they do not want our help – piss off!"

'Big Man (Big M.A.N.)' is a brave rant against the macho world from the male point of view, and as such must have presented a significant challenge to a large part of their audience: "Keep your myth of manhood, it's been going on too long". Although it was a truly revolutionary moment on the album, and of live sets played to hordes of white males, often wearing big bovver boots, it was probably misunderstood. "They'd sing along to it as well," remembers Steve Ignorant. "Ninety per cent of the Crass audience was men. The failing of punk rock to me was that it didn't bring men and women together – you still had that male-dominated thing ... maybe girls just don't like gigs? You go to America and it's totally different – more like 50-50. And also punk rock didn't bring black and white people together – which I really hoped it would do."

Nevertheless, 'Big Man. . .' was a significant step in the right direction, as Steve Ignorant notes. "At least it got *me* thinking about it, my life and how I was looking at things. And for the audience I think it actually kicked off a talking point. It had never really been covered apart from people like Germaine Greer, and the separatist 'cut men's balls off' brigade. Now it was young people and other blokes trying to write anti-sexist lyrics."

If proof was needed that attitudes were still far from perfect, consider this letter written to *Sounds* in May '79: "Your paper should be called Gay News, what with all those 'Whangers Of The Week'. Are most of your readers perverts, poofs, womens lib or what? Why not give your straight male readers a treat and print this picture I took recently of a great band called Bitch."

'Demoncrats' continued in the female spoken poetry vein of 'Reality Asylum', and is in many ways a more satisfying affair. 'Walls' even tiptoes to the disco, albeit a punk rock disco. The beat is initially provided by the sound of a radio dial being whizzed to and fro. It sounds like – and indeed is – a precursor to the scratching movement that would begin in a few years. On vocals, Joy De Vivre's voice sheds the harsh growls of 'Women' on the first record to display a folky smooth tenderness, with a highly unusual explanation: "That's cos I can't shout! I can't sing-scream like Eve could. Singing in a folky way is much more me. It's a song that's so not disco in its wording."

For Crass to essentially parody their idea of disco raises some interesting presumptions on their part, and indeed on the wider part of the feminist movement. For all Crass' feminist leanings, it's indisputable that most women felt infinitely safer and more comfortable at a disco than they would have done at a punk gig. And songs like Gloria Gaynor's 'I Will Survive' talked a lot more clearly to women in supremely 'disco wording'.

Penny Rimbaud: "'Walls' is a very avant-garde piece of dance music. There was a lot of experimentation just beginning to happen."

Stations also stood to reaffirm that Crass was keeping the faith. The 'difficult second album' was often the fork in the road for punk bands

143

who didn't have a second album's worth of material in them, as an opportunity to showcase their 'new direction', which was often straight to the bank to open Gold accounts or straight to the building site to plead for a job. Instead Crass reiterated their commitment to the ever-increasing number of punks who weren't going to change just because a few peacocks in London had declared punk officially over.

One of Steve Ignorant's few regrets about Crass surfaces on the track 'Hurry Up Garry (The Parsons Farted)' – a rather bitter attack on Garry Bushell and Tony Parsons for having the temerity to give *Feeding* bad reviews. "Just because it gives him too much fame really," explains Steve.

'I Ain't Thick, It's Just A Trick' is the real concession to rock'n'roll here. A barnstorming singafuckinglong that rails against the usual forces of repression, it's there to keep the narrower-taste punks on board, as Rimbaud willfully admits: "Most people wrote what they wanted to and when they felt like it. I was the 'jobber'. That's what it turned out like. Initially, I said I wasn't going to write anything after Steve had shown me 'So What', which was a direct reaction to my *Christ's Reality Asylum* (the book, not the song). He'd managed to put it into common parlance – mine was a massive incomprehensible tract . . . [so] I adopted a different way of writing . . . and enjoyed doing it. 'I Ain't Thick' . . . sounds awfully contrived, and it was (and actually I think it's the worst song I ever wrote) – but I wrote it because I thought we hadn't got a 'boot song' on that album. I thought, hey, this album hasn't got an anthem, and we need one. You could almost say it was cynical commercialism. It's quite interesting that it became one of the most asked-for songs . . . inevitably."

Stations also sees Crass come into their own with lyrical eccentricity, made all the more entertaining by their apparent lack of awareness of the fact. The 'jock rot heavy metal leg-iron gush' sits proudly beside the 'crap-lined pit'; phrases sung without a hint of humour or self-conciousness, making them all the funnier.

And then there's the live side, which is uniformly awful. Notable only for a segue between songs that borrows a couplet from the Buzzcocks' 'Everybody's Happy Nowadays', it's a pretty much unlistenable combination of songs from *Feeding* and songs available elsewhere on the album. So it's kind of pointless too, thankfully.

It would probably be true to say that in terms of the entire band the input on *Stations* was much more general – a greater reflection of all of the personalities in the band. As was now the norm, *Stations* stormed to the top of the alternative charts where it stayed for the foreseeable future.

Throughout this period, punk gigs were dogged by crowd violence. While it's true to say that not all skinheads of the time were violent, it's equally true to say that if a gang of skinheads turned up at a punk gig – which they often did – then the chances of Nazi salutes and violence kicking off were increased greatly.

"People forget that in those days the minute you stepped out side Central London and went anywhere slightly suburban, you were in danger," says Steve. "One of the worst gigs for trouble was when we played Epping."

Stevenage was another bad gig for Crass and Steve Ignorant in particular when he got arrested for ABH. "We played at Bowes Lyon House." He says. "The security were friends with the local skinheads. It kicked off and Gee went to confront them. One of them slapped Gee round the face. I jumped offstage and managed to clump him. At the end of the gig, the police turned up and arrested me."

Though the arrest eventually came to nothing, it certainly wasn't the end of trouble for Crass. Violence, or at least the threat or rumour of it, would dog them throughout the rest of their playing days. Crass themselves finger the starting point of all this to be a benefit gig they did at this time for Persons Unknown, with Dutch band The Rondos.

Persons Unknown were a group of anarchists who'd been arrested by the police on the vaguest 'Conspiracy to incite' charges. Effectively, this means that no crime needs to have been committed; simply the thought that one might be at some point (in places unknown, conspiring with persons unknown, hence the name of the case).

Dave Morris, then a part of the Persons Unknown support group remembers:

"The police claimed they were going to kidnap Princess Anne! Then they dropped that and said it was about armed robberies. In fact it was all about Special Branch trying to manufacture some public hysteria to try to justify their own existence."

The venue for the gig, the Conway Hall describes itself as "a landmark of London's intellectual, political and cultural life", and as such has been promoting leftist events from its inception in 1929 to the present day. Crass had found themselves a fitting venue to play in London and played several times there without (much) incident. On one such occasion, they showed the Anthony McCall piece *Four Projected Movements* during the silent break in 'They've Got A Bomb'. As the music performed an emergency stop, the wedge of light was projected from the back of the room at head height towards the stage. It then began a slow circular movement. It would be interesting to know how many punks in the audience realized it was more than just a lighting effect.

For the Persons Unknown gig, as was often the case, a Crass gig had attracted a gang of skinheads who purported to be of the far right. Band members believe they were establishing a healthy dialogue with these people as time went on, but this time they were playing a benefit gig for the 'traditional' anarchist cause and certain elements weren't so tolerant. The gig was trashed and the skinheads with it.

Steve Ignorant: "I couldn't put my finger on it, but I wasn't sure about The Rondos. We went to the gig and there was a lot of rumours going around that the British Movement were turning up. As usual! We got that at every gig. I remember being backstage and this roar went up. All of a sudden there's this full-scale battle going on and all I could do was watch from the stage – I didn't know who was thumping who."

Phil Free: "The Rondos were Maoists – bloody heavy. Jesus, they were frightening. Serious! They made us look like a vaudeville show! They're probably still doing time for something!"

Eve Libertine: "That was horrible. I just remember swathes of people, somebody covered in blood."

Steve Ignorant: "Apparently what had happened was the SWP had had a meeting up the road and had been given reports that loads of skinheads had been seen going into the Conway Hall, so they all came down to do the skinheads."

One of the security team that night has written an account of the trouble from a different perspective. A flavour of the evening can be garnered from the forthcoming book *Anti-Fascist, London* by Martin Lux, an account of street confrontations with the far right during the seventies:

"Around forty plus British Movement skinheads had barged in and were gathered inside the main entrance exuding menace. It didn't take long to evaluate the situation. Hopeless. A dozen of them were large brutes, evil looking bastards, real hardnuts, with another dozen or so inner core. The remainder were merely runty followers, but dangerous if mob-handed or tooled up. The organisation of the gig had collapsed, Nazis ruled the roost. The only thing holding them back from rampage was that they were waiting for Crass to come on for the finale, then they'd rush and take the stage.

"Abandoning the door, I tried to further suss out the opposition. Like the bullies they were, the boneheads were amusing themselves by insulting the punters, punks and anarcho-trendies who avoided dialogue or body contact, wise under the circumstances.

"I'd managed to gather around half a dozen lads, most of whom had accompanied me on previous jaunts, could be depended on, and were willing to have a proper go. The trendy anarcho-types were no good in a fight, unless of course, it involved the missus. Besides, they were always hinting, if not stating outright that there was only a marginal difference between us anti-fascists and the Nazis themselves. Now faced with such a raw situation, no longer able to afford the luxury of such pontificating, they kept their traps shut.

"I was called over to the door, asked to step outside; someone had been enquiring after me by name. Curious, I stepped out into the chill October night to be met by a couple of anti-fascists who were attached to the SWP. I'd joined these characters on many a past expedition against the Master Race. Someone had been on the blower as these lads had everything well-sussed. 'Can you keep the lid on it for a couple of hours? We're gonna get our crew together, steam 'em real heavy.'

"'It'll be difficult,' I mused, 'But I'll do my best. I know they're waiting for Crass to go on so they can storm the stage. Crass are headlining, so they won't be on 'till last.'

"'You and your mates don't mind us having the bastards knowing that Crass won't get to play?'

"'Far as I'm concerned,' I retorted, 'This gig's been fucked from the beginning. I don't give a monkey's what people think so long as these

Nazi fuckers get what's coming to 'em. Anyway, you'll be doing my eardrums a favour. I can't stand this racket.'

"They departed for the warmth of a nearby pub. "We'll send word when we're ready. See you outside.""

Steve Ignorant: "It would have been alright but the *Guardian* reported it as fascist skinheads started the trouble, which it wasn't. So our very tenuous relationships with the skinheads went right out the fucking window. And that's when all the *real* trouble started – people being chased down trainlines outside the Moonlight Club and getting ambushed on the way to gigs: retribution took place."

Eve Libertine: "Usually with the skinheads, there'd be one who had the suss, and the others would do whatever the leader was doing. If the leader was taken away, they wouldn't be sure what they were there for, quite honestly. I know there were problems, and I know stuff was going on but they were just like, 'Look, I'm a Nazi', but it was more like, 'No, you're not, you're just an idiot.'"

Steve Ignorant: "We weren't going to start not letting skinheads in – I used to be a skinhead!"

Eve Libertine: "They were a pain in the arse and we had a lot of trouble with them after that. Before that, they used to come to the gigs and there wasn't trouble. OK, so we're singing 'Big Man' and they're singing along to it – do they not listen to the words? But there was no saying you can't come in because you're not a pacifist or anything"

Joy De Vivre: "One thing that was important to me was that very occasionally we got through to somebody who was really right wing without actually giving them a hiding. There was an idea that if you could get through to people without beating them up, get through their thick skins and influence them … if they were there in the audience, maybe you'd have a chance to reach them in some way."

Bob Short: "I think the big difference is that in that era there was so much that you didn't want to remember. I look at the period between '78 and '83/84 as one of the few modern wars without correspondents. There was the birth of a thriving (and genuine) counter culture that almost completely eluded the possibility of corporate manipulation and takeover. Unfortunately, it was set against a backdrop of violence that most people I now know have little comprehension of."

"The punk of '76/7 was a wild energy rush but by '79 it had definitely split into a battle between the reactionary and the creative. The rise of the large squat estates created a genuine cultural identity. The rise of the British Movement gave it a dark mirror and a wolf at the door."

Lots of punk kids had flocked to London and ended up living in squats, the exodus from the provinces becoming the beginning of punk as a way of life and a movement. Often these squats would be viciously attacked by organised gangs of skinheads. Stories of gang rapes and people doused in petrol and threatened with being set on fire abound. As Tony D points out, for all their faults, the SWP didn't go round in gangs attacking innocent people like this.

"It is not the National Front or the British Movement that represents the right-wing threat; they, like the dinosaur, are all body and no brain and because of that will become extinct."
Penny Rimbaud – *Last Of The Hippies*

The punk squatters saw the reaction of Crass to the Conway Hall incident as a clear case of Crass being out in Epping and out of touch with their everyday lives in London. Some I've spoken to are incensed that Crass could even think this, given how heavy the violence was at the time. An example: "Penny Rimbaud … what a wanker. He probably thinks broomsticks shoved into unwilling anal cavities are wizard pranks much like what he used to get up to in public school, whato."

Alistair Livingstone: "As members of a post-sixties intellectual avant garde privileged elite, living in their Safe Epping Forest Home, Crass adopted the style but not the substance of punk. Dial House was never a squat and its inhabitants never had to confront the 'in yer face' reality which the survivors of the punk squatting scene had to as part of their daily life."

Joy De Vivre, on the other hand, recalls a relatively recent incident when she & Phil Free were spotted by a middle-aged ex-National Front skinhead in a café: "He said if he hadn't have come across you guys, he'd have been a complete and utter thug, he'd have never got out of that trap. There was, perhaps naively, an idea that you didn't go round beating the shit out of people, you actually tried talking to them. Maybe that wasn't particularly wise or even realistic, but just occasionally it worked. I think the Conway Hall gig was a point at which it might have worked."

Joy DeVivre: "Of course there's an honourable tradition of beating up the fascists, but how did they become fascists? There's such a load of full stops everywhere and I guess a lot of our stuff was just trying to erase the full stops and start people seeing each other."

On the subject of skinheads, Penny Rimbaud credits himself with having started the movement back in the sixties: "When I was at art school, I found this barber. He'd learnt his hairdressing in the Polish Army, where he shaved a lot of heads. I decided I'd have my head shaved. Then I got a bluebeat hat, which was my dad's trilby cut down. We had an American student staying with us who had a pair of desert boots which he gave to me. Then the building department boys at college – who were the hard nuts – really fancied the gear, so they started wearing it. I definitely think I was one of the prototype skinheads."

The Conway Hall gig also boosted one of the more extreme fanzines of the day. *Toxic Graffity* (sic) had been lined up as the benefactor of the next gig Crass was to play at the Conway Hall, but since they were now understandably persona-non-grata, they offered instead to give the fanzine a new track 'Rival Tribal Rebel Revels' – partly inspired by the Conway Hall events – for inclusion as a flexi-disc for the next issue. This proved such a popular move that *Toxic Graffity* sold tens of thousands, where purchasers were treated to page after page of anarchist ranting and newspaper cut-out invective. It was possibly a sign of one of the failings of the movement that the intelligent and eloquent young man who put the fanzine together considered constant dumbing-down and clichés as the best way to get his message over.

"The extreme left is largely made up from educated and privileged people who, because of their social background, are able to infiltrate organisations, from schools to the media, in which they can push their propaganda. The threat that they pose to the development of radical creative change is far greater than that of right-wing organisations. The right, because it lacks any true political ideology (at least, that which it does have is so laughably transparent) and because it rarely has the 'social respectability' of the left, relies on its appeal to a small group of people who,

finding themselves on the bottom of the social scrapheap, rejected by leftists and liberals alike, take the only option that is on offer to them – violence. So-called 'right-wing violence' is generally not politically motivated at all, but is simply an end-of-the-line reaction against seemingly impossible odds made by people who are offered nothing by society but a life of slavery.

The left-wing 'threat' is an organised and calculated attempt by generally priv-ileged people who to gain power and control will use those who are less privileged to fight their causes. Those that do not conform to their leftist requirements they label as 'fascists'. At the same time however, they would happily recruit those so-called 'fascists' to achieve their own ends – in violence there is no morality.

We have the strength, by simply refusing to be used as tools to other people's desires, to overcome oppression; but do we have the personal courage to stand alone, without our 'party membership card' or 'Little red book', and demand our right to live?"

Penny Rimbaud – *Last Of The Hippies*

Martin Lux: "I suppose in my heart of hearts the reaction following the Conway Hall bloodbath didn't really surprise me, although I was taken aback for a while. After years of abuse, insults and cold-shoul-dering from many in the anarcho scene, it came as no great shock. Even so, it infuriated me. The group Crass and their support band The Poison Girls, issued weighty statements. There were shock horror reports of the carnage in the *Guardian* and *Time Out*. The BM Nazis were treated as sacrificial lambs, despite them outnumbering us over two to one. We and our friends from the left were 'Red Fascists', a 'Football Gang', 'their leaders appeared to be Scots', even in the sup-posedly liberal press of the day a by-word for 'nutter'. Such parochial-ism – even the Nazis would blush. The odium was heaped on me and others, but I withstood it with the usual fortitude, a couple of minor outbursts aside. After all, my critics would soon disappear into the halls of academia, respectability, the Labour Party, the media and property-owning classes. Fuck 'em."

Following this incident, and the protagonists' subsequent ostrasisation from the anarchist and Socialist 'establishment', Martin Lux and his fellow 'comrades at arms' would go on to form Class War and Red Action/AFA, the respective histories of which have been since well documented.

"Freedom without socialism is privilege and injustice. Socialism without freedom is slavery and brutality." – Mikhail Bakunin

In 1979, an event took place that was to mould and almost dictate Crass' activities for the final years of their career together. The Conservative Party inevitably won the General Election and Margaret Thatcher was sworn in as British Prime Minister on May 4.

Somewhat unfortunately, with the luxury of hindsight, Crass was busy pontificating on the uselessness of voting and shouting lines like "left wing, right wing, you can stuff the lot". Regrets?

Steve Ignorant: "I do regret it actually. This might sound a bit weird, but I wonder how different it would have been if people had voted and kept the Tories out. I was like, fuck it, whoever you vote for the government wins. But fuck me, what a government we got."

Pete Wright: "We were actually sided against Callaghan. When Thatcher got in, we moved smoothly to siding against her outfit. It's a conceit that premiers in the G7 have much power. I think I pointed out the machinations that pushed the British government into the Falklands attack. The culprits are usually hiding round the back pulling the strings. Buckminster Fuller said that the power of the president of the US approximates to zero."

Steve Ignorant: "At that time, I didn't give a fuck, and that's what I regret. I wish I'd taken a bit more interest."

Mick Duffield: "I think with nation states that anyone who gets into power gets bent into a mould very quickly and you can't work outside of that within the political establishment so I think it's valid to say that the differences between (the left and right) are so minimal that they're not worth considering. If you take the left far enough, you end up with an authoritarian, bureaucratic horrific state, like Russia – so how are people better off? How is anything there worth pursuing? In western democracy, it might appear that the left offers a slightly softer alternative to what the right has to offer, but in reality, where it leads is no better."

Crass recorded their only John Peel session in January 1979, recording 'G's Song' (with a long free jazz/classical music intro to emphasise further the contradictions), 'Mother Earth', 'Shaved Women'. "Shorter than the single I think and perhaps more effective," said Peel, for some reason or other.

The final song was 'Bomb'. Where a Peel session would be an important career mark for most bands, it was essentially a non-event for Crass. "Well that was Crass – I bet you thought I'd gone home in the middle of that," Peel quipped, referring to the weird gap.

"Hope lies in the proles" – George Orwell, '1984'
"I've met the man in the street, and he's a cunt" – Sid Vicious, 1977

Though few foresaw it at the time, the election of Margaret Thatcher as Prime Minister signalled a new phase in the class war that had been simmering in Britain throughout the seventies. One of the flashpoints lit up when teacher Blair Peach was killed at a demonstration in Southall where the Special Patrol Group were called in. The SPG, as they were known, was the most feared elite corps of London's Metropolitan Police, and if the 'Met' were out of control, the SPG were their Gestapo. Thatcher responded with pay rises for them and an increasingly politicisation of the role of the British police as time wore on.

The Government also announced it had agreed to host American unmanned Cruise missiles in the UK, starting off at Greenham Common airbase near Newbury. This effectively entertained the possibility of a 'limited' nuclear war between the superpowers using Europe as its chessboard and obliterating its population as a side-issue.

The age of 'beer and sandwiches at No 10' – referring to regular meetings between Labour Prime Ministers and Union leaders in the seventies – was more than over. In its place came a woman who was not only hostile to Unions, but hostile to the concept of society and to the very rights of the working man and woman that Unions had been set up to protect. Though Thatcher is popularly portrayed as a bastion of the middle classes, it was the interests of the ruling class that she championed. The class war in Britain was as alive as ever, but now the tide had turned in favour of the bad guys. It was a war that would explode in largely unprecedented ways over the next decade.

Class, of course, was one of the sticks that Crass was beaten with increasingly regularly by both the press and certain punks. Crass was not just hippies, but *middle-class* hippies to boot. The aura of privilege perceived to surround them suggested that only those born into favourable economic situations could afford (in any sense of the word) to 'drop out' and go and live in a commune in the countryside.

Phil Free: "I was an upper-working class, lower middle-class background. My old man was a bank clerk, and with four kids, that meant no money. But there were certain middle-class aspirations – we did have books in the house."

Joy de Vivre: "I didn't have a fantastically privileged upbringing. Compared to some people, yes, but it wasn't marvellously middle-class – my parents were very working-class. We were a very mixed bunch."

Punk bands were an increasingly mixed bunch too as they waved goodbye to the seventies. Some of the more imaginative bands were beginning to break through, with The Slits releasing the classic dub-tinged 'Cut' and Siouxsie & The Banshees 'Join Hands'. The UK Subs were still going strong with their first album release and bands like The Jam and The Undertones were embracing the mainstream. The Jam clearly weren't punks, but lines were a lot more blurred at the time. On another front, journalist Garry Bushell was having increasing influence at *Sounds* writing about punk bands like the Angelic Upstarts, who were representative of a new and altogether harder (more macho) steel toe-capped strand of punk that was waiting in the wings.

The year of 1979 was possibly the last that all these diverse strands – from The Psychedelic Furs and the futurists that played at the Futurama festival to the emerging Cockney Rejects and Cure, Bauhaus and The Swell Maps – would be considered punk. For the time being, they were still just about appearing side by side on bus stop graffiti and the backs of leather jackets, but punk as a multi-faceted movement was dying, to be replaced by more narrowly defined sub-genres. One of these – the 'Crass bands', followers and fellow travellers, would be called anarcho-punk.

421984

Those who would contend that punk in the UK had well and truly died a death by the start of the eighties could do worse than leaf through the ever self-consciously trendy *NME*. It had taken the Crass style white stencil lettering on a black background as its central style theme for section headings. The indie top 10 charts featured Spizz, Dead Kennedys and Stiff Little Fingers. But it's the adverts that are the true gauge of the market — look there and there's still as much punk gear being sold as all the rest of the fashion ephemera put together.

Across the globe, punk was still growing and getting even bigger — from the United States, where the lack of a Pistols/Grundy moment had allowed the movement to grow more organically at its own pace, to the Soviet Bloc countries, where punk was a purer and more dangerous (and heroic) act of political defiance, to the North of Ireland, where punk was seemingly the only movement going beyond sectarianism. If punk had undoubtedly lost much of its imagination and become more of a uniform — with all the paradoxes therein — it was also turning into a social movement, a movement of the streets, a movement for social change. And in the UK, social change was beginning to happen. In the wrong direction. Thatcher had won the minds of a significant part of the people. The party that most advocated selfishness was on the march, preaching virtue in social conformity and the scapegoating of those who defied it: fascism–lite, available now at your local democracy.

Believing that the streets were where response was most needed, Crass decided to try and popularise the graffiti campaign they had been waging with a leaflet urging others to follow in their spray can-steps, a much more feasible activity in the days before big brother was literally watching you via CCTV.

"This is a sample of some of the sprays that we use for various graffiti projects," they wrote in their leaflet. "If you cut these stencils out, perhaps it would be better to copy them onto thin card first. You could use them for decorating clothing, in which case silver spray is the best to use if it's onto black clothes, or if it's onto any other light colour any car spray paint will do. You can buy alphabetical stencil kits in most shops that sell art material. You can also buy craft knives which are the best type for cutting stencils. Some of these stencils are the ones that we use on posters etc to let people know that we don't agree with the shit that they promote: it's a good way of spending an evening, but don't get caught. Graffiti is a really effective way of letting your opinions be seen: if all the army recruitment offices in the country were sprayed with a 'fight war' stencil maybe the message would get through a little."

But what message? The clues are scattered around the living. . .

"In 1914, just before the curtain rose on the trench slaughter of World War 1, Aleister Crowley and his mistress Leile Waddle hosted an event in London called the Rites Of Eleusis. Over some four or five nights they presented a quasi-masonic ritual, music poetry dance and drama. Actors pronounced that God was dead with a ponderous Nietzschean finality, readings were given from the Tibetan Book of The Dead *and, on the final night, the audience received, communion-style, the 'Elixir of the Gods' – in fact, red wine generously spiked with mescaline. As the punters tripped out, a chorus announced the dawning of the New Aeon based on Rabelais' law of Thelema: 'Do what thou wilt'. Sound familiar?"*
Mick Farren – *Give The Anarchist A Cigarette*

Farren is, of course, drawing a parallel with the hippy movement, but years later both Adam & The Ants and Crass would be singing songs advising 'Do what you wanna do / be what you wanna be' (Ants – 'Dirk Wears White Socks') or even 'Be exactly who you want to be, do what you want to do' (Crass – 'Big A Little A'). Elsewhere in his book, Farren states: "In theory, in a place like The Roxy, 'Do what you will should once more have been the law, but ... the punks were far less tolerant of deviance and aberration than the hippies had ever been, unless said deviance and aberration conformed to their own norms of perversity."

Writing in 2005 on his website messageboard, old Sex aficionado and Adam And The Ants guitarist Marco Pirroni attempted to explain the contradictions that ran rife through punk rock: "It was just a big promo to sell trousers, it was a working class social revolution, it was an art school prank, it was a posey fashion experiment, it was all about the music MAAAN, it was a record company marketing campaign, it was left-wing, it was neo-Nazi, it was fascist, it was apolitical, it was anti-drug pro-amphetamine anti-sex shag-fest, it was racists who loved reggae, it was against disco, but danced to Donna Summer, we came not to praise Elvis but to dress like him, we hate Pink Floyd, we love Pink Floyd ... boredom with a passion, the worse it is, the better it is ... if I have to explain, you can't understand."

The delicious beauty of punk was that it was all those things and more. As time moved on, of course, people cherry-picked the parts that appealed to their personal dogmas and all decided their own version of punk was the authentic model. This is how we've arrived at a position where punk died at various moments in 1976 and 1977, but kept going until the mid-eighties and indeed is still alive and vital (as well as being dead and long-gone) today.

Reviewing *Stations Of The Crass* for *NME* the previous year, Graham Lock picked apart the Crass view of punk: "'Punk was once an answer' they claim on 'White Punks On Hope', already idealising and distorting the past in an archetypically regressive manner. Punk was a gesture, a fart in the face of authority – it was never an answer. At best it was a beginning, opening up possibilities which people are still exploring in a variety of ways."

Crass and Adam & The Ants were the two big underground punk bands of the era, both massive compared to everyone else. In the new fashion of the time, they were the two bands on the back of every leather jacket. Both trumpeted the power of the fanzine over the music press and both had written songs complaining about it – 'Hurry Up Garry' from Crass and 'Press Darlings' from the Ants, both of which name-checked Garry Bushell.

Tony D remembers selling all 1,000 copies of the first issue of his fanzine 'Kill Your Pet Puppy' at a London Ants gig around this time. It had the fanzine equivalent of three scoops on the front page: Ants / Tuinol / Crass – the two biggest bands and an article about the drug that was threatening to ravage the London punks the way that heroin had seen off the Haight-Ashbury hippies.

Unfortunately, tragically even, the Ants and Crass seemed to see each other as detestable rivals. Adam Ant filled in a fanzine questionnaire for *Panache* fanzine: "Hates: Hippies, Crass. . ."

Crass responded with equally juvenile posturing, though to be fair this wasn't until Adam Ant had become a teenybop idol. "I'm sure if I bumped into the bloke we'd get on fine," says Steve. "A bit like Joe Strummer – 'CBS promote The Clash' etc – but I never stopped loving them. I always knew that I'd still buy the records."

While both the Ants and Crass attempted to split their audience in some kind of musical sectarianism, the audience itself remained remarkably bi-partisan. Neither player was bigger than the club, even if both clearly considered themselves so. Essentially, Adam & The Ants were the far better band both live and on record, but – as various derided but essentially perceptive journalists noted early on in their career – Adam's integrity was always shaky at best. What Crass lacked in Adam's professional and showbiz technique, they more than made up for in honesty and their genuine belief in punk rock as a social movement and not just a consumer database. Indeed, this belief itself influenced the future of punk in that direction once Adam Ant had shown his contempt for the punk fans. Given the problems it is now clear Adam was always struggling with, the whole thing seems easier to understand and tolerate, but at the time it just felt like treachery.

Crass wasn't the only band with a vestibule of honesty, of course. Other bands were pursuing punk-as-communication/dada/avant garde in successful left-field styles, notably The Au Pairs, The Pop Group, Gang Of Four and The Fall. Both Scritti Pollitti and This Heat emerged from the squatting scene with a great awareness (conscious or otherwise) of avant garde values. "Anything was potentially a source of music," This

Heat drummer Charles Hayward told Simon Reynolds in his book *Rip It Up And Start Again*, echoing John Cage once more.

Pete Wright: "In the Sixties, the hippies were the new radical movement that shook things up. That's basically the same with any new movement. It's a basic feeling, and punk gave a great contrast. It meant different things to different people. The punks that emerged in '76/77 were bought off very quickly and by the winter of '77, London was a bit of a wasteland where nothing was really happening. There was a sense of loss and that we were left with nothing. We knew we'd have to build things from scratch. Punk was made mainstream. History has been re-written – it always happens, you have to take things in context. It provides the uncritical element of actually being involved in the movement. You get to understand things in a more mature way, Crass fell into the trap of having narrowed itself down to a linear message. Constantly had to defend itself. The intentions were more about energy and combating propaganda."

Pete's comments about the linear message ring an uncomfortably familiar bell – it still remains a mystery why Crass, given the same space that punk created in which to do as they pleased – 'This here atmosphere where everything's allowed' (as Patti Smith put it) chose to do, of all things, straightforward punk, which was virtually a deliberate denial of the imagination they so clearly possessed. Given that most of them were middle-class and equally not punk fans, you'd expect them to have used a more experimental path. Whatever, there was a second generation of younger punk rockers waiting for the anarchist call. . .

In his book *Harmony In My Head*, Buzzcocks guitarist Steve Diggle opines that, "If punk rock in its truest form had started to peter out in 1978, it's safe to say that, by 1979, it had all but vanished."

Safe to say that, yes, but was it (in its 'truest' form) true? If so, are we to accept that hippies didn't survive beyond the UFO club or the Merry Prankster acid tests?

Alistair Livingstone: "The alternative point of view is to see such initial situations as the cultural equivalent of a nuclear chain-reaction. Here the initial impact breaks up an unstable particle into many particles which in turn initiate further reactions which in turn trigger more reactions in an explosive process which only dies away when all the unstable elements have been used up – or where an external force (carbon rods inserted into a nuclear reactor) intervenes to absorb and contain the energy of the chain-reaction."

In 1980, there were still many kids dressing like punks (if you can pardon the inherent flaw in that sentence); there were many kids going to punk concerts and buying punk records. What was lacking was new punk bands coming up to fill the spaces left by the original bands as they split up, jumped ship or sold their souls. This is where Crass fitted a niche perfectly. Because of their overview that punk was part of a wider maelstrom, almost a direct descendent of the previous counter culture, they saw no reason whatsoever to abandon what they saw as the huge potential of punk just because it was being challenged in the fashion mags by the Mod and Two-Tone revivals.

"Hates: Hippies, Crass. . ."

That questionnaire by Adam Ant still rankles. Much of the evidence suggests that Crass was more correct than people admitted about the close relation between the seventies 'hippy' scene and punk rock. The popular image of punk as some kind of year zero wipe-the-slate-clean movement coming straight out of nowhere and impatient to get back there isn't really born out by close inspection. Steve Jones, Sex Pistols guitarist, in their film *The Filth And The Fury* describes where the early fans – those who wouldn't go on to make a career out of being such – really came from: "I remember in High Wycombe, opening for Screaming Lord Sutch, seeing some faces there with long hair, and then a week later we'd be playing at the Nashville and I'd see the same people with their hair cut short wearing a ripped up t-shirt. Every gig, you'd see a few more and a few more, people who just got converted."

The same people with hair cut short . . . indeed, when Johnny Rotten gave his first interview to the music paper *Sounds*, his sneer "I hate long hair. I hate hippies" gave the impression that he'd never had long hair or listened to Hawkwind, both palpably true with the luxury of hindsight. And if you want to deface a Pink Floyd tee-shirt with 'I Hate. . .', it follows that you've got to own a Pink Floyd tee-shirt in the first place.

So, it can be pretty safely assumed that the schism between 'hippies' (or 'freaks', as Pete Stennett would have it) and 'punks' was a blind alley. In other words, Crass was right and Malcolm McLaren was wrong.

Reflecting on his time searching for help during the Wally Hope hospitalisation saga, Penny notes in *Last Of The Hippies*: "The most useful and compassionate help came from organisations like Release and BIT, underground groups, some of which still operate today helping people over all sorts of problems, from housing to arrest. Critics of the 'hippy generation' would do well to remember that the majority of such organisations, plus alternative bookshops, printing presses, food shops, cafes, gig venues etc., are still run, for the benefit of us all, by those same hippies; old maybe but, because of the enormous efforts many of them have made 'to give hope a chance', not boring."

Of course, what constitutes being a hippie – or being a punk for that matter – could remain a debate for eternity. But it's worth bearing in mind the old maxim that history is always written by the winners. So it is with hippie and punk – we are told with all the authority that celebrity can muster that 'it was like this' or 'it meant this' by a select group of people who owe their fame and media standing to their particular movements. They appear on late-night talk shows and documentaries telling everyone how it was – what it was. And for them, so it was.

But the 'foot soldiers' often have a very different – and unheard – story to tell. Alan Bream's book – *Rehearsal For The Year 2000* – tells a very different tale of the hippie scene than the images that usually spring to mind. His is a world of crash pads, of people helping each other via voluntary groups, of alternative visions and possibilities. A world where 'hippies' were simply normal, fallible people struggling with themselves and society to keep smiling and holding on to loving ideals despite their own shortcomings and those of their surroundings; of being pro-active in organising alternatives to straight society simply to help their fellow man and attempt to set an example. This is a very different reality to the archetype served up with your daily cliché, and there's precious little to 'never trust' about it other than the sense of terminal boredom if you don't take drugs. That said, it wasn't perfect...

Pete Wright: "I think I was as guilty as anyone else in the return to shamanism. It's as good as any other uncritical approach until the going gets rough. I remember seeing a sticker in the back window of a car in the sixties, 'next time your house gets broken into, call a hippie'. It made me think. Of course, testing the nature of your own self-imposed restrictions can be a fruitful path. One of Penny's best lines was, 'Big Brother ain't watching you, chum, you're fucking watching him.'

It should be said that all socialisation is based on prohibition, which is mainly self imposed. It is an easy option to think that most prohibitions are redundant, while living safe within one's own insulated environment."

Tony D: "Bands like The Derelicts and The 101ers were anti-dropouts and layabouts. The dropouts and layabouts called themselves hippies as an excuse for doing nothing. Then there were the others who were hippies because they were political activists, still living in squats. They were all tarred with the same brush – the 'never trust a hippy' thing was probably a slogan from the early '70s from the activist types."

Whether or not Crass were 'hippies', Steve Ignorant is adamant they never thought of Dial House as a commune. "That's one of the worst things ... Pete Stennett (Small Wonder) said to Graham Lock (*NME*) that we all lived together in a commune. We didn't, we lived in this house. Because the minute you say 'commune', my instant vision is of a pregnant bra-less woman slopping about in fucking Jesus sandals – dog on a rope, tepees and what have you." Steve warms to the theme: "Beds in a row in a dormitory, Grey blankets with those red lines on them. All getting up to do the washing up and rinse out the soya beans for the daily tofu.... So, no. We did *not* live in a fucking commune! It was a house where we all lived together and ate meals at the same time."

That said, everybody did share money, perhaps one of the technical definitions of communal living. Steve Ignorant: "The only person who had a bank account was Penny Rimbaud, so all the money that we got from Crass used to go into his bank account, and then it would get doled out. When it started, we really didn't know what to do with it. In those days, it was bad form to have money. So, it was, like, how do we get rid of this stuff?! We had an allowance each of £500 a year – I remember having that and thinking I was rich! That's £10 a week!"

Steve Ignorant: "What we'd tend to do is put the money in the kitty, cos it tended to turn out cheaper that way. It was *commun-al,* I'll give you that, but it wasn't a 'commune'. I take the piss out of it, but it made sense for what that place was, and it *did* work. It worked pretty good. And still does actually. There weren't any rules or regulations, but the washing up always got done – even when there was 15 people and 23 cats. The place was never a shithole."

Despite this, Penny says he was unaware of the Commune movement in Britain until the early seventies. "I've never accepted that we're a commune." He says. "My idea from the start was that we had an open door policy, and that's how it has operated, and continues to do. This isn't my home, in the sense that we understand it in the West. It's where I live, but I never know who's going to be here at breakfast or even who's going to be in my bed at night – in the sense that my shed has been moved into by people once or twice in the past. I've had to say, 'Excuse me!'

"The place has been designed to accommodate any number of people at any time. Having been in the managerial position for the best part of 40 years, I really have learnt how to manage. I know there are certain combinations of personalities which would be dreadful for everyone concerned. Every hotel manager probably knows exactly how to deal with certain types of people: how to nudge someone into the other bar so they avoid someone else."

When the music press – particularly *Sounds* – started ridiculing Crass for being hippies, Steve Ignorant would be almost beside himself: "That used to drive me right up the fucking wall! I hated that. I don't know how people are going to take this, but it used to wind me up more than people thinking we were fascists. I can understand people mistaking us for fascists because we wore black, and the symbol and everything. But the hippy thing used to drive me mad because I never was a hippy and never will be. I mean, I had long hair when it was fashionable, then I had a David Bowie haircut, then punk came along. Before that I was a skinhead. So that used to really bug me, because it took it away from being punk. It took away *my* thing.

"But I won't knock Dial House, a lot of it I liked. It was a gorgeous place to live. There was always food on the table, always a roof, it was always warm, people were always friendly, the door was always open … hippies or not, I respect that. Lovely house, lovely garden, always clean. But I hated being called a hippy and I think the way I dealt with that was to put myself over as being even more working class and yobby than I was."

This begs the question, what's wrong with hippies? Punks all feel they instinctively know but they all struggle to put into words. "I find hippies really boring and dull," says Steve. "What I remember of hippies is from my brother's time – he was a hippy – *The Old Grey Whistle Test* and stuff like that. All you'd see was an acoustic guitar and a mass of hair with a centre-parting. Wittering on about some Donovan-y type thing. And all this 'peace and love' thing – it was so obvious it wasn't going to happen. The Summer Of Love never happened on the council estates of Bolton and Dagenham, the areas I can talk about. It's like the Swinging Sixties thing. . . I like the sixties black and white films, but I can't stand people saying the Swinging Sixties was a great time. Yeah, if you lived in a flat just off the Kings Road in Chelsea and you had mummy and daddy's money to do it. But if you were just an oik working on the dustbins out in the suburbs, there was no fucking Swinging Sixties, there was no Summer Of Love, there was no magical rebirthing time of David Bowie. The only good things to come along for me were skinheads – cos that was real – and then the punk rock thing. That was the best thing – suddenly it was so obvious – if I can't afford to go and see a band, I'll do my own. If I can't afford to buy that tee-shirt, I'll make my own. It was obvious – why hadn't I thought of it before?"

Dave King: "I don't think you could really call anyone who was there a hippy – there was some long hair. . . I don't even know if anyone had bell-bottoms . . .there was vegetarianism and the organic garden, raising animals. There weren't any drugs. If you were at art school in England in the sixties, you were probably a piss artist and that was about it."

Similarly with punk, the stereotype wheeled out now with monotonous regularity is that post-1977, punk had degenerated into some kind of psuedo-skinhead morass where it was hip to be thick and macho clowns ruled the day. This was nowhere near the truth despite the vested interests of those who wouldn't let the truth get in the way of a good story.

"In the Crass definition of punk," opines Mick Duffield, "what was worthwhile was political. There were some interesting angles to punk that were more art-orientated that didn't have the more political dimension, who'd been around on the art scene, like Throbbing Gristle for example. They were another extreme aspect of punk. There was room for quite a broad idea."

God forbid that broad was ever that narrow. Just before the second wave of punk really took off with big-booted 'real punk' and Oi music, most punks had a broader taste – from Crass to the Ants via Killing Joke, Stiff Little Fingers, The Pack, The Wall, Bauhaus, Joy Division, UK Subs, The Au Pairs, The Cure and Gang Of Four, and lots of others too, of course – too many unknown soldiers to mention, too many to know.

What really set Crass apart from many of these bands in the eyes of all the young punks was Dial House. It was the ace up their sleeve inasmuch as people were gradually realising that here was a band who weren't just talking about it. In Dial House, they were living the dream, both as an everyday pseudo–utopian reality and as an example to others that it was possible. Anarchy in action, as the press once vividly called it.

As Penny Rimbaud muses: "The very fact that we were living proof – even if only to ourselves – that you could live in a certain way, that you could produce your own food, you could live for very very little, was why we thought as we did.

"This place was, and is, key and central to Crass. I don't think Crass would have had the physical environment in which to be created, it wouldn't have had the background on which it based its creation. But not only that, the very fact that it was a very secure environment which had minimal upkeep and costs, which had sufficient room for a large number of people to live for bugger-all made it central. It was, and remains, a central facility. It offers space, and now we own it, a very secure and very cheap place to be.

"You can't possibly divorce Crass from Dial House. Because Crass without the fact that we were living proof of what we were talking about – I mean the way in which we talked about was very aggressive, it wasn't very listenable – who the fuck would have picked up on that? Anyone who came here was always quite devastated by the degree to which this place rounded the edges. They were devastated, in a very positive way, by the sheer beauty of the place, being so much in contradiction to the manner in which we publicly appeared. We were the most angry band of the time, because it was genuine, we weren't trying to entertain."

As they once wrote, they trusted in the wind to carry their words. But it only did that because the wind included inspired tales of a Garden of Eden out in Essex. Religions have been selling themselves on such promises since the year dot. Of course, it could seem odd to be so angry when you are surrounded by such beauty. You could be forgiven for wondering why the prevailing atmosphere wasn't more the kind of satisfaction we all feel after a good day's physical work.

Penny Rimbaud: "We were angry because we knew the possibilities. And that is the greatest anger of all. If you know that through co-operative living; if you know that it's possible to grow your own food, make your own bread, to share and nurture each other. If you know that's how we *can* live . . . and we were the living proof of it."

The greatest anger of all? As much as being an inspiration for anyone lucky enough to pay the place a visit, the Dial House/Crass camp was looked at from another perspective completely by parts of the music press and, it must be said, many punks as well. They were perceived as public school toffs hailing from privileged backgrounds playing at being punks. It would hound the band throughout their years.

Penny Rimbaud: "I remember Bushell saying that we were a University band, that we were all obviously degree holders. None of us were – Pete might have been but all the rest of us certainly weren't."

Eve Libertine: "I was brought up middle-class. My father was a head-master. If you think that's privileged to be middle-class, then, yes. But I found it quite the opposite. If you were working-class at my Further Education college, where I was doing drama and art . . . there were a lot of middle-class people who started talking *like that*," says Eve, slipping into a cockney accent. "I just thought it was ridiculous, pathetic. It was *cool* to be working-class."

Steve Ignorant – a bona fide working class geezer for those who acknowledge such concepts – comments: "The trouble is that most of the people that I like were public schoolboys – John Betjeman, Vaughn Williams, classical composers . . . it's like, poor sods, they couldn't help it any more than I could help where I went to school. That's why I never agreed with Class War. Am I not meant to read Wilfred Owen because he went to public school? Fuck off, do me a favour . . . Andy and Pen never used that public school thing against anybody apart from other public school people.

"Pen can really put on that public school thing, which can be really great if you're talking to policemen or solicitors or people like that – instant respect!" Steve also notes the other side of the coin: "You look at Penny Rimbaud in a pub, and he doesn't know what to do. I can walk into any pub and I can mingle."

"The music press is guilty of making endless attempts to divide and thereby control the energies of the bands from whom they make their parasitic living. Through the 'gossip columns' and carefully edited 'interviews', they fabricate differences and animosities between bands that in reality may well not exist. In their capacity as servants to the music business, they separate and divide bands who without their intrusions would probably be able to work together. Bands are often totally unaware of the aggressive and dishonest tactics used to promote sales and hype charts by the record labels to which they have signed. As the labels get richer the bands invariably remain penniless; hyped by the business and lied about in the press, they slowly sink into a helpless position where the honesty with which they might have started their band is lost in the compromises that are forced on them by others.

"It is essential that we prevent people like Bushell from stealing our energies and making them into this week's media joke; we don't need him and others like him ripping us off. Punk is not a media fashion, it's a way of life – it's up to us to tell the music business Mafia and their parasitic lackeys in the press to fuck off. We can, and will, manage on our own. Punk's the peoples music . . . let's keep it that way."
Penny Rimbaud – *Last Of The Hippies*

Given this kind of talk, it's interesting to read Gary Bushell comparing Conflict and Crass in the first ever feature on Conflict in *Sounds* (entitled 'Guy Fawkes Was Right'): "Anarchy ain't a word to toss around lightly. Even as punk's calling card, it meant (and means) a hundred different things to every hundred different people who paid it lip-service. For Rotten, it meant self as social incendiary device, for The Damned, one long endless custard pie fight, for Wattie Buchan apocalyptic chaos and survival of the fittest, for Crass, more traditionally, an absolute social/political alternative to the way things are.

"Young Eltham band Conflict work from the latter interpretation, but whereas Crass seem trapped by their (ho ho) 'classless' communal lifestyle, Sixties hippy drop out / cop out ineffectualism dressed in nihilistic puritan black rather than narcissistic promiscuous technicolour, Conflict have the potential to mean much more because they follow the Pistols ultimatum of being the poison *in* the machine, keeping their dissent on the streets, arguing with people instead of bellowing at them from any safe Epping Forest bunker."

Andy Palmer told Radio Tees: "We don't deliberately shun the publicity, but our policy in the past has been to try and develop a relationship with a potential interviewer before we commit ourselves to doing an actual interview. If somebody from the music press rings, we'll say well, it seems a bit abstract to not even know where you're coming from . . . come and see us for an afternoon and we'll find out a bit more about each other and then we'll do the interview after that.

"It's happened repeatedly in the past that the person has come out to do that run-through and the result is that there's been some sort of derogatory thing printed in the press before the time that the interview was meant to come out, so the trust that we might have developed in that situation had disappeared."

While in most areas Crass was wonderful and caring, they could miss the mark so completely sometimes, perhaps suggesting that in some ways they really were cut off out there in Epping.

Penny Rimbaud: "The main attack came from the more lefty element, because we weren't playing that game. Not so much the media game, it was that we weren't prepared to stand out in support of, generally speaking, the people who were outside just playing at punk – the fun side of punk thing, which was great, a good bit of rock'n'roll – people who aspired to some sort of political position were expected to toe the leftist line and that's something we virulently would not do. The net result of that was that the leftists (in the music press) took exception to that.

"There is also the element that the press represented corporate interests – in those days we'd have probably called it capitalist interests . . . we didn't use that word in those days. If we didn't let the mass media do interviews, then the only available interviews were through fanzines, and that meant that if a lot of people wanted to read about us – and a lot of people did – that meant those people managed to sell their fanzines. That was keeping it within our own culture. That was without question a successful and very valuable contribution to make to the overall movement. It was the only place people could find out about us."

Eve Libertine takes perhaps a more practical view of the press animosity: "They didn't like us because we weren't personalities. They couldn't get a person out and say what kind of underpants they wore." (Though black ones would have been a pertinent guess!). "We didn't want them and they want people to want them. They just used to write rubbish, stuff like the women writing poetry and doing needlework – it was beyond belief. And that thing that I couldn't be a feminist because I was attractive. I mean, where were they at? Would I do an interview with someone who thought like that? No."

"One does not establish a dictatorship in order to safeguard a revolution; one makes a revolution in order to establish a dictatorship."
– George Orwell

In May 1980, Crass released a split single with Poison Girls. With their 'Bloody Revolutions' track backed with the Poisons' classic 'Persons Unknown', the proceeds from the record were to go to the formation of an anarchist centre in London. Being the idea of (the now famous Irish author) Ronan Bennett, it may well have been inspired by the anarchist centre in Belfast. Initially there was talk of UB40 doing a benefit single, as Ronan Bennett had met a brother of one of the band in prison – which is probably what earned UB40 their surprise MI5 file.

'Bloody Revolutions' was the best Crass song yet – what appeared yet another rant against the ambitions of the far left had taken its inspiration from the Conway Hall violence. Slices of *La Marseillaise* and parodies of the 'Revolution No. 9' introduced Steve Ignorant's Beatles take-off: "You talk about revolution, well that's fine / but what are you going to be doing come the time? / Are you gonna be the big man with the tommy gun? / Will you talk of freedom when the blood begins to run /

Well freedom has no value if violence is the price / I don't want your revolution, I want anarchy and peace".

From thereon in, Steve Ignorant's terrace growl interplayed with an extraordinary, almost folky, vocal performance from Eve Libertine that perfectly married punk rock to the avant-garde and showed the band at their most imaginative. It could almost have been Lee Hazelwood and Nancy Sinatra. The Poison Girls track was equally inspired, subverting its title to comment more widely on alienation. The sleeve notes contained a beginners' guide to anarchy as Penny Rimbaud saw it and an explanation of the idea of the proposed anarchist centre for which the record was a benefit. At this moment, the punk movement met the traditional anarchist movement. But they didn't like each other much.

Contrary to what Rimbaud has written in *Shibboleth*, it wasn't Ronan Bennett that met up with him regarding the benefit gig for Persons Unknown as he was in prison at the time. "We had a big debate, cos we didn't know – we thought, well, if they *are* making bombs then we shouldn't really be supporting them," says Penny. "We turned a bit of a blind eye to the possibility they might have been. Suddenly we were hoisted by our own petard – we'd been playing around with it to some extent until then – using the anarchy flag just to get the left and the right off our backs. We weren't looking at what it might otherwise involve ... that was the crossover point – that was when we stopped being just a band with something to say and turned into something which was much more politically hardline and out there in the political arena."

Rimbaud denies the idea that Crass built up an ideology on the fly as people asked them about the meaning of 'anarchy and peace'. "No, because there was a fundamental ideology which was fundamentally anarchistic that I had. From organising the first Stonehenge festivals to Exit to all the things that have gone on here, it was part of my ideology. I was posing the question: do I actually look at serious anarchist tracts to see to what extent I can defend them? I actually chose not to. I thought bollocks, my anarchist tract is my life. I'm not actually interested in what Bakunin or Proudhon said. I have read bits and pieces – more than bits and pieces since. There was this fear of being drawn into something we couldn't control – not in the sense of being control freaks, but we didn't want to suddenly find ourselves publicly allied with something that we couldn't wholeheartedly support. I was very nervous about Persons Unknown."

Also in 1980, a small but perfectly formed era ended when Pete and Mari Stennett decidedto call a halt to their label Small Wonder Records. In the three years since their inception, from their debut with 'Mucky Pup' by Puncture, Small Wonder had leant a helping hand to an impressive roster of artists. Aside from Crass, they gave us Angelic Upstarts, Cockney Rejects, The Cure, Patrik Fitzgerald, Leyton Buzzards and Punishment Of Luxury.

Small Wonder Pete told *NME*'s Graham Lock: "We'd have a bit of money, a guy'd come in with a tape and we'd say, 'Fucking great, we'll put it out!' But it's not like that anymore, punk's a decaying thing. The energy's gone." Interestingly, Stennett cited one reason for the demise of the label as the influence, and therefore immense and centralised power, of John Peel, something Crass may have liked to reflect upon with their own label.

Pete Stennett: "Like, Peel took a shine to the Cockney Rejects' single so he played it nearly every night for quite a long time and we sold 13,000 copies. Another single we put out about the same time, which we thought was just as good, Peel played just once and we only sold 1,200 copies. We can't survive with sales like that because we're losing money and the bands are getting nowhere. So there's this one guy, who I respect and admire very much, but he's affecting not so much my business as my whole life." Graham Lock finished his obituary by describing their decision to quit as "a sad loss for everyone who values independence and integrity in a business where such qualities are rare."

On the upside, *Sounds* had started featuring a 'DIY corner', full of homemade record and cassette releases. Whatever the quality, the width of the DIY movement was startling as the punk rhetoric became reality.

Still, there were still other independent record labels taking up the mantle. A chap called Mike Stone left Beggars Banquet and started Clay Records, releasing the wonderful but ignored twelve-inch 'Style Wars' by Product and the altogether less ignored Discharge. Strange though it seems in hindsight, Discharge shared a mantle with Crass for a short while in 1980 – the emergence of 'real' punk. Though the phrase sounds horrible now – conjuring up images of bovver boots, violence and general thick conformity – back in 1980 there was a brief but real sense that a second wave of punk could make a more creative and lasting contribution than the first. The first two Discharge records – 'Realities Of War' and 'Fight Back' – were powerful slabs of pure punk; fast, hard, dark walls of sound that would have frightened the life out of Phil Spector, with song titles that suggested both intelligence and a similar anti-war/religion/system line to Crass.

Any suggestion of a genuine alliance, however, was shattered when members of Discharge ridiculed Crass in interviews ("I'm going to boot the bald bastard up the arse"), and any suggestion of a genuinely invigorating band started to lapse as further releases – despite the use of John Heartfield's 'Niemals Wieder!' imagery of a dove impaled on a bayonet – showed the band up as a one-trick pony, writing the same song over and over again.

Given the extraordinary popularity of Crass, it was inevitable that big business would show an interest, and so it proved when they were approached by Tony Gordon, manager of Angelic Upstarts and future manager of Boy George. At the time, Gordon was organising 'Pursey's Package', a proposed punk tour to feature Crass and Angelic Upstarts.

Penny Rimbaud: "There was nothing he could offer, but we were very interested to see how it worked – an insight into the music business. We went up to his Mayfair offices. It was a basement office and he'd got sewage problems – the whole place stank of shit, not just music business shit, but real shit! There was a ghastly desk covered in Laura Ashley fabrics. He was trying to be impressive but it was all so cheap and shoddy. It was so transparent and corny: the classic 'I can market revolution' line. And when we told him to piss off, his line was that he'd see to it we'd never play London again. All the 'I can make you and I can break you' bollocks."

Still, perhaps unwittingly, making Crass in a big way was *Sounds* journalist Gary Bushell. An undoubtedly talented writer, Bushell was probably the most influential music journo in the UK at the time. His apparent dislike of Crass seemed to border on the obsessive, which paradoxically did the band no harm whatsoever.

Penny Rimbaud: "He served us very well. There's no better way of building up a name and a reputation than the sort of stuff he was slinging at us all the time. You have to be good if someone's saying you're that bad. More than anyone in the main press, he helped our cause."

The reality appears to be that the music press simply couldn't comprehend the fact that Crass, unlike almost every other band on the planet, didn't conform to the accepted rules of engagement between rock performers and the press. "I think it was more a case of *Sounds* and all the other music papers being, even in the days of punk, remarkably conservative rock-papers written by and for boys as well as girls who liked what boys liked," says David Tibet of the band Current 93 who was also writing for *Sounds* at the time. "Crass couldn't and wouldn't offer any freebies except stencil kits, and served up a genuinely revolutionary attitude, as opposed to the whole sad and tired 'drugs+sex+guitars up to 11+cheekbones=revolution' schtick that was being yet again re-marketed in new clothes as 'punk'.

"*Sounds* was remarkably corrupt in its favouritism, myself included. I would always give good reviews to my friends and those whom I admired, whether I had heard the record or not. Occasionally I would invent records by friends to give top reviews to. Bushell certainly hated Crass with all the hatred of someone who had loved them before he found they didn't think much of invading lumps of rock on the far reaches of the Empire, which Bushell held to be a great thing to do, as long as he himself wasn't confronting the Argentines or their ferocious sheep.

"But Crass, equally, didn't want to engage with the music papers – so one could hold that Crass was conspiring in not playing the papers' game. Crass would not have benefited for playing the moronic papers' game; Crass was better and wiser than that and they knew it too. It worked better for Crass than for the papers which all went to the circulation Hell that God had created for freebie-guzzling liggers. I was certainly the only person at *Sounds* who admired Crass. Everyone else mocked their 'earnestness' and conviction, and said they were middle-class. Like, of course, all the journalists there. Crass wasn't hip, which of course made them hip to anyone who a brain and heart."

"They're not evil, but they diminish things," says Eve. "We were working *bloody* hard. I would (theoretically) always want to see what was written before it was put up, because you can change two little words and the person and what they're saying come across as totally different. It's so easy to fuck people over in the media – why would we want to bother with that? We didn't need to ... people knew who we were."

Garry Bushell: "Yes, I'm fairly sure I gave the *Feeding Of The Five Thousand* a bad review. There were several reasons for that. Most importantly I didn't like the music. I liked the anger of their sound, their refusal to compromise and their strong image (an echo I always thought of Woody Woodmansey's U-Boat's stage look). But I thought that their early stuff was willfully unmelodic. I also disagreed with their ideology as I was coming from a Trotskyist (they might say workerist) background. To me Crass were hippies, and I never had much time for hippies. Communes and Greenham Common, it was all too middle class for me.

"My view on punk was that it should be the poison within the machine. Crass initially preferred to be snipers on the outside. I was more impressed by some of their later high jinks. I quite liked 'Hurry Up Garry', though. My band, The Gonads, recorded our own Crass inspired song in 1981: 'Annie's Song' which concluded: 'I wouldn't give you tuppence for your Crass commune, old iron, old iron.'"

Pete Wright: "Well, dear ol Gary was certainly a poison within the machine. As such, he fitted in perfectly. He was also our main publicist, luckily for us."

Bushell remembers that Crass tried to set him up once with punk singer Honey Bane. "One of Crass brought her to a Covent Garden pub I drank in," he says. "It was some kind of Honey trap, but I was in there with Skully from the East End Badoes and we saw right through it."

Crass did indeed attempt to scam Gary Bushell via an interview set up with him. Also present was Andy Palmer, pretending to be a representative of the A&R department at EMI. Palmer was also secretly recording the interview, a tape of which still exists. It begins with Honey Bane slagging off EMI, at which point Andy Palmer intervenes on behalf of his supposed benefactors. From thereon Bane and Palmer to and fro, playing out a scenario where Honey is endlessly complaining about

EMI's attempts to turn her into a commodity. Bushell is a silent, and presumably bemused, onlooker throughout the exchanges.

Bane mentions the relationship between EMI and weapons manufacturers Thorne, which may have been the long lost point of the episode. She then asserts she wants to go and record an album on an independent label.

"We don't make any bones about it," says Andy in his EMI persona. "We have involvement in missiles, in the armaments industry, whatever you want to call it. You read it all over the bloody place."

The point of all this is forgotten by all concerned (on both sides) and impossible to grasp from the tape. But it is hard to shy away from the impression that it leaves the Crass scam looking pointless at best and Gary Bushell looking like a nice bloke, which is presumably why Crass didn't feel moved to publicise this particular ill-conceived episode.

"If you'd have had five or six singles that had been top ten, do you think you'd feel the same as you are now?" asks Bushell, completely reasonably.

"I think I'd feel worse," answers Bane, "because I'd be even more changed. I don't give a toss about making money."

Bane tells Bushell she wants to start making political statements again, and is interrupted by a cynical Palmer wearingly challenging "yeah yeah yeah..." and accusing her of naivety. More Bane/Palmer arguments follow, interspersed with reasonable, if bland, questions from Bushell every now and then. It's vaguely unpleasant to hear how smoothly Andy Palmer plays his false role.

As a result of their ongoing war with the music press, Crass turned instead to fanzines. Originally a vibrant and vital part of the early punk scene, fanzines had developed their own clichés and unintentionally become magnifying glasses for the more professional but different standards of the mainstream music press. Crass would inject the then diminishing fanzine scene with a new energy and, equally importantly, a new way of ensuring sales. At the start of the eighties, pretty much every fanzine seemed to have a Crass interview in one of its issues. It was easy to get in touch with them and — in stark contrast to their attitude towards established music press — they always agreed to do the interviews. Having Crass' name on the front would guarantee sales.

Eve Libertine guesses, almost certainly correctly, that some of the interviewers never were from fanzines; more likely they were fans who claimed to be writing a fanzine as a ruse to meet the band, who would benignly welcome them whatever. It makes you wonder why the music press didn't pretend to be from a fanzine – maybe they weren't quite as dishonest as the Crass worldview suggests.

As a result of Crass' support, a second wave of punk fanzines exploded onto the scene. Sitting beside the more general punk fanzines were a swathe of anarcho-punk 'zines inspired by Crass and the wider anarcho-punk movement. Most of them were indescribably dire examples of people's inability to communicate their own ideas and instead ape the Crass stance like good little foot soldiers. On the positive side, you could say that it was great that these people had the confidence to share their output, but existentially and essentially, it was usually barely worth sharing.

The next single release was 'Nagasaki Nightmare'/'Big A Little A', which was delivered in the traditional wraparound sleeve, covered in information carefully collated about the peace and war movements.

'Nagasaki Nightmare' featured Eve and Joy on vocals, mixing punk with cod-oriental sounds, again building on their avant garde twist to punk. The B-side (inasmuch as the concept applied) 'Big A Little A' was the most anthemic song they'd ever written. Dangerously close to rock-'n'roll, it began with children singing the playground song of the title before crashing guitars announced Steve Ignorant:

"Big A Little A Bouncing B, the system might have got you but it won't get me."

Half way through the song the power chords suddenly stop and we're faced with Crass almost getting funky. Unlikely as it sounds, the whole thing works a treat, Crass proving they were still growing and reaching out to an ever-increasing audience without the slightest dilution of their ideas.

In the same spirit, Crass' phenomenal record sales had left them with a massive surplus of cash. After some debate, they decided to widen the Crass Records label to include output by other bands. Later they would also run a second label – Corpus Christi – to expand upon the ideas of Crass Records.

Steve Ignorant: "It was just a way of giving people we liked a foot in the door, a way of keeping the faith. We were making money – apparently for tax reasons you needed to get rid of it, put it into things so you don't have to pay the taxman. It was as bitchy as that. So we bought a new van and new gear."

"I think it was just a way of giving people like Honey (Bane) and Annie (Anxiety) a chance," says Steve. "It didn't cost much in those days, and you were pretty certain that if it had that logo (records on Crass Records all looked the same) on the front, people were going to buy it. And it worked."

It also gave Crass an unhealthy, Peel-like power over the whole scene. Releases on Crass Records sold and Crass effectively became arbiters of choice, with the power to alienate as well as promote. "Crass Records, and later Corpus Christi, gave exposure to bands that might not have got it otherwise," says Pete Wright. "Who knows? It certainly gave a sense, along with all the other independants, that something was going on. Christ, we used to agonise about everything – and with good reason."

Early releases on the label were promising. Honey Bane's EP *You Can Be You* featured 'Girl On The Run' and was recorded when she really was on the run. Other releases by Zounds, Poison Girls and The Mob were fantastic snapshots of English punk in the early eighties. But like the anarcho-fanzine market, there were plenty of bands who were little more than Crass tribute bands – regurgitating the Crass style and rhetoric.

Disappointingly, Crass appeared to encourage this by releasing records that sounded like parodies of their own, an image exacerbated by their insistence on heavily stylized record sleeves that made any Crass release instantly recognisable as such, much like the corporations they despised. It was a tactic that not even the major labels used, and the fact that bands failed to object didn't inspire much confidence in their supposed integrity.

Penny Rimbaud was largely responsible for selecting the acts they would record. "It was me who had my ear to the ground. I didn't look for what was commercial, I didn't look for rock'n'roll, I looked for people I could and would believe in.

"I enjoyed their attitude more than their music. I've never been that enthusiastic about punk as a musical form. I thought the Pistols were a fantastic rock'n'roll band, and The Clash were quite a good rock roll band. But I don't see what that's got to do with punk. What always mattered to me was that peoples' attitude was right.

"I think Hit Parade were brilliant – musically and politically they were absolutely spot-on. I think Kukl[1] were stunning. But I think a lot of them had one good track."

In London at the time, the choices Crass made for record releases, and equally the choices they didn't make, served only to increase the perception of them as being out of touch out in Epping. Despite living on the London Underground, they really didn't appear to know what was going on in the underground scene they sang about, and in which they were thought of as big players.

"Being in the band was fairly all-consuming," says Joy. "I don't think we went to see many other bands. We just did our thing and weren't particularly involved . . . which I think is a shame in a way."

"We lived out in Essex, so we were out of the London loop," agrees Phil. "We had these time constraints and huge financial constraints."

Indeed, this is yet another aspect of their situation that sets Crass apart in attitude; considering themselves too impoverished to attend gigs while at the same time having sufficient funds to release records – often at a loss – by other bands. For better or worse (and there are arguments on both sides), Crass preferred to stay in Essex and release records by bands that came their way rather than be part of the (far) wider anarchist punk/squatting scene in London where they could check out what was going on.

There were seemingly two anarcho-punk scenes going on at the time. In London and some of the other bigger UK cities, people were doing it for themselves. They appreciated the effort Crass was making, but they didn't *need* them. However, in many of the smaller, more remote areas, people seemed to be waiting for Crass to take the lead. While this may be an exaggerated generalisation, in London at least, Crass was perceived

---

[1] Kukl included Bjork and Einar Benediktsson who went on to form The Sugarcubes.

to be out of touch with what was happening 'on the ground'. Their reaction to the Conway Hall incident had cemented this in many eyes.

Phil Free: "It was largely because we weren't up on the musical side of things: none of us had particularly been in bands beforehand so there was no connection with that. We were playing outside the band circuit. . ."

They were also seen as being peripheral to the culture, despite their generous influence on it, partly because of where they lived but also because of their ages. "We weren't 16 or 20," says Phil. "And because you weren't in that loop you were very nervous about that. You didn't talk to people, partly because you didn't know what to say to them. And you know you're not going to be able to talk chord progressions. I remember the gig we played where John Peel was doing the disco (Northampton), and you couldn't go and talk to him because you're shy. . ."

Joy De Vivre: "And everbody thinks you're being snooty! It is a peculiar thing though, because I think a lot of the music we did was brilliant – quite stunning. And yet we always say that the politics came first. But I think the effectiveness of the music carried the politics."

Phil Free: "We went on tour with some bands who were straight punks and some, like Zounds or Poison Girls, were a bit more musically orientated. They'd sit round and jam – *I* couldn't jam. I knew what chords I knew and I could play you a Beatles' tune, but I couldn't jam. So what do you do? We couldn't talk to musicians because they all want to jam or talk about music. So you end up talking to people about political situations.

"You're very stand-offish because you're *scared* of talking to a musician. Obviously you like music and you like what you like, but you're a punk so you've got to be careful about what you say. So the whole thing binds itself, things get tied in. Like the way the black (clothes) started off fairly relaxed but then slowly tightened up."

Crass firmly deny any idea that the power they assumed by having their own record label made them 'leaders' in any way. "It didn't make us leaders," says Penny. "It was a fantastic opportunity to offer people the chance of selling thousands of records where if it came out on any other label, it wouldn't have stood a chance. The only people who broke with our cover policy were The Poison Girls and The Cravats, and their sales suffered as a result . . . it was their choice, but sales did suffer, they halved. Because people like collecting.

"There was a diversity within the music on the label because we were trying to say 'punk's a way of life, not a way of music, not a style.' Someone like Annie Anxiety is every bit as much a worthwhile statement within the genre as Conflict are.

"When we toured with Dirt, the audience enjoyed that a lot more than when we toured with The Poison Girls, who were actually a far better band. But people didn't want that – they weren't dealing with the issues that kids on the street wanted to know about. They didn't want to see their mum singing – that was their attitude. And that was the very reason we toured with them; to expose the audience to a different set of ideas."

More to the point, perhaps, The Poison Girls weren't making thrash music almost exclusively for young white men.

In 1985 Penny Rimbaud told *Mucilage* fanzine: "I think that our anger is our passion and on a superficial level people may not be able to recognise the anger, a lot of people who have parodied us have effectively come across with an aggressive stance and have really, in my view, been exposing their emptiness. I don't think we've ever been aggressive, we have been extremely angry and extremely passionate and we still are."

A perfect example of how tightened up the whole situation had become came when Crass Records released a compilation album of 'artists' that had sent them demo tapes. *Bullshit Detector* was a very, ahem, challenging record indeed. Depending on your viewpoint, Crass released a compilation album that was either a) the worst record in the world ever, or b) the most illustrative of the DIY scene, or c) both.

Bullshit Detector was so far beyond bad that it's difficult to do justice to a description of its incompetence. It was certainly full of 'straight punks', whichever way you choose to interpret that description, and featured an assortment of bands that – with a couple of notable exceptions – had recorded their offerings on tape recorders without proper instruments. This can be seen as a noble DIY crusade, a fart in the face of prog rock, or an extension of Dada, but it's difficult to believe that many people listened to it more than once.

It was the clearest indication yet that DIY was a myth, that not every-one *could* do it themselves. Or perhaps more accurately that they could, but no-one would feel compelled to listen, and who could blame them? In his *NME* Crass interview the following year, Paul Du Noyer claimed the record was "great fun (really), highly recommended", which must go down as a mystery on a par with JFK's assassination.

Another aspect of Crass' anti-capitalist stance was their refusal to sell any merchandise. Badges were given away with replies to letters and at concerts, while t-shirts were shunned completely – by the band that is. Other t-shirt manufacturers saw the gap in the market immediately and Crass fans were eager to purchase them regardless of the band's requests not to do so. In effect, Crass was handing over the profits from mer-chandise to capitalist touts.

In the summer of 1980, Crass tried to play the Stonehenge Festival that Penny Rimbaud had, in part, helped to start. It was a disaster. A biker gang, under the impression that Stonehenge was 'their' festival, decided to introduce all the young punks to their version of anarchy by viciously attacking them. The same weekend found The Stranglers jailed in France for inciting violence at their gig in Nice University.

'Bikers Riot at Stonehenge' announced *NME*, describing the scene: "The evening began peaceably with music from Nik Turner's Inner City Unit, The Mob and The Snipers, but when punk band The Epileptics took the stage they were greeted with a hail of flour bombs, cans and bottles. Their lead singer was knocked to the ground by a bottle."

Gurts DeFreyne, of Inner City Unit, described the night as "horrible . . . the bikers were pulling punks out of their sleep bags to beat them up, it was really disgusting."

"Our presence at Stonehenge attracted several hundred punks to whom the festi-val scene was a novelty, they, in turn, attracted interest from various factions to whom punk was equally new. The atmosphere seemed relaxed and as dusk fell, thousands of people gathered around the stage to listen to the night's music. Suddenly, for no apparent reason, a group of bikers stormed the stage saying that they were not going to tolerate punks at 'their festival'. What followed was one of the most violent and frightening experiences of our lives. Bikers armed with bottles, chains and clubs, stalked around the site viciously attacking any punk that

they set eyes on. There was nowhere to hide, nowhere to escape to; all night we attempted to protect ourselves and other terrified punks from their mindless violence. There were screams of terror as people were dragged off into the darkness to be given lessons on peace and love; it was hopeless trying to save anyone because, in the blackness of the night, they were impossible to find. Meanwhile, the predominantly hippy gathering, lost in the soft blur of their stoned reality, remained oblivious of our fate.

"Weeks later a hippy newsheet defended the bikers, saying that they were an anarchist group who had misunderstood our motives – some misunderstanding! Some anarchists!

"If Phil and the first Stonehenge festivals were our first flirtations with 'real' hippy culture, this was probably our last."
Penny Rimbaud – *Last Of The Hippies*

Eve Libertine: "Poison Girls were there and they had their ambulance – they were hiding people in it, and had towels and hats to put over heads so the spiky hair didn't show. It was very frightening – you didn't know what was happening because it was dark and people were screaming. They didn't want us because we were different. I was thinking 'I wish the police would come in.' They were staying out. It got to the point where you just didn't know what was going to happen."

Although Gurts DeFreyene thought "maybe this is the end for Stonehenge", in a couple of year's time, punks would infiltrate the Stonehenge crowd as surely as the ravers would at Glastonbury Festival at the far end of the decade.

As Penny Rimbaud remembers it, the bikers weren't the only ones bemused at the presence of punks at Stonehenge: "There was this animosity towards punk, not just from the bikers but from the old hippy elite. I think we were a real challenge and a real threat to their 'alternative supremacy'. And it was interestingly the same crew that had been the Windsor (festival) crew. They did see themselves as a hippy elite, and probably continue to do so. They're actually quite bitter people. I liked Heathcote (Williams), but I never particularly got on with Sid (Rawle). There was something quite small and mean about them. I remember being at Stonehenge and Sid was sitting in his mammoth tipi. A couple of street kids from Liverpool had got down there with their tiny cotton tent, and Sid was saying, 'It's easy man, you just get your tipi and move on out.' Telling that to these kids, who'd made this stupendous effort to get down to Stonehenge was just bullshit, because there's no way in a million years they could have..."

Steve Ignorant: "I've never really enjoyed being outside, with fires and the smell of smoke and people being drunk – I've always preferred it indoors. The reason we played it was because it was something that Wally Hope had set up. Wally would have been turning in his ... wherever he was. But the funny thing was that punks kept going back year after year..."

Mick Duffield: "It was free and wasn't a commercial operation and really the dying embers of the hippy thing. I was never there for the entire duration. I never enjoyed it that much."

Nor did former cabinet minister Lord Peter Melchett, who announced he was planning to raise in the House Of Lords claims that 300 people at the Festival were strip-searched by police in front of passers-by. Crass soundman and erstwhile manager John Loder also complained to the press that the police were "totally uninterested" when he'd complained to them about the biker violence.

Meanwhile, back in the cities, the punk rock tower block chic of The Clash and their ilk was being viewed as little more than symbolism. But the rhetoric had taken a firmer root in the minds of many, and the second wave of punk gave birth to a group of bands that Garry Bushell would lump together and promote heavily in *Sounds* as a movement called Oi. Crass clearly took it seriously, not least because of its many shared fans.

"Rock cannot be politicised, despite what followers of Oi, or Marx, might say. Rock is about all of us, it is the collective voice of the people, not a platform for working-class mythology or socialist ideology. In rock 'n' roll there aren't any workers to 'wet' about. Rock is about freedom, not slavery, it's about revolution of the heart and soul, not convolution of the mind. To say that punk is, or should be, 'working class' is to falsely remove it from the classless roots of 'real rock revolution' from which it grew. Punk is a voice of dissent, an all-out attack on the whole system, it as much despises 'working class' stereotypes as it does 'middle class'

ones. Punk attacked the barriers of colour, class and creed, but look at how it is right now, do you really think you're freed? Oi and, more recently, Skunk, have been promoted in the pages of Sounds as the 'real punk', real suckers maybe, but not real punks. Whereas punk aims to destroy class barriers, Oi and Skunk are blind enough to be conned into reinforcing them.

"Oi's spokesman, Gary Bushell, who, like Marx, romanticises working class life whilst, in all probability, never having done a day's manual work himself, claims that 'only the working class can change society' — presumably he realises that his 'professional' and privileged status as a 'journalist' prevents him from being in a position to contribute to his own pet theory — he wants to have his cake and eat it.

"Bushell's idea of what 'working class' means is nothing but a 'middle class' fantasy about a type of person who, except in the media-forms of Alf Garnett and Andy Capp, just doesn't exist. His unrealistic view of workers as cloth-capped, beer-swilling, fist-waving jokers, is a complete insult to working people of whom he, clearly, has no understanding.

"Oi would have been harmless enough if its comic-book caricature of the 'workers' hadn't appealed so strongly to the elements that, inevitably, were drawn to its reactionary views — the so called 'right-wing'. Rather than rejecting its new and possibly unwanted following, Oi appeared to revel in its image of being 'nasty Nazi muzac for the real men'. Defending the trail of blood and bruises that it seemed to leave behind itself wherever it went, the 'new breed' claimed that 'they weren't advocating violence, they were just reflecting the way thing are'. Despite repeated evidence of Oi inspired violence, it became increasingly obvious that Oi the Bushell and Oi the Bands were either perfectly happy with 'the way things were' or totally incapable of controlling the monster that they'd created.

"At a time when something could have been done to change the image, the 'Strength Through Oi' album was released, but rather than making an effort to shift the 'right-wing' emphasis, it deliberately promoted it. The attractive cover sported 'yer average skinner' about to land his 'cherry-reds' up someone's 'khyber' — but that week "yer cherries' also left their mark on an old aged pensioner's face; but no matter, you can't win 'em all.

"Get wise lads and what few lasses can stomach your exclusively male reality, you're being used by the system and the media that serves it in the way they've always used people — like suckers. Oi and Skunk are simply Bushell's way of dividing something that he and his media cronies just can't control — real energy,

real punk. Whatever they are labelled, the 'real' punks are first and foremost one thing – themselves. The system and the media set out to contain us within their labels – if you fall for that trick you'll fall for the circled 'A's in the Total Chaos Column – what a joke!"
Penny Rimbaud – *Last Of The Hippies*

Garry Bushell: "I had a lot of time for Conflict; Colin Jerwood and Big John were the working class wing of it all but again the music was a bit impenetrable. The Oi bands wanted to be accessible. They had better songs and were struggling towards a more coherent ideology. By the time of the second Oi conference in May 2001, the bands had moved from a vague pro-working class 'having a laugh and a say' stance to a commitment to playing benefit gigs for strikers and the unemployed. Southall queered the pitch, of course, but as anyone who was there knew our real problem was football related not racial politics. Crass saw it as 'Rival Tribal Rebel Revel.' It was a problem we were getting to grips with, post-Rejects. Look at some of those songs like 'National Insurance Blacklist', 'Suburban Rebels', 'Jobs Not Jails' etc. There's no mistaking the radical pro-working class political stance that was evolving. Some elements of Oi were naturally inclined towards the Class War end of the anarchist spectrum."

At the time, in a quite literal sense the working class was shrinking rapidly in direct proportion to the rise of the 'underclass', this largely due to the spiralling unemployment Margaret Thatcher was raining down on her poorer subjects. In September of 1980, even *Sounds* ran a multi-page feature on youth unemployment. While *NME* made a habit of lefty forays into stuff not strictly music-related, it's a far bigger indication of the times to see *Sounds* dipping its toes in the same water. Writer Phil Sutcliffe is clearly impassioned as he writes of youth unemployment: "In whole regions . . . the figure is up to between 20 and 30%. In black spot districts within the major cities, it peaks at 50-60%."

Less than two years into the Thatcher regime, Sutcliffe is almost pleading:

"A generation is being dumped, spat on and trampled by cold political economists in government and industry in pursuit of immediate power and profit – the future wreckers."

It's also worth remembering that the dark Dickensian future predicted because of this milestone in unemployment was because the figures had risen to above two million for the first time since the thirties. There were far darker times to come.

But as Rotten's 'no future' dictum appeared to be taking shape, it's worth remembering that unemployment was a doubled-edged coin for many in the full time punk scene. Thatcher used unemployment and the threat of it to decimate working-class communities and families while lining the pockets of the better off. But she also unwittingly created a space for legions of punks and assorted dropouts and layabouts to go on an invisible strike, taking up the 1968 Paris cry of 'Ne Travaillez J'amais' and getting on with their lives without becoming a cog in the wheel of capitalism (apart from signing-on once a fortnight).

The Clash had sung about "Monday coming like a jail on wheels" and warned that a factory was "no place to waste your youth", but Crass – particularly in the lyrics of Steve Ignorant – took it a stage further and hinted that a lifetime of shirking was a viable way to live. With unemployment so high, it was relatively easy to convince the Social Security that you couldn't find a job, even if you weren't looking for one. For once, pink hair and torn clothes were a practical advantage.

Sometime later, with unemployment even higher, a handout was circulated advertising one of London's anarchy centres. Put together by Tony D of Ripped and Torn/Kill Your Pet Puppy fame, it declared "National Tragedy: 23 Million People Still Employed!" and shouted "abolish wage slavery". Many anarchist punks – though by no means all – preferred this reasoning to the message of traditional labour from the traditional left.

Pete Wright and Steve Ignorant, on stage, 1982. *(LFI)*

Pete Wright, Andy Palmer and Phil Free, live, 1982. *(LFI)*

Penny Rimbaud, producing in the studio, 1982. *(Dial House Collection)*

Eve Libertine, Gee Vaucher and Joy De Vivre, pictured outside a service station, 1983. *(Dial House Collection)*

On the road, 1983. *(Dial House Collection)*

Penny Rimbaud, Annie Anxiety, Pete Wright and others in Iceland, 1983.
(Dial House Collection)

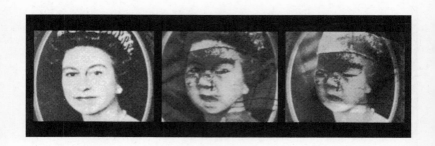

Artwork, 1983. *(Dial House Collection)*

Various members of Crass – including Phil Free, Joy De Vivre, Gee Vaucher, Eve Libertine, Andy Palmer and Steve Ignorant – with others in the garden at Dial House, 1983. *(Dial House Collection)*

Dial House – taken over by Penny Rimbaud in the late sixties. *(Dial House Collection)*

Crass members double up as sound crew before the gig. *(Dial House Collection)*

Phil Free on stage in Iceland, 1984. *(Dial House Collection)*

Crass handouts, 1984. *(Dial House Collection)*

The band off stage in Iceland, 1984; left to right: Gee Vaucher, Andy Palmer and Steve Ignorant. *(Dial House Collection)*

321984

Despite the appearance of a blanket ban on interviews with Crass, one journalist who did pass the necessary requirements was Paul Du Noyer at *NME*.

"I don't know why Paul Du Noyer was privileged," laughs Eve, at her choice of words. "I think he probably proved himself to be intelligent."

Crass was given a full-colour centre spread for the piece on February 14, 1981, though typically there were no photos of the band, with *NME* instead mimicking Gee Vaucher's political collages to surprisingly good effect. "You come across Crass in every place you look," opened Du Noyer, possibly raising an eyebrow towards *NME*'s designers. "They rarely play and hardly ever advertise. They live outside the music business but they're far more successful than most people inside it."

As introductions to the band go, Paul Du Noyer's was considerably more accurate than most: "They don't need to promote themselves because their following does that for them. Their logo's on a hundred thousand black leather jackets and their name is sprayed on town halls and bus stops from Amsterdam to Aberdeen. Crass records regularly sell well in excess of the figures achieved by outfits whose faces adorn the megastore displays and the pages of this paper ... yet next to nothing is known of them."

NME went on to make a decent stab at redressing the balance, and at the same time offered an all-too-rare glimpse of what one of the original punks thought of Crass, with Du Noyer transcribing an extract from a conversation with Joe Strummer:

"PDN: It's strange, all these '*real punks*' who seem stuck inside 1976.

"JS: Yeah, and that's worldwide. There's Crass fans in Europe, you wouldn't believe it!

"PDN: I met them, the other week, Crass.

"JS:Yeah? What are they like?

"PDN: Mm, nicer than you might imagine.

"JS: They've done it the ultimate way, haven't they? Self-sufficiency. I'm surprised they don't make their own guitar strings. But I always thought it was self-defeating, cos you gotta be *heard* ...Y'see, the thing about Crass is , ultimately it's all self-defeating, cos it's all kosher. No-one gets to hear about it.

"PDN: They won't go out for publicity y'know. But you've got to respect that integrity.

"JS: But it's no bloody use is it. If it's not available

"PDN: I don't think they trust go-betweens.

"JS: (Shrugs) It's a storm in a tea cup then. Title of their next album, *Storm In A Mug...*"

Du Noyer eloquently summed up Crass' situation when he wrote: "For thousands of young punks, who are bored/angry/lost, this band offers excitement and passion and maybe hope. But for others like me whose tastes and attitudes lie elsewhere, then Crass are at best a challenge and at worst an ugly row, impossible to take.

"You can't just tolerate Crass: you must either reject them outright or else prepare to get every idea in your head radically shook up – they probably won't 'convert' you but they'll sure as hell confuse you, and often that can be the healthiest effect of all."

Not for the first, nor for the last, time, Crass had received a glowing tribute in the pages of the established music press, something they would airbrush from their worldview.

The next slice of mainstream publicity that Crass enjoyed brought with it an element of farce. Confusion certainly reigned supreme at *Loving* magazine when they were tricked into giving away a Crass flexidisc to their teenage girl readership. "How a teen mag's bullshit detector let them down," squealed *NME* in delight. "Crass leave *Loving* at the altar."

Marriage, and even monogamy, were not sacred cows in communes. Everything was up for question and everything was up for grabs but if that was the reality in the alternative society, 'straight' society was plumbing new depths in the exploitation of teenage angst and loneliness. *Cosmopolitan* magazine may have started in an age of wild and often brave experimentation, but it also opened up a space eagerly filled by those who sought not to explore but to exploit. There was an abundance of teenage magazines aimed at cashing in on the problems of being a teenager in love, and selling false dreams of a 'happy ever after' fairytale.

Loving was one such magazine. *NME* reported: "Flicking past 'Dreamy Wedding dresses And Magical Make-Up', past 'How Revealing Is Your Underwear – What Does Your Choice Tell About Your Character?' . . . your eyes might have alighted at last on *Loving*'s 'fabulous record offer' – a free seven inch flexi called 'Our Wedding,' sung 'for you' by one Joy De Vivre."

As part of the recording process for their new album *Penis Envy*, Crass had recorded a jokey version of Eve singing the old American 50s song 'Lipstick On Your Collar', renaming it 'Lipstick On Your Penis'.

Penny Rimbaud: "It's such a shame we never kept outtakes because Eve's performance of it was absolutely killing. A fabulous performance. We were rocking with laughter – we must have done about eight takes . . . none of them we could use because every time we were just cracking up."

Eventually the band decided to ditch the idea, calculating that the inevitable lawsuit wasn't worth the trouble for what was little more than a schoolboy joke. But having got this far, with a painstakingly arranged backing track, the band didn't want to waste what they'd got.

Penny Rimbaud: "We thought let's see if what we can't salvage it. So Phil & Joy offered to go off and write a banal lyric, still with the idea of it just being the final track on *Penis Envy*. They came back with this infantile piece of crap, a nice little commentary on the banality of weddings and the social bullshit that surrounds them. By then Eve was incapacitated to perform so Joy did it. Very fortuitously because Joy's got this very sweet girly voice, so it suited very well. As we were recording it, I was thinking there's a heist here. So we got the idea of trying it out on one of these teeny magazines ... cos it sounded so disgustingly convincing!"

Phil Free: "We realised we had to get the schmaltzy lyrics to fit the schmaltzy song."

Joy DeVivre: "Terrible words for terrible music! It had to fit a number of things: it was supposed to pass the idea of being on the *Loving* magazine flexi, so it had to be a believable piece. There was such an anti-marriage thing in the band."

The song itself featured Joy's normally saccharine voice really laying on the syrup as she did her best to sound like a fifties Stepford Wife: "Never look at anyone/ anyone but me / never look at anyone/ I must be all you see". Sung over layers of keyboards that cheekily include a church organ and wedding bells, the package was convincing until you found out whodunnit. All traces of lipstick had been carefully removed from the scene of the crime.

Steve Ignorant: "We'd eat, then we'd sit around and then the discussion would start. It could go on till three in the morning. That's how the *Loving* flexi came about – a conversation over the dinner table: 'Oh, wouldn't it be a laugh if...?'"

The track was duly passed on to *Loving* editor Pam Lyons who fell for it hook, line and sinker. Crass pretended to be a rather more conformist outfit by the name of Creative Recording And Sound Services (CRASS) and approached a number of magazines with the idea of a free flexi release. Loving had taken the poisoned challice bait. When the scam became apparent Lyons roared: "This is a sick joke. We've turned *Loving* into a responsible and authoritative magazine" (what was it before, you wonder?) "and then this happens", to which Penny Rimbaud responded by calling *Loving* and similar magazines "absolutely obscene and despicable. They exploit people in an aggressive and unpleasant manner", adding that Crass was out to "expose the people who promote and produce the paper as emotional charlatans. They way they trivialise love and relationships is scandalous – it's teenage pornography."

Predictably (and perhaps not accidentally) the *News Of The World* picked up on the story and, equally predictably, postulated indignantly about Crass under the headline: "A BAND OF HATE'S LOVING

MESSAGE". Their exposé was squeezed between two rape stories and a cartoon of Titus The Newt. It also revealed that the track was taken from an album whose title was "too obscene to print".

Journalist Jad Adams – at that point working at the *News Of The World* – had called *Loving* magazine to inquire whether they were aware that their bonus giveaway track was actually featured on an album called *Penis Envy*.

Penny Rimbaud: "The *News Of The World* was actually more interesting in exposing another Fleet Street journal than the content of what they were exposing ... the serious side was that we had made a feminist album about exposing a woman's view of the world. That statement was a serious statement: people like Loving *do* exploit teenage fantasy and create untenable and unacceptable models for young lonely girls to get lost with."

Perhaps frustratingly for *Loving*, Crass hadn't broken any laws and no action could be taken against them.

That summer, the summer of 1981, England exploded. Margaret Thatcher's economic policies had brought about high unemployment, especially in England's inner cities. The Iron Lady had also given the police carte-blanche to treat these same kids – especially black kids – as criminals and hassle them with impunity. As a result the police were perceived not as a body that served the community, but one that ruled it. Finally the bubble burst. Brixton rioted and other cities all over the country followed suit. England was burning, not with boredom but with righteous anger. The press screamed about 'anarchy' and, using the fruits of the 'Bloody Revolutions' single, London's first anarchy centre was established.

The Autonomy Centre, as it was known, was set up in a warehouse in Metropolitan Wharf in Wapping. The space was suggested by workers at the anarchist Little A printers who worked in the same building. Although it was rented, it had much in common with subsequent squatted venues in that there was no music or drinks licences. You don't need permission for anything, as Rotten once said.

"It was a good try," says Penny. "We'd made all this money to defend Persons Unknown and it wasn't needed. I think it was something in the region of ten grand, which was a lot of money in those days. Ronan Bennett came up with the idea of putting it into a centre."

For the duration of the centre there existed an uneasy tension between the old school anarchists and the anarcho punks. The punk element put gigs on every Sunday, where you could see six bands for a pound, whilst the Puppy Collective ran a bar, the profits from which were ploughed into free food.

Steve Ignorant: "I fucking hated it. I went in there maybe twice, and what I didn't like was the elitist side – all sitting in a circle with chairs drawn up talking about Bakunin. This ain't go to the bar, have a beer, natter about this and that then maybe watch an anarchist film or something. No, it was this full-on . . . I didn't like the way they spoke, I didn't like the way they looked at me. I felt it really flopped. That's one regret, that we got involved with that – that tarred us with a brush, and that's when the anti-Crass thing came along, other bands having a pop. We'd been ruling the roost for too long."

Ironically, one of the best evenings at the Wapping centre was when Crass played a 'secret' (that is, not advertised in the music press) gig. For once there was no axe to grind and a fun time was had by all, particularly Steve Ignorant who played a significant part of the set with his trousers round his ankles.

The coming together of all the disparate punks under the equally disparate flag of anarchy was largely unsatisfactory. Cliques and factions quickly developed and the place could have won awards for how unfriendly many of its visitors were. Within this melee, perhaps seeking some kind of stability through moral superiority, there was also an atmosphere of political correctness in the air.

Steve Ignorant: "The bands that came after Crass out-Crassed Crass by being even more scruffy and dirty and being even more square and even more miserable than we were meant to be. They became even more politically correct. And I didn't like a lot of those bands that came out because they were parodies of what we were doing. For me, some bands were too heavy on the anarchy bit. It was like, Jesus Christ, you're fucking boring! I don't want to go out for a drink with you – calling me comrade – yawn! But I don't think it was all our fault."

The Autonomy Centre closed down after six months or so and wasn't really missed. The seeds for such spaces remained sown, however and over the next few years several squatted venues would crop up: the Ambulance Station in the South London's Old Kent Road became an arts centre that also put on gigs; Mollys Café in Upper Street was a squatted nightclub; the Bingo Hall in Highbury & Islington was a gig venue (and still is today, called The Garage). There were others spread all over the country and all over the world – you can't kill the spirit.

Whether or not Crass contributed to the instinctively unlibertarian PC groundswell, there was the beginning of something of a backlash against Crass as a band. Nobody, it seemed, was neutral about Crass, and the people that didn't love what they were doing hated them with a venom.

Steve Ignorant: "For a long time it was cool to like Crass, but then it got to a point where were other things to listen to, like Cockney Rejects, who were doing far better punk rock music than we were. And who wants to read another interview bangin' on about this and that. Even I got fed up with it. [There was a] horrible, dark dismalness of the Thatcher years and that skinhead BNP stuff, but also a lot of the interviews were just so fucking boring – every interview is saying the same thing. If I'd been a 16-year-old punk rocker wanting to read a Crass interview about 'what do you do if you leave home because my mum and dad piss me off' and then got all this fucking jargon – 'don't drink beer, drink tea' – fucking hell, y'know? And then you get the Exploited coming along just out for a good time – take speed and have a laugh – I think I know which one I'd have gone for. I'm not saying that what we did was shit, but I can understand why that split happened. At the end of the day, when you go to a gig, you want fun – you want to have a laugh."

"We were too serious," says Penny. "And because I think people are very threatened by commitment because it actually challenges their own commitment. Stewart Home is famously known for hating us because we injected the politics into punk and took the fun out of it. I think it made people feel guilty – the people who weren't prepared to buy into punk as a way of life, as a movement which is about opposing the system at every level as a revolutionary front. It's like when people get aggressive about you being a vegetarian. Why? I'm not asking them to be a vegetarian, I'm just saying I am one. People get aggressive because they feel uncomfortable about eating meat. If they don't, they don't say anything. I'm just reflecting their own discomfort."

Alcohol always seemed to be conspicuous by its absence around Crass, a vague pseudo-abstinence that got blown way out of proportion via the Chinese whispers around the anarcho punk scene.

Steve Ignorant: "Obviously you could have a few beers before you went onstage but don't get out of it. The local bobby was taking an interest and people coming to visit were being hassled by the police, so there was no drugs in the house. It'd be stupid to get busted for that. We used to drink but . . . not in the house. I seem to remember only me doing it, so I got a reputation in Crass for being this hardline boozer: 'Fucking Igs is drunk again.'

"Alright, I could go outside and drop some blues and have some beers – usually with Conflict. But God, if you're the only one who's out of it on speed and the rest of them are dead straight – and it's Crass! – that ain't gonna be much fun is it? Probably better with your mum and dad!"

Steve realises he missed some rock'n'roll fun by being part of a band that put responsibility at 100%. "From Crass, I don't have any of those anecdotes – 'Oh there was this night we got the fire extinguishers etc' – which is the stuff people love to hear. We didn't have none of that. Just cups of tea and staying round peoples' houses being polite to their mum and dad."

Phil Free: "At the time, there was very little money, so you couldn't even go and buy a bottle of wine. It wasn't a common thing – we weren't all lads out down the pub on a Friday night. . ."

Joy De Vivre: ". . . but we weren't teetotal. It was just that we didn't have the money for it."

Unfair as it might have been, it was for these reasons that Crass developed a reputation as being somewhat dour, puritanical even.

Steve Ignorant: "Not puritanical, but it got to the point where we took ourselves seriously. If anything came up then it was discussed and it was taken seriously. For example, I decided to have a short haircut, and we had to cancel a gig because of it cos it was decided we might attract a skinhead following. It had me in tears. Bonkers, isn't it. But that actually happened. Crass actually cancelled a gig because I had my hair cut too short – and I was a skinhead.

"There was also the issue of whether the cats should be vegetarian. Should we be buying meat for the cats? It was extreme. And if it was discussed and you agreed on it, it was quite diplomatic. So I never used to drink indoors and not take drugs indoors – I'd go out and do it.

"I always used to feel a bit embarrassed. I remember The Business came to visit one day – after the Southall riots. They came round because they wanted to write a thing about it. So there was Lol Pryor, their manager, Steve, their guitarist, and Mickey Fitz, the singer. I remember being so embarrassed as they were offered cups of tea, and it's obviously these south London geezers. I said, 'Do you fancy a beer?' I think I had two cans of beer and we shared them. Punks would turn up with their six-pack and be told, 'Actually, there's no drinking in the house' or they go to roll a spliff and be asked not to. You'd see their faces and I'd think, 'Oh my god, they're gonna think we're right fucking twats!'

"But in a way it did make sense, because we didn't want to give the impression . . . people were writing to us and saying they wanted to start the equivalent of Dial House and we were saying, 'Look that's fine, but you've got to make sure you don't get pissheads living there, or junkies.' If that's the rule, you've got to take your own medicine."

Joy De Vivre: "It was just cigarettes. There were no substances that would change your state of mind. But it never felt puritanical. There were enough mind-bending, head-fucking, shit conversations without alclohol!"

In June of 1981, Crass played at the 100 Club in London's Oxford Street, where the Pistols had famously built up their reputation five years earlier. Edwin Pouncey covered the event for *Sounds*, neglecting to mention that he had a tenuous connection with the band inasmuch as his own punk band, The Art Attacks, featured John Haney on drums, before he left to drum for the even better Monochrome Set. Indeed, the two were introduced by Joy De Vivre, who was at art school with the journalist, and was John's sister.

Pouncey's reflections on the gig offer an interesting snapshot of the times and how music journalists perceived the culture surrounding Crass: ". . . a mass of multi-coloured hair twisted into spikes . . . leather jackets spray-painted or Humbrol enameled, many with great artistry, utilising the names of the groups that support the cause that many have written off as being dead."

Observing the supporting line-up of Annie Anxiety, Flux Of Pink Indians and Poison Girls, Pouncey clearly fails to live up to Crass' belief that the press is their enemy: "What has impressed me most about the evening's proceedings has been the organisation of the entire event, the way each performance merges into the next leaving no tiresome time-filling gaps. . ."

This live review stretches over one and a half pages of the paper, the sort of space normally given only to megastars on the first date of a world tour, which gives some insight into just how many extra papers could be shifted by featuring the band. And like other reviews, it doesn't really fit into the portrait of the press painted by Penny Rimbaud in *Shibboleth*. Edwin Pouncey views the gig as "a sign that Crass are beginning to bloom, steadily adopting a new musical alternative of getting the message across rather than that of just heavily-meshed punk thrashing (which they still do, in case you're wondering), just seeing them in action makes much more sense. The musical side is superbly and disturbingly illustrated with a graphic bombardment of cutting room floor, film montage bludgeoned into your senses with a cruel yet deceptive wit."

By the end of the evening, if not before, Pouncey is a fan, and is considering the issues that have been thrust in his face: "All these effects are fitted together to form a terrifying portrait of what could happen tomorrow should the right madman get it into his head that today's the day . . . I hang around to socialise and sip après-gig cups of tea. Crass have turned the little canteen to the side of the club into a veritable cup of tea factory. The best drink of the day never tasted so good. It felt great to be alive."

Reviewing the same gig, *NME*'s Chris Bohn made some pertinent points, particularly in comparison to Poison Girls: "Their deliberately crude playing may have offered a way out of rock's restrictive standards, providing both themselves and listeners with a key to upset the mechanism, but to allow it to become a new and established order is lazy and damaging: today their incompetence only trips them up . . . Poison Girls give the impression they're in a constant state of flux, Crass that they've reached a stasis. Poison Girls bare themselves to the world — it's a two way communication. But Crass plainly attack it . . . Crass have become just another station on accepted rock routes."

Though the sixties are usually thought of as the decade of change, this was really only the case with the (London) liberal intelligentsia. Change for everyone else — and particularly woman — occurred far more in the seventies.

Since 1970, the birth rate in the UK has dropped by more than a quarter, doubtless due to abortion, the pill and the changing social attitudes that enabled more women to work for a living rather than just being housewives and baby machines. In 1970, only 10% of marriages ended in divorce, not least because divorce was still a dirty word and many women felt unable to escape bad, even abusive, marriages. There were also the financial implications: in a world where you may be earning half the wage of man in the same job, feeding the children was a very real issue. One big change was the 1969 Divorce Reform Act, which encouraged far more relaxed attitudes towards divorce.

In the seventies, radical feminist ideas enjoyed something of a heyday, with the launch of *Spare Rib* magazine contributing to the ever-growing debate on women's rights. By 1975, the introduction of the Equal Opportunities and Sex Discrimination Act was the biggest positive law introduced for women in the UK since the suffragettes had won the vote in 1918.

Crass, of course, were far more concerned about the truth on the ground than the theory handed down from Parliament, and the truth was that many punks were as macho and old fashioned in their attitudes as their grandparents had been before them. It's not hard to see how this could happen: Britain still harboured a very macho culture wherein 'queer bashing' was still a socially acceptable pastime in many areas. For every kid that was enlightened when David Bowie put his arm around Mick Ronson whilst performing on *Top Of The Pops*, there was a whole gang who denounced him as a 'poof'.

Punk itself had gone from being a decidedly non-macho, gay and woman friendly movement to a place where men strutted around in big boots, leather jackets and Mohicans in a barely related parody of what they thought punk was originally about. But whereas many of the original punks – often gay disco regulars, whatever their sexuality – had scuttled off in disgust at this sea change, Crass decided to respond with a feminist concept album.

The third Crass LP, *Penis Envy*, was a radical departure from the first two albums and as such represents something of a milestone. It was released the same week as the *Loving* flexi scam, proving Crass were no idiots in the promotion department.

Penis Envy is "the misuse of one of Freud's more absurd theories", as described by Penny Rimbaud to a radio interviewer in 1983. "When we first started, we were seen as a male boot band and this record certainly puts that straight – that our sensitivities are much wider than just that element." In this respect, *Penis Envy* could be thought of as Crass' first truly self-conscious recording. Having had plenty of time to reflect on the position they found themselves in, *Penis Envy* is the sound of the band trying to achieve something tangible and pre-conceived.

The band heralded *Penis Envy* as their big feminist statement, though in truth it covered a broader range of topics, and with considerably more generosity to men than other feminist acts of the time. Indeed, it could be argued that the real theme of the record is love itself. The cover featured a packaged rubber doll, none too subtly juxtaposed with back cover artwork of an animal being cut up in a slaughterhouse, and a collage of women in bondage.

The album opens with a woman's voice: "Little girls of about six or seven asked: what do *they* want to do? Some time later, they were asked what do *little girls* like to do." Then it steams straight into 'Bata Motel' – one of the most effective songs that Crass ever wrote, and the one that would later land them in court under laughable obscenity charges.

Overall, *Penis Envy* builds on the band's experimentation, though the absence of vocal contributions from Steve Ignorant or Pete Wright gives it a narrower palette from which to paint. Nevertheless, working solely with female voices, as well as reaffirming the feminist thread of the project, lends the music a softer, more melodic feel, and is all the better for it.

"We're trying to push ourselves and we trust that people want to come with us," said Penny. "They don't want the same old thing time and time again. That's why we put out records as infrequently as we do – we don't put a record out until we've got something to say."

Eve Libertine illustrates the bands stubborn reluctance to play the game: "The previous record was *Stations*. People would want more of that, so we'd do something different."

Indeed, it's probably at this point in the Crass ascendancy that it really becomes obvious that the band have developed self-consciousness. Aware of their popularity and the platform from which they can advocate social change, *Penis Envy* differs significantly from *Stations Of The Crass* in this, knowing, sense. It's as though the band are thinking, 'Now we've got a bit of power, how can we wield it?'

Penis Envy showed the band at their most musical, with less 'obvious' lyrics that explored feminism, love and the concept of marriage. The music had more room to breathe, and for once Crass played with melody and gentleness.

Eve Libertine: "I think it just came out of the fact that it was women singing so we could use our voices more. And because of the lyrics."

'Bata Motel' sees Eve Libertine on vocals as Crass give a vague nod to powerpop in music, if not lyrical direction: "Today I look so good / Just like I know I should / My breasts to tempt inside my bra / My face is painted like a movie star / I've studied my flaws in your reflection / And put them to rights with savage correction."

Through 'Systematic Death' and 'Poison In A Pretty Pill', the theme continues – a punky pop-backed feminism that attempts and largely succeeds in letting in the macho hordes who would buy the record without compromising the ideals. There were some cute lyrics too: "Poor little sweety, poor little filly / They'll fuck her mind so they can fuck her silly"; "I want so gently to remove your mask".

The next track pulled all the experimental punches. 'What The Fuck' began with ten seconds of the sound of a turntable needle being scratched over vinyl –which must have had many a listener sprinting in panic to their record player, before almost a minute of about six different voices all talk at once, each rendering the others intelligible. This was almost Throbbing Gristle territory. When the song finally started in a musical sense, it was a slow jazzy rant against the minds of those who "would destroy the earth, dry the river beds... Why must I share your fear of breath, light, life, PEACE?"

The neatly titled 'Where Next Columbus' attacked the main philosophical influences that shape today's reality: Marx, Sartre, Einstein and, predictably, Jesus. 'Berkatex Bribe' subverted the Berkatex Bride adverts of the time with the most poppy track of the album, attacking the apparently limited vision of marriage with gauntlet "Does the winner take all? What love in your grasping? / What vision is left and is anyone asking?"

'Smother Love', with lyrics from Gee Vaucher, took the concept a stage further and almost certainly a stage too far, attacking love and romance themselves: "The true romance is the ideal repression". Whilst it contained neat lines and sharp critiques of straight life: "We can build a house for two with little ones to follow / The proof of our normality to justify tomorrow", it also seemed to suggest Crass were on some evangelical mission to get us all to take our boring clothes off and indulge in free love. In a hackneyed attempt to think beyond relationships, they resorted to calling love "another social weapon", which surely failed to strike a chord with anyone.

Joy DeVivre replaced Eve libertine on lead vocals for 'Health Surface', plodding along as it married Joy's angst regarding (one presumes) hospitals and her experiences therein to an almost defiantly snail-like beat. Eve returned for 'Dry Weather' to finish the album statement saying "I don't want these games..."

Unannounced, the bonus track was of course 'Our Wedding', reproduced faithfully from the *Loving* flexi, but with the wedding bells outro suitably tampered with to make yet clearer the parody.

Whereas in the past Steve Ignorant was in the forefront of proceedings, he was now relegated to a less significant role. He wasn't entirely pleased about it. "I was quite happy going along with it being the front man, being Steve Ignorant the front man – being outrageous, shirt off and diving and all this stuff. In the meantime, there are people in the band actually thinking, 'Next move – what's it going to be?' Not to make money, but thinking, 'OK, now we're going to be a bit more avant-garde...

Such matters fell upon deaf ears, as far as Steve was concerned: "Those

200

conversations were so boring. I could stand them for about 15 minutes and then I was off. As long as I could still do 'So What', and 'Owe Us A Living', and 'Banned From The Roxy', I don't give a shit! As long as I've still got my bit and I can still wink at girls in the front row. By this time, I'd become a vocalist... Crass wasn't my band anymore, it was all these other people."

In an *NME* review – coincidentally next to a review of old nemesis James Chance & The Contortions – Graham Lock described *Penis Envy* as showing Crass "developing a more sophisticated form of punk and realigning their attacks on society from a radical feminist standpoint."

Eve Libertine: "I'm a bit wary of the terms. When people ask are you a feminist or are you an anything, I'd like to know what they mean by that before answering. But I guess, yes, it is. I have heard from women that they really appreciated it and got a lot from it. And men who hadn't thought of stuff before."

NME wasn't without its (again, pretty fair-minded) criticisms of the record: "Crass songs are still great angry wordy splurges, all banners and thumped tubs where a swift guerilla raid might be more effective. They could also do with more, well, *joi de vivre*."

In the same week that *Penis Envy* was released, three members of fellow punk band Discharge were fined £600 for 'working' (if being in a band can ever be called that) and signing on. In due time, Crass would also be facing the wrath of the law for accusations of obscenity regarding *Penis Envy*, more of which later. But for now, the feminism that Crass had aligned themselves with was making big waves in the UK.

"Women started to appreciate themselves as not second class citizens – punk made that clear" – John Lydon, Sex Pistols, *The Filth And The Fury*.

Both the feminist movement and the peace movement were at the front of public conciousness at this time, thanks in no small part to the energy punk had injected into both. The two would meet most famously at the Greenham Common peace camp. Initially mixed, the men at the camp were 'voted out' early on and the camp became women only.

Eve Libertine: "I thought it was great as a tactic, a very good idea. I don't like the whole thing of shutting out men, or saying 'men are shit'.

But I think in that situation it was very good to have women there, because as a tactic – if there had been men there, there would have been more aggression, no question. Not necessarily because the men would have been aggressive but because the people on the other side of the fence would have seen the men there and then relate in a different way."

On the radical end of things, a hardcore element within the feminist movement had started taking their stance to an extreme of dubious logic by putting on women only gigs.

Eve Libertine: "Sometimes I think women have just wanted a place where they could go and have their own energy – that's fair enough. But I wasn't into that particularly. I was involved in the feminist movement quite a way before Crass, in the mid-70s, marches, groups, that sort of thing. 'Consciousness-raising' was the big phrase – there was a lot of that going on. I personally found some of that quite difficult, because within that there were quite a lot of women who didn't like men and blamed men for an awful lot of stuff. Some of them were quite afraid of men, they'd had bad experiences. Intellectually I could relate to that, but emotionally, I couldn't, because I'd never had that experience with men."

The Greenham women and other peace camp people apart, consciousness-raising often appeared to be the sole (pseudo-)point of the mainstream peace movement. The peace movement was also particularly adept at ignoring the war on its own front doorstep in Northern Ireland. But in 1981, no-one could ignore it any more, as Irish Republican prisoners started dying in hunger strikes. The various movements for social change in Western Europe, of which Crass were a part, were challenging the status quo, but it was in Ireland that the status quo (especially when fronted by Thatcher rather than Francis Rossi) would show its true colours.

IRA Commanding Officer in the Kesh Bobby Sands was the first to refuse food. In April of that year, he was elected to parliament and so now an MP. Still, with rioting now commonplace in Northern Ireland, the Iron Lady would not return the prisoners their rights. Thatcher had started smashing her way through anyone that opposed her – the lady was not for turning, not matter who got hurt. Or killed.

The subsequent death of Sands and nine other young men shocked the world. There were riots in both Northern and Southern Ireland.

There was also much international condemnation. Most significantly, there was a massive upsurge in violence and support for the IRA. Even Winston Churchill hadn't gone this far with Ghandi (though recently released records show he wanted to). If Penny Rimbaud had discovered the ruthlessness of the state via the Wally Hope experience, the rest of Crass might have considered this their wake-up call.

Out on the streets of the UK, Crass was also encountering a different sort of problem. Their increasing fame and notoriety had given them a wide and often quite young fanbase. As with everything else in their set up, Crass toured without the usual rock'n'roll circus. Despite being significantly older than most bands, they had no roadies, preferring to lug all the equipment themselves. Rather than stay in hotels, they stayed in peoples' houses – often at kid's parent's houses and often without beds. Instead, all the door money would be diverted to a plethora of good causes – almost every gig was a benefit for something or other. Their values deliberately represented a mirror image of the hippy capitalist popstars who flaunted their excesses in front of those whose poverty they continued to shamelessly ignore.

Phil Free: "A number of the members of the band were starting at the age where most bands are reforming, and had lived without any great money or jobs ... so it wasn't like we were starting out and here's somebody showing us some money. We were quite happy as a lifestyle getting by – someone would always be bragging about who got the cheapest bit of army gear and so on."

It was inevitable this integrity would be misunderstood by younger fans and lead them into uncomfortable areas marked celebrity and responsibility. While Crass would take up the mantle of responsibility with almost unprecedented, er, responsibility, it would be a chore that would tire them out. Years of explaining how anarchy and peace could be reconciled to earnest young men must be more tiring than relaxing with a beer and a spliff backstage. Things like the quandary of signing autographs – you're damned if you do, damned if you don't. Sometimes time would be taken pointing out the inherent flaws within the concept, but not always...

Steve Ignorant: "Because you just got so pissed off with trying to explain ... you'd have more bloody arguments ... does it hurt? Have I sold out? I remember in Holland a couple of girls wanting to shag me. And I wanted to shag them, but I couldn't, because I was with Crass.

"In England, however, I was looking round thinking, 'Where's all these blonde girls throwing themselves like the Sex Pistols got?' None of that, because we were talking about feminism. No, it tended to be people coming up and wanting to talk to you really deeply about what you were saying. Very quickly it became obvious to me that I can't just get offstage and have a beer and fartarse about and be an idiot and roll about. No, I've got to carry on the gig afterwards and talk in-depth to people who were interested. It was like I had to have a clipboard: how can you have anarchy & peace? Der-der-der-der-der-der Why did you say in an interview der-der-der-der-der-der."

While keeping the band credible to their increasingly demanding fans, the Crass ethic of doing it all so differently, particularly on tour, was beginning to take its toll on their health and general wellbeing.

Eve Libertine: "Touring was really hard work because we didn't eat well, we didn't sleep well, we had really long journeys to do, we didn't have roadies – everything was done by us. So it was really tiring. Someone would ring up and ask us to come and play in Aberdeen. They'd organise the gig and put us up. It was a great way of working – setting up a tour with people who like what we do. But it was very hard work.

"I remember a gig in Wales where the men had to sleep under the billiard table and the 'girls' as the dad said, the 'girls can sleep on the couch!' It was a curved white leather sofa, so we were sleeping in a curve. We were starving when we got there and we were given something like half a bun each – that was a bad night!

"We'd hang on till we got home then we'd just flake out. The band would often end up at peoples' parent's houses: amazing people," reflects Eve, somewhat understandably when you picture the scene from the parents viewpoint, "very accepting."

"I remember one in Scotland. I was feeling quite sick all the way in the van. I couldn't do the gig. We went back to someone's parent's house and they had a fitted tartan carpet. I got a single, made-up bed. It was like bliss! I just got into that bed – because I'd just been lying in the van while they'd been doing the gig. I could hear people going, 'Eve, are you in there? Are you in there?' I was like, 'Oh go away, I'm going to throw up!' In the morning, there were oat cakes and I felt better."

For Christmas 1981, Creative Recording And Sound Services was cranked back into action with a comedy Christmas single: 'Merry Crassmas'. Featuring an end of pier organ playing a medley of Crass songs, a cheery Santa voice wishes everyone a Merry Christmas at the end, adding that if they were munching on a delicious turkey as they listened, "I HOPE IT FUCKING CHOKES YOU."

221984

1982 saw the release of the Crass' piece-de-resistance record, *Christ – The Album*, an ambitious double set, presented in a beautiful, all-black box. It comprised two 12″ albums, an enormous – and wonderful – collage poster featuring Margaret Thatcher laying a turd, and an album sized 28-page pamphlet entitled *A Series Of Shock Slogans And Mindless Token Tantrums*. Of the two albums, the first was 'the new album' – all new songs that had clearly taken a lot of time to record in the studio. The addition of keyboards from (erstwhile Hot Chocolate man) Paul Ellis gave some tracks an almost orchestral feel, though the return of Steve Ignorant on vocals after his absence on *Penis Envy* meant a return to a punkier sound as well.

The second disc was more ambitious still. Ostensibly a live album featuring tracks from the previous year's 100 Club gig, it featured all manner of cut ups and collages with Zen poems, random noises and the aural paraphenalia of everyday life. It was clearly more of a John Cage influenced avant-garde record than anything to do with punk; you certainly wouldn't have got this from an Exploited live album.

Steve Ignorant: "We'd realised that we'd arrived. We had loads of bands on our label, we were selling more records than AC/DC, people like Paul Weller were saying that they respected Crass, so that was a foot in the door. Sade said that she liked Crass and so did her management. It was filtering through from all these people. So we thought for once we'll take time over it and produce our piece-de-resistance."

In between each song on the album there's a segue featuring aural collages of various TV quote people, cleverly assembled to make you question . . . well, just about everything.

The record opens with Steve singing Penny Rimbaud's 'Have A Nice Day', another self-defence song in which Crass needlessly lambast the music press one more time: "If you don't fucking like it, fucking tough!" Poor erudition from someone who could so obviously do better and had done many times – Crass had some peculiarly pointless obsessions. Largely the album retreads traditional Crass themes and punk music, albeit with better production and a more 'grown up' presentation of their ideas.

Next song is 'Mother Love' – wherein Steve Ignorant states of his family: "I didn't fucking need them with their love and family ties". "That's a song I really don't like," he says. "It was just a bitter attack on parents. I wrote that because I went to see my mum and dad. Now I look back, I totally got the wrong end of the stick. I went there and they weren't interested in seeing me – they never played any of my records, hadn't ever listened to them. They weren't really interested in what I was doing – I was in a pretty successful punk band by that time. My mum actually went out and bought that *NME* with me in it, but that quickly got thrown away with old tea leaves in it. It was just an attack on that really. I realised that all they'd been waiting for was for us kids to leave home, so they could have their little life together . . . which is actually fair enough. Later I realised they were just two people who loved each other dearly and just wanted their own life, like we all do. So I regret writing that – it's just too bitter and nasty."

In the segue, news reports of the previous years riots are intercut with Thatcher commenting on them, introducing 'Nineteen Eighty Bore': "The army occupy Ireland, but the boot will never fit". 'Reality Whitewash', with an almost classical music feel, is one of the more tender songs: "The grey man at the wheel / looks around to see if there's some skirt he can steal / he doesn't really want to, he's just acting out a game / and in their own fucked up way, most people do the same / she cleans the bathroom mirror / so she can line her eyes / an expert in delusion, an artist in disguise."

Elsewhere, 'The Greatest Working Class Rip Off' paraphrases a Cockney Rejects song title to criticise the burgeoning Oi movement promoted by Garry Bushell in *Sounds*. Joy De Vivre lends her usual gentility with 'Sentiment (White Feathers)' and 'Birth Control' whilst Eve Libertine is relegated to backing vocals, squad rotation style, for the album.

'Major General Despair' is a new song with an old title and might be the best song on the album, a summation of the anger of the anarcho movement at the connection between the arms trade and the starving millions, both kept in place by the same people: "We're looking for a better world but what do we see? Just hatred, poverty, aggression, misery / So much money spent on war when three quarters of the world is so helplessly poor . . . ."

The song – and the album – end on an upbeat note: "The earth was our home, the wind and the air, the blue sky the grass and the trees, but these masters of war, what do they care? Only sentiments, these / It's our world but through violence they took it away, took dignity, happiness, pride. / They took all the colours and changed them to grey with the bodies of millions that died. / They destroy real meaning with their stupid games, make life a trial of fear. / They destroy what values we have with their aims, make us feel wrong if we care / Well we do care, it's our home, they've been at it too long, if it's a fight they want, it's beginning. / Throughout history we've been expected to sing their tired song, but now it's OUR turn to lead the singing. . . . Fight war not wars / make peace not wars. . ."

On its release, *Christ The Album* felt in many ways like it was the bands final offering. The *Token Tantrums* booklet thanked all the bands that Crass had played with over the years and the *Last Of The Hippies* section read like it was looking back after the fact.

Penny Rimbaud: "I think we were aware that within the framework we were working, we couldn't have gone much further. It's not impossible that had the Falklands War not started, that it would have been our final album. Artistically, that's where I would have liked to have bowed out. If it hadn't been for the Falklands, we wouldn't have known what to do, because we'd said it all. And I don't think the band – any of us – were about to start repeating ourselves."

Despite the time taken over the whole affair, there are still aspects Steve doesn't like, particularly the production: "Still for me, that album still hasn't got that deep bass that other punk bands had – that real get up and go – it's so trebly and tinny. But yeah it was great – we've arrived! And at some point we'll be invited to these parties with the lines of cocaine and the limousines and the paparazzi . . . never happened."

Like so many people, Paul Du Noyer, reviewing the album in *NME* seemed to be teeming with respect while edgy with frustration: "At worst you'll be exasperated by just how wrong-headed and clumsy some of the onslaughts are. At best, on the other hand, there's always something exciting about such raw passion; anger which hits you so hard that – if you're prepared to give it a listen at all – every idea in your head gets shook up, violently. I've never come out the other end of the experience agreeing with Crass – but they challenge your cherished preconceptions so fiercely that you're absolutely forced to re-examine where you stand."

The page before the review, a centre spread was devoted to the thoughts of an (anonymous) ex-soldier talking about the reality of fighting in occupied Northern Ireland. These were political times, times where it was clear that music and politics did indeed mix.

Possibly a bigger influence than either of the records, however, was the booklet that accompanied them. Du Noyer agrees: "Reading the booklet in its entirety, its impossible to come away preserving the protective shield of ignorance which so many people erect between themselves and what Crass really are. Rummage through wreckage, the black box holds some answers."

The title of the booklet was inspired by a piece written by Steve Sutherland in *Melody Maker* (on one of the few occasions it deigned to acknowledge their existence): "Crass by name, even worse by nature, like it or not, they just won't go away. Crass are the distempered dog end of rock 'n roll's once bright and vibrant rebellion. That they're so unattractive, unoriginal and badly balanced in an uncompromising and unhumourless way, simply adds to the diseased attraction of their naively black and white world where words are *a series of shock slogans and mindless token tantrums* to tout around your tribe and toss at passers by."

"We know that they are not fit to rule our world, yet we allow them to do so. We allow them to build around us a hideously dangerous environment; Britain is at risk of be coming little more than a launch-pad for American missiles and a

practice ground for Russian ones. Thatcher's government intends to spend twelve and a half thousand million pounds this year, 1982, on the military alone and that doesn't include the other thousands of millions on war-related expenses, from communication systems to government fall-out shelters and nuclear power stations. The British coastline is becoming dotted with potentially lethal nuclear power stations that produce very little electricity, about ten per cent of yearly UK requirements, and very big bombs. The first 'power stations' were built solely for the production of nuclear bombs; there is little to suggest that those being built now are for anything but similar purposes. The air, the sea and the land are becoming increasingly polluted with nuclear waste; the Irish sea is the most radioactive stretch of water in the world, people and animals have already died as a result of this mindless litter-bugging.

"Do we have to wait for the accident that will and must happen, that kills people by the thousands, before the authorities accept that there is a little bit more at risk than their self-important reputations? The nuclear programme has enabled the authorities to intensify enormously the development of their 'security systems'. So not only do we have to suffer the insecurity of the threat of nuclear war … we also have to contend with the added insecurity of living in what is fast becoming a police state. Nuclear establishments have at their command an armed force who answer to no authority but their own. The government recently approved plans to set up a new style 'Home Guard': a force who will be specially trained to deal with 'domestic problems' and that means me and you, so don't be fooled by tales of 'Dad's Army', this one isn't a comedy. The authorities are increasingly prying into our private lives. From phone tapping to census forms, our lives are becoming files in their dark offices. The authorities have just purchased a computer system capable of linking together all the other computers that store information about every man, woman and child living in Britain.

"At the press of a button, the authorities will be able to have details on our lives, from birth to the present time – fifteen years ago, we were claiming that computers were going to enormously limit individual freedom; naturally, we were accused of 'being paranoid', but, none the less, that's exactly what they have done. Now, with the development of the 'micro chip' there is no way that anyone could imagine the effects that these new technologies will have on our privacy and freedom. 1984 has become a memory, a clumsy hypothesis that fell hopelessly short in its failure to allow for the horrific escalation in technological 'hardware'. Private life is becoming a memory – we are becoming nothing but *numbers in some bizarre lottery game and when your number is called run like fuck, but beware, they'll probably have a print-out on where it is that you're running to.*

"As the authorities increase military expenditure, the money for the so-called 'social services' is decreased. We are expected to live on less and less as the government spends more and more on their 'war games'. In Great Britain, 1982, there are people who are suffering from malnutrition because they can't afford food; they are almost freezing to death, many actually are dying, because they can't afford heat; they are being made homeless because they can't afford the rent; they are being moved into half-way houses because the councils can't afford decent homes, where they are suffering from malnutrition because they can't afford food; they are almost freezing to death, many actually are dying, because they can't afford heat; when the deprivation finally makes them ill, they are being moved into hospitals where the authorities can't afford to properly treat them. They'll probably die young, but most people die eventually anyway. Meanwhile, Her Majesty's Government is spending twelve and a half thousand million pounds this year, 1982, on the military alone and that doesn't include the other thousands of millions on war-related expenses, from communications systah, blah, blah, blah, hello, hello, is there anybody there?"

Penny Rimbaud – *Last Of The Hippies*

As well as Penny's unforgettable piece, there was a startling diatribe from Pete Wright about education and mind control and a considered essay on pacifism and its strands of anarchism from Mick Duffield. It was the most effective of all the Crass multimedia efforts and *Last Of The Hippies* in particular had a profound effect on many people who read it.

Whatever the influence or artistic merit of *Christ – The Album*, the band felt an acute sense of failure at having been overtaken by events. By the time of its release, the Falklands War had been started and finished, complete with the needless death of 1,100 young men.

In March 1982, Argentina occupied the Falkland Islands, to which it had long claimed ownership. Margaret Thatcher duly sent a task force and a war was fought with Britain emerging victorious by June. Neither side had actually declared war, so like Ireland, Thatcher was fighting a war that dared not speak its name.

The tabloid press, particularly *The Sun*, was disgusting in its jingoism.

Front page headlines like 'Gotcha!' and the continual reference to the Argentinians as 'Argies' showed no respect to the dead of either side whatsoever. The British public, however, lapped it up.

Penny Rimbaud just managed to slip a small piece into his *Last Of The Hippies*:

"Since writing this article the 'Falklands Crisis' has developed graphically illustrating the complete madness of rulers. What should have been little more than a minor territorial dispute requiring discussion and diplomacy has blown up into a tense world situation where hundreds of young men have already died for the arrogance of their 'leaders'.

"Around one hundred and fifty years ago the British stole the Falklands so that they could maintain access into the Pacific ocean; since that time the Argentinians have made repeated attempts to negotiate a return of the islands to their control If it had not been for the discovery of oil and mineral deposits in the area Britain would have handed back the islands without a second thought, but, because of the enormous wealth to which they gave access, Argentinian claims ware ignored. Eventually and inevitably the Argentinians re-invaded the Falklands and the British government, seizing it as an opportunity to divert attention from its enormous domestic problems, launched the country into war — however understandable the Argentinian aggression might be, it is as unacceptable as the British response. Violence breeds violence.

"Historically Britain has no 'right' to the Falklands; it seems easy to criticise the Argentinian action, yet it was by exactly the methods that Britain now so self-righteously condemns that the islands were originally stolen. Thatcher, her government and other governments before her couldn't care a fuck about the British people on the island, couldn't care a sod about sovereignty — it's the oil and minerals that they care about, the wealth and the power that they can exploit and if that means that hundreds of people are going to die for that privilege — tough shit! The nationalistic fervour that has been whipped up is just a crude cover that enables those in power to send young men to premature death and that creates an atmosphere in which it becomes 'acceptable' to brutally murder the so-called 'enemy'.

"Thatcher talks of 'peaceful solutions' whilst ordering the slaughter of five hundred young men and claims that 'our people' need protection whilst already having been responsible for the murder of over thirty of them — she is a bigot, a hypocrite and a liar.

"Obscene articles have appeared daily in the press. The dehumanising term 'Argie' has been coined to make the death and mutilation of fellow human beings appear 'commonplace' and 'ordinary'. Page three pin-ups have appeared wearing an assortment of nationalistic insults. Desperate sweethearts flashed their knickers as the QE2 sailed away with its cargo of gun-fodder. Britain relived the 'war years' rallying to its blood-stained flag in some dreadful memory of a power that once held half the world in its imperialist grip – now that grip is a weak wristed fantasy that, through sheer arrogance, would risk the safety of the whole planet. How long must young men continue to die for the greed of governments? How long must young women exploit their bodies to support this psycho-sexual fantasy of war? The big bang, big fuck – enough. WE MUST LEARN TO SAY 'NO'."
Penny Rimbaud – *Last Of The Hippies*

The feeling of having been left at the starting blocks would alter the band mindset in a crucial way. From here on in, everything they did was re-active – all artistic output was dictated by external events. On *Christ* ... they'd sung: "Throughout history we've been expected to sing their tired song / now it's our turn to lead the singing". It was an almost triumphalist statement, as if the band feel some kind of critical mass is about to be achieved in conciousness. If that was the intention, the Falklands War, and especially the almost total lack of vocal opposition to it, would show it was naïve in the extreme.

George Mackay: "There was something of an eschatological imperative in the air at the time, this sense of doom, ending, nuclear eschatology. That was all there in the zeitgeist."

Pete Wright: "I think it was about 1982 when I came across an article by an Australian scientist/scientific journalist who suggested that if all the nuclear weapons in the world were launched, arrived and exploded at the same time – an unlikely worst case, but go with it – then the net result, excluding the highly improbable occurrence of a catastrophic crust split or some such, would be that most of northern Europe and parts of north America would be a wasteland. Since most people in the world live south of the equator, and the weather systems north and south hardly mix, the result for this majority would probably be a move to the right in their governments and a marginally increased radiation count.

Our big bombs just weren't that big. The Apocalypse which we projected on the rest of the world was our local apocalypse, limited to ourselves. "We are the world." Oh yeah? It's the same today. Me is everything."

George Mackay: "It struck me as the confirmation of everything that they feared – that we were now slipping over. There was a grand conspiratorial side of Crass – the system will get you, everything was the system ... but in that moment the state was mobilised and the army went out and killed people, and got killed. Young men. I don't think they were overdramatising – I thought Crass understood how important it was for the British establishment to have a victorious war."

The Crass response to the Falklands had been pretty much the loudest vocal opposition outside the usual suspects in Parliament. Their first response was a flexi 'Sheep Farming In The Falklands', a rather cheap and nasty jibe at the British Army that envisaged soldiers fucking sheep and relied on the double-entendre 'the Royal Marines are coming'.

"I think we did 20,000 of them," says Penny who played the radio commentator in the style of Monty Python. "We wanted to get something funny and vocal out there. It was actually before the Belgrano went down that I wrote it. When it just seemed like a joke, because no-one had been hurt at that point. I remember we were on tour doing 'Sheep Farming' ... we had a huge banner with all the words on it. Eve would go along with a stick and the idea was everyone sung along – it was great fun. We were actually on tour when the Belgrano went down and the whole thing wasn't funny any more ... it turned into something which was costing lives. We really had a big problem – do we go on doing this song? We did, but the whole colouration changed.

"There was reference to the sinking of the Sheffield – at that point we were still too nervous to make it a clean public statement. We decided that in the event of anyone pinning us down on it, we could say it was a bootleg – someone must have recorded us at a gig – 'nothing to do with us mate'. Rough Trade agreed to stick it in any old album – that's how we got it out."

It was also possible to simply go into Rough Trade and ask them for the new Crass flexi, which they simply took off a pile on the counter and gave you.

Steve Ignorant: "Would I sing that now? I don't know. Even as a joke, I just didn't find it funny. Penny's sense of humour has always been different to mine. I remember thinking at the time that I didn't mind taking the piss out of skinheads or whatever (Rival Tribal Rebel Revel), but with soldiers – those people have got cars and could drive and do someone. And I don't think it's very clever to take the piss out of people who are going to war. How do you justify that? You can't. In hindsight, I should have refused to do it."

Mick Duffield: "Britain was involved in war again ... all jingoistic inter-nation-state, with potential for escalating into something more widespread and dangerous. It cannot not be overstated that with two world wars already this century here we were limbering up for a third with another exercise in mass-jingoism – it was horrendous."

Having had a bit more time to consider their response, Crass released another single: 'How Does It Feel To Be The Mother Of A Thousand Dead?' A direct attack on Thatcher, it came in a black sleeve decorated with white graveyard crosses. When, during Prime Ministers Question Time, Thatcher was asked if she'd heard the record, things were getting serious.

The Conservative Party attempted to fight back, as the *Guardian* reported:

"The Attorney General, Sir Michael Havers, has been asked by the Conservative MP for Enfield North, Mr. Tim Eggar, to prosecute an Anti-Falklands war record under the Obscene Publications Act. The record 'How Does It Feel To Be The Mother of 1,000 Dead?', by the group Crass, which also owns the record company Crass Records, which released it, is said to have sold 20,000 copies since it was issued last Saturday. It refers to Mrs. Thatcher and the decision to send the Task Force. 'You never wanted peace or solution, from the start you lusted after war and destruction ... Iron Lady, with your stone heart so, eager that the lesson be taught that you inflicted, you determined, you created, you ordered ... It was your decision to have those young boys slaughtered."

Tim Eggar was the brother of Robin Eggar, a *Daily Mirror* columnist who had previously written in his column: "Rock music is often used by the young to voice their protests. However distasteful the Sex Pistols appeared to be in 1977, their songs were a chilling warning of the coming recession. But anarchist band Crass have gone too far. They released last week the most revolting and unnecessary record I have ever heard. 'How Does It Feel To Be The Mother of 1,000 Dead?' is a vicious and obscene attack on Margaret Thatcher's motives for engaging in the Falklands war. It bears little relation to reality. Retailing at only 75p it has already sold more than 28,000 copies."

Crass themselves escaped any direct threat from the state. "We didn't actually get any of it," says Rimbaud. "There's no question at all that that was a policy." Rimbaud cites a circular sent around the Tory party after MP Timothy Eggar opened proceedings against 'How Does It Feel?' which stated that "on no account must they respond to any form of provocation from us".

A hilarious LBC radio interview ensued, where Tim Eggar debated with Andy Palmer and Pete Wright. Eggar is clearly angry fit to burst before he even starts, and – sounding like a clichéd public school Tory – starts off by blustering that the record goes "beyond the acceptable bounds of freedom of speech, being the most vicious, scurrilous and obscene record that has ever been produced". One can only presume he hadn't heard *Reality Asylum*.

The presence of Andy Palmer here is a masterstroke. Just when the general public might expect a sneering punk rocker saying they didn't care, we instead hear Andy replying in a calm and considered manner – and with a voice every bit as posh as Eggar's – that the real obscenity comes not from the record but from the death and destruction caused by the war. An outraged Eggar goes on to quote some of the lyrics, his voice and disgusted tone lending an unintentional hilarity: "It starts off 'You slimy shithead got it all. . .', and then it gets worse from there."

As the voice of opposition, Crass started to receive letters of support from Labour MPs, among them Ray Powell, Andrew Faulds and Frank Allaun. This was not a game.

Steve Ignorant: "I was shit-scared. I started sleeping with half a pool cue next to my bed. We started getting letters from the House Of Commons – once politicians start writing to you, then you've suddenly come to the attention of the powers that be. 'I don't know that I want to be here'. Once that headed notepaper came, I thought we were in the shit. And I was ready to back off very quick."

"I remember going to the Victory Parade with Gee – she wanted to take photographs. Coming out of the tube station, there were Union Jacks everywhere, and tanks and soldiers waving at people. I remember thinking, 'Keep quiet or you'll get lynched from a lamp post'. I've never experienced that public fervour. It was really quite scary, because you were against the whole thing but you couldn't say so."

Crass also found themselves privy to information about the war that wasn't circulating in the public domain. This information had come from a member of the Armed Forces who was out in the Falklands on one of the ships.

Steve Ignorant: "I received a letter from a sailor calling us anti-English bastards. I was incensed and wrote back to him. The bloke replied and apologised, saying he was off to the Falklands. When he came back, he got in touch and said that he wanted to meet up. So me & Pen went to meet him and brought him back to Dial House. He told us how a lot of the English equipment didn't work, how most of the blokes on the ships were puking and shitting themselves physically every day cos they were so fucking scared."

The meeting took place in a café near Victoria Station. It was all cloak and dagger stuff, as Rimbaud recalls: "Oh yeah! If you look at what happened to that bloke in Israel … it says something for the methods used by the British Secret Services that we never got copped for that. And the fact that that has never yet come up as an issue. There was virtually a mutiny after the Sheffield, because all the sailors knew what had happened. And that's why the flagship (HMS Invincible) was so long coming back. There would have been a massive de-programming."

Steve Ignorant: "The Coventry, which was his ship and the ship that Prince Andrew was on both sent up foil but the Sheffield didn't, so that was used as a decoy for the Exocets to go in. Conspiracy or not I don't know – that's the trouble with conspiracies, you can never prove them.

"I remember beginning to feel that this wasn't why I joined a punk band and wondering what the fuck we were getting into. If someone asks me about it, I can't explain it, I can't defend it, I can't justify it … but it was anti-establishment so I went for it."

Crass reflected on the Falklands in a handout entitled *The Party's Over:*

"Over 1000 dead. 1000 young men pointlessly murdered. 1000 lives that are no more. Over 1000 dead. Young men mostly, tragically, pointlessly and prematurely sent to their deaths by two unbending arrogant governments to whom the death of young men is nothing but a tool in the machinery of power. It is no longer funny to speak of the 'Iron Lady', Thatcher has proved herself to be a dangerous and uncaring lunatic – her violent treatment of the H Bloc prisoners in Ireland last year was indication of her cruel mind, the Falklands was proof of her madness…

"… Thatcher has been able to con people into believing that Britain is great again (was it ever?), that military violence is right and justified (just like Ireland and strike-busting and riot control). Don't be fooled, that same squad of Falklands heroes will be smashing your head when you finally realise that you've had enough of her madness. The public responded to the Falklands in a festival of World War Two memories, we were at war again, all pull together against the Hun etc etc. The difference was that the Argentinians had got a cause (even if their manner of dealing with it was unacceptable) and the Nazis had no cause except greed and power. Even in the wildest of imaginations the Argentinian invasion can hardly be compared with Hitler's plunder of Europe. Thatcher has through the atmosphere of war, made the reality of nuclear war that bit more possible. The peace movement must realise that resistance to installation of American missiles in the UK will now be far less acceptable to the General Public. Our work has been put back possibly ten years – IT'S TIME TO FIGHT BACK

This partially welcome publicity served to make operating more awkward for Crass in various ways.

Penny Rimbaud: "I think it was a policy right from the start. After we had that raid by the Vice Squad over *Reality Asylum*, which was in the first year of our existence, their policy was quite clear. Within days, we were hearing that shops all over Britain were being raided – never anything confiscated but being told, 'You sell that and you're in trouble.' Which wasn't true at all. Throughout our history, we'd have a tour of, say,

14 dates and we'd have seven of them pulled. We'd normally lose about half the gigs we set out to do because the police would go along and, in some cases, just say you're not doing that. I remember that happening in Bournemouth . . . they'd make people aware they weren't happy about it, which is normally enough for people to pull out."

As well as the lives of all those involved and their friends and families, The Falklands War would change Crass and their whole approach to their art. Penny Rimbaud explains: "From then on, everything we did was a tactical response – if something happened, we'd get something out as quickly as we could. We didn't think about any of the artistic merits or values. Which is why that stuff is bitter and craggy, and . . . interesting in a historical way. We were getting desperate, we didn't know how to deal with it.

"It seemed like up until that point we – the punk movement – had been on a winner. We all thought we were going to break through with something. That war knocked it all on the head, and then the miners immediately afterwards, confirmed it."

Always willing to at least try to back up words with actions, and aware that people could do with something to lift their spirits, Crass' next move was to organise a squat gig in London. The result was a free one-day event featuring a dozen bands – disappointingly the usual suspects from the insular anarcho-punk scene. Of all the bands that played, only The Apostles and Youth In Asia were not on the Crass label.

The original venue was supposed to be the Rainbow in Finsbury Park. "We had hold of the Rainbow for three days," remembers Rimbaud, "realised it wasn't going to happen because there was too much police presence, and had the Zig Zag as a back-up. We moved into the Zig Zag the night before the gig. Andy did the break in – he'd had quite a bit of squatting experience.

"We felt at the time we needed a celebration. We felt it was time we had a lark – things had got serious and a bit isolated. We needed to celebrate not just what Crass was up to, but what all of us were. We needed to get together with as many people as possible who were a part of that sense of . . . movement, as could come along."

A touching piece of graffiti appeared on a wall during the gig – a vertical line, a horizontal line and then the two conjoined – 'we control the vertical, we control the horizontal, we control the Zig Zag'.

Steve Ignorant: "It worked very well. The police were outside and they accepted it – they said that if anything happened in the street people would get nicked double-quick, but we took care of what happened inside. So there was some sort of understanding. The people who actually broke in – God bless 'em, worked really hard. If it hadn't been for them, we wouldn't have got in.

"It was a real party atmosphere – people were going out, getting more beer, sharing it. We had soup on the go, people would rush out, go home and bring things back. It was great but not in a hippy-dippy way. When we went onstage, I've never heard such a roar – it was a bit like Freddie Mercury at Live Aid!

"Someone booted in the door to the cellars downstairs and there were six untapped barrels of beer. So, someone decided that it shouldn't be opened because everyone would be too drunk and fuck it up. Everyone else was saying no, it's not your squat. So all the beer came out, no-one got out of it.

"Everyone went home nicely afterwards apart from a few hardliners who decided they wanted to keep the squat going. We said no, the point is that you go in – bang! – out – you don't stick around. I remember thinking that perhaps it *can* work – the anarchist thing, it really inspired me."

In a (successful) attempt to inspire others into setting up similar actions, Crass released the customary handout:

"We came up with the idea of squatting a venue as being a step towards taking back what is <u>ours</u>. The day was a success. Fifteen hundred people turned up and proved with a bit of common sense and trust in each other, you can do something together, without having to shit on or be shat on by anyone else.

"There are a lot of people who don't want to pay £2.50 on the door so that they can dance and forget. The pain and suffering won't go away just by ignoring it. They are here to stay unless we get off our arses and do something about it. That day at the Zig Zag proved we can.

"Most of the property in this country is owned by only one per cent of the population, the rest of us are expected to sit up and beg. The Zig Zag had been

empty and unused for over a year before last Christmas. Now it is boarded up again more securely than ever. Homes are almost impossible to find. 3 million people are unemployed. That's 3 million who can't pay the price, whether it be in rent or on the door at a gig (not that many would want to even if they had the cash). It's a liability to walk out of the front door, if you've got one, for fear of being abused by one 'authority' or another. We are offered nothing by the system that expects us to work and die for its progress. The healthy and privileged have neither sympathy nor understanding for the vast majority of the population. They assume that they are in control. And they are until we show them otherwise. We pay for their privilege. Not just in money- money is the meanest form of energy. Human energy should have no price tag. We will be ripped off, for as long as we let them rip us off.

"What happened at the Zig Zag, we hope, was one step towards reclaiming what is ours – freedom. Free food, free shelter, free information, free music, free ideas. Freedom to do whatever does not impinge on the freedom of others. The idea of 'squat rock' is not purely another way of doing gigs, as we hope this handout explains. Hopefully it will have been, and is, an inspiration to other people to open up more places, whether it be for gigs, to live in, whatever..."

The leaflet went on to explain in detail how you could squat somewhere, from the tactics on getting in in the first place, to the legal situation once you're there.

"By theft and murder / They took the land / and now everywhere around the walls spring up at their command"
– The World Turned Upside Down – Leon Rosselson

"Think of this as a window"
– Graffiti painted by squatters on to the bricked-up window of a derelict house.

To say that squatting has a long history would be like saying organic food has been around for a while: that is to forget there was a time when it was the only way people lived. Squatting is the oldest form of tenure in the world, of course, and everybody on the planet is the direct descendent of squatters. As time went on and the laughable concept of 'owning' land somehow became accepted, people like Gerard Winstanley of the Diggers movement in the 17th Century declared: "The poorest man hath as true a title and just right to the land as the richest man."

After the Second World War was over, many war heroes returned home to find no home to return to, and a big wave of squatting began. Over 30 service camps and disused military installations were squatted in just two days as homeless families figured that they were due a bit of the freedom they'd fought for.

In the sixties and seventies, squatting became even more widespread as people took over disused houses and buildings and returned them to functioning spaces. Sometimes whole streets would be taken over, turning them from derelict emptiness to vibrant communities overnight. Squatting was enthusiastically taken up by the hippies, and then by the punks. Rough Trade − now famous as an independent record shop and record label − was started by Geoff and Steve, both squatters.

In *Last Of The Hippies*, Penny Rimbaud saw squatting as part of the bigger picture of an alternative future:

"We can open up squats and, from them, start information services for those who want to do the same, or we can form housing co-ops and communes to share the responsibility of renting or even buying a property. In places where we already live, we can open the doors to others, form tenant associations with neighbours and demand and create better conditions and facilities in the area. We can form gardening groups that squat and farm disused land or rent allotments where we can produce food for ourselves and others that are free from dangerous chemicals and grow medicinal herbs to cure each other's headaches. We can create health groups where we can practice alternative medicine, like herbalism and massage, that create healthy bodies and minds rather than the drugged-up robots that are the results of conventional medicine; we can then, maybe, learn to love and respect each other's bodies rather than fearing them. We can form free schools where knowledge can be shared, rather than rules laid down. Education, rather than being little but state training in slavery, can become a mutual growth and a true enquiry into our world where everyone is the teacher and everyone is the pupil. We can start community centres where people have an alternative to the male dominated, money orientated atmosphere of Britain's only nightly social event, the pub. Centres could serve and further the interests of the community, rather than simply being there to finance

the brewer. In Scotland, a group of people found an unused site hut which they squatted and having soundproofed and decorated it, put on gigs and discussion groups. The local council were so impressed by their efforts that they have been given official use of it. We can run food co-ops that buy and distribute foods that have been grown by people that we know, or have been brought from sources who we trust are not exploiting the people who produced it. A lot of supermarket food is grown in the Third World where the workers are paid next to nothing so that the middlemen can make huge profits – food co-ops can break down that chain. At one time we ran a food co-op from our house that supplied over twenty other homes with food that had been produced outside the capitalist system. We can form 'work banks' where we can exchange our individual skills for the skills of others. If enough people are prepared to join a 'bank', money becomes almost redundant. The only limitation is our own imagination."
Penny Rimbaud – *Last Of The Hippies*

In October 1982, Crass played two concerts at the Belfast Anarchist Centre. The A Centre had been 'reopened' especially for the two gigs, in a gay disco borrowed from owner Jeff Dudgeon, who had fought for several years for gay rights in Northern Ireland through the European civil rights courts.

Tensions were high in Belfast as Crass played the first night, due in no small part to the IRA assassinating a prominent loyalist MP that day. During the gig, "NF adorned skinheads" started trouble, which was duly expanded by the police, who set about some of the punks.

Reviewing the gig in *NME*, Adrian Maddox reflected: "In the Crass shop, there's no browsing allowed – you buy or get out. And like a hard porn or horror flick the Crass camera moves in close, focuses in, holds, spares you nothing. In that sense, it must warp, must shut out so much else … there's more thoughtfulness, informativeness and persuasiveness in just one of Crass' pamphlets than in their entire rant of a set."

The second night passed without incident, leading Penny Rimbaud to ruminate "whether perhaps the different factions in the Troubles took Sundays off, a kind of godforsaken truce in a thoroughly unholy war". After the gig, they received an invitation.

Penny Rimbaud: "When we did our gigs in Belfast, we were invited to this pub, which I didn't go to. We were invited to go along to thank our protectors, who were the IRA. They'd been 'looking after us' for the time we were there. I don't know what that means. . ."

Steve Ignorant: "All the punks were interested in doing was eating (magic) mushroom sandwiches and getting out of it. They weren't interested in political things. . . . I hated every second of it. I thought it was a frightening, ugly place. I didn't like seeing soldiers walking round, I was just glad to get back home. The gig was good, but it was frightening having the RUC come in with their guns. But the people were great. The time I enjoyed was in the pub with the Irish punks, drinking Harp lager.

"The best night was being at what I think was an IRA-funded drinking club and dancing to all the Abba records and stuff like that. Then we were really accepted into the whole community. There was a cage on the door, the bloke shook our hand, blah blah blah, IRA, yeah, whatever. And it was like a Saturday night in a pub – mums and dads out, dancing to the disco . . . IRA connection? It could have been, I don't know. All I saw was young people getting totally smashed out of it in a way that I never had. But then what did they have to look forward to? Cos there's tanks and soldiers and, if you don't agree with it, kneecappings and shit."

After all the publicity the band got from their Falklands record, the offers started to fly in, but not from the record companies, who were presumably wise to the band by now. No, Crass were attracting far more serious customers.

Penny Rimbaud: "Throughout the Falklands thing we were pretty nervous because we were so vocal about that. By then we were getting stuff coming in from all over the place – from the remnants of Baader-Meinhoff, the IRA – all sorts of dissident organisations."

Now it was the turn of the Russian Secret State.

Penny Rimbaud: "A Russian literary magazine whose name I don't remember and in my view didn't even exist, wanted to have a little chat, so we were invited to this apartment off the Cromwell Road (in London). It was obvious from the start – there were people wearing Trilbys and raincoats with their collars turned up behind lampposts; curtains flickering. It was obviously a KGB pick-up point. . . Because they knew that we'd got information on the Falklands. *The Observer* had printed that information on HMS Sheffield, which no-one's ever done anything about, they quite rightly thought that we might have access to more damaging information."

There was also a visit to Dial House from people claiming membership of the German Baader-Meinhoff gang.

Penny Rimbaud: "A woman turned up here with her young daughter, who looked like her young son. By then, Baader-Meinhoff had all but collapsed, but there were still cells. She and her daughter did bank jobs. They turned up one day on pushbikes. They were having a relax in Britain, and in Germany they were doing bank jobs, to finance the cells."

They informed Crass about this, which in the circumstances seems a ridiculously foolish thing to do. Penny continues: "People did openly tell us things. Because of our reputation, we were privy to that sort of information. People told us things, which often we didn't want to bloody well hear."

Meanwhile, of all the movements for social change, the rise of the peace movement in Western Europe had led to its mainstream wing, CND, enjoying a massive rise in popularity and influence.

George McKay: "Around that time, there were a number of different music contributions to the movement. One of the big ones was Glastonbury Festival. From 1981, Glastonbury was organised through National CND offices – through CND's national structure and organisation – and that's one of the key reasons why Glastonbury became successful ... remember, there were only three Glastonbury festivals held during the seventies, and the one that most resembled what it became, the 1979 event, a fundraiser for the UN Year of the Child, was something of a financial disaster. Over the eighties, the usual figure quoted is that Glastonbury gave CND something like a million pounds, and that really helped support things."

George McKay: "Because Crass bolted the CND symbol onto the anarchy symbol, they made that connection more explicit. But there were a lot of other things going on too – in November 1983, there were 102 peace camps up and down the country, inspired by Greenham Common women, for instance. Crass had a role to play, but I don't know I'd want to overstate it."

Of all those involved in the peace movement, Crass were among the most aware regarding the powers of the parliamentary left to co-opt it and the liberal left to neuter it.

"The present rebirth of interest in CND runs the risk of once again going up the political arsehole. Socialist power seekers have already moved in on the hard fought for peace platform. Speeches at the two Trafalgar Square rallies were directed more towards vote catching than peace making; when the issues weren't so fashionable, the leftist doves were happy to be sharing peanuts with the rest of the pigeons in the square. Now they are promising to refuse to allow America to install cruise missiles in Britain; is this just another vote catcher that they'll back out of once they're elected in? The Labour Party will sell CND right down the river and sink it without trace if it's allowed to do so. Nuclear disarmament and the wider issues of peace must not become political soap-operas in which the power hungry can play their insincere games...

"...To put it in the words of a little-known Welsh anarchist, 'Eat shit you fuckers. Apart from the obvious threat of political exploitation, a very real danger to the long-term existence of CND and its allies is the current interest being shown in it by the music business. Peace has become a saleable commodity, a trendy product, and established record labels, the music press and bands alike, who four years ago dismissed those who opposed war as 'boring old hippies', are now bending over backwards to be seen to be supporting the cause. The only cause that they're supporing is their own; it's good promotion, good sales, good business sense, and they'll bleed it dry as long as it's 'this year's thing'; when it isn't, they'll drop it, as they did RAR, like a ton of hot bricks."
Penny Rimbaud – *Last Of The Hippies*

Pete Wright looks back on Crass' pacifism with a less than complete satisfaction: "Crass fell into the trap of having narrowed itself down to a linear message... It really comes back to the way we excised people like Class War from 'our' fold. Had we been more inclusive or even more indifferent to people with a different angle from ours, the 'peace movement' might have stayed a 'change movement'. It's ironic that I went to some pains to warn E.P. Thomson of the dangers of cutting the punks out of CND, especially after these same punks had revitalised it, when I was doing precisely the same thing hamstringing the 'movement' with evangelical pacifism. Egg on face."

"Old and strong / She goes on and on
You can't kill the spirit / She is like a mountain"
Greenham Common song

On December 12, 1982, a remarkable demonstration took place at
Greenham Common airbase, hinting that radical ideas could indeed
flow into the mainstream.

Just fifteen months since the peace camp had been set up, more than
thirty thousand women came from all over the country to demonstrate
their opposition to it. BBC newsreader Fiona Bruce poignantly remembers, "We had to be divided up into who would be arrested and who
wouldn't."

'Embrace the base' was the slogan, as they held hands, making a circle
around the outer limits of the base. The importance of the demonstration wasn't lost on the *Daily Mirror*, who devoted their centre pages to it
the next day, interviewing women such as Mary Stevens, a wheelchair-
bound multiple sclerosis sufferer who'd travelled all the way from
Birmingham, and told the paper: "Nuclear weapons are the most frightening thing this world has ever known or will know." Perhaps
poignantly, she was at pains to point out: "I am not a fanatical women's
libber or a loony professional demonstrator. I don't belong to any political group. But I want to make sure the future is safe. One day I'm
hoping to have grandchildren and I'm doing this for them." Women
symbolically and somewhat disturbingly placed baby clothes and pictures of children on the perimeter fence.

The *Mirror* hailed the day: "Last night celebration bonfires were
blazing to mark the women's greatest day in their campaign against
Cruise Missiles." The Cruise Missiles hadn't moved an inch, but maybe
public opinion had. It could, however, be looked on as naïve in the
extreme to think that public opinion was anything that kept Margaret
Thatcher awake at night.

121984

O n New Years Day 1983, the Greenham Women invaded the base, unsure whether bullets or guard dogs awaited them. Neither did however, as a group of 44 women held hands and danced in a circle round a silo in the early morning mist, like a scene out of the *Wicker Man*. Despite the Falklands fiasco, the movement was on the move.

By this point, Crass was receiving "easily 200" letters a week from fans asking for advice, political opinion or just badges. Each week, Tuesdays were set aside for the band to sit down and reply personally to their mail, again setting them apart from the vast majority of bands. Wednesdays would be set aside for the endless stream of fanzines queuing up to either interview the band or simply pretend to as an excuse to meet them and visit the house. A principle reason for this deluge of mail was the highly unusual fact that they always replied to them; not with a signed photo and a fan club press release, but with a proper handwritten letter and usually some leaflets and badges as well. Sometimes, the letters imposed a great sense of responsibility.

Phil Free: "We'd have all these letters to answer and there would always be in this stack, one letter from someone who was talking about suicide. Suddenly, you stop talking about anarchy in the UK and you start talking about real lives. I assume every band gets suicide letters? Given the stuff we were talking about, it didn't seem that unreal to feel suicidal, and we were old enough to know that there are a lot of sixteen year olds out there who feel like that. But when somebody writes to you and you sit down to reply and this letter is three months old. . ."

Penny Rimbaud: "There were seven of us and we'd be dealing with an average of 20-40 letters each on that day."

To this day, Dial House still receives about ten letters a week to do with the band, often from new fans. Some things clearly still matter.

Still shocked at the silence surrounding the Falklands War and left feeling very isolated, Penny Rimbaud decided to write an open letter to musicians, which he sent to the music paper *Sounds*:

An open letter to rock 'n' rollers everywhere
"I am writing this letter in the hope that it might inspire reaction or, more importantly, action.

"Last year the Falklands War demonstrated how easy it is to drift into a war, a war that in the nuclear age might easily develop into the *war, the war to end all war. The cold, calculated way in which Mrs. Thatcher guided this country into what only good fortune prevented from being that final war is a grim warning of the kind of future that may be in store for us all.*

"For years we have been witness to horrific oppression, by government forces, of the people of Northern Ireland. More recently, in the riots of Brixton, Toxteth etc., the discontent of the poor, who are expected to live on less and less as the ruling elite grow ever richer, was viciously responded to by those same forces. Violence is becoming the accepted 'method' for the State to deal with the social problems that it *creates. Thatcher has adopted Victorian 'gun-boat diplomacy' to deal with both national and, unbelievably, international problems. The appalling degree of that violence has been demonstrated time and time again in Northern Ireland; the Falklands War only confirmed Thatcher's doctrine of 'the sword being mightier than the pen' and showed her up as the spiteful, malicious and revengeful person that she is.*

"It is quite clear, in the light of what is now commonly available material, (see One Man's Falklands *by Tam Dalyell), that Thatcher, against the advice of her own staff in both the Foreign Office and the forces, deliberately escalated the Falklands 'dispute' into the Falklands 'war'. It is transparently obvious that her actions were designed not only to impress the British public with her dynamic and therefore vote-worthy character, but also to cover over increasingly glaring problems on the home front, recession, depression and unemployment, on both counts she*

was highly successful; for her own political neck Thatcher couldn't afford not to have a war. Had the British public been aware of the real facts, things might have been different.

"It is evident that the sinking of the Argentinian cruiser Belgrano was an unwarranted act of aggression by Thatcher designed to abort the very strong possibility of a diplomatic solution being found through Peruvian and American negotiation. Thatcher personally ordered the sinking of the ship and with it, the escalation of aggression that led to the sinking of HMS Sheffield. The real war had begun, not the Falklands War, but Thatcher's War.

Throughout the war we were told by the woman directly responsible for an unemployment figure of over three million to 'support our boys in the Falklands'. What has she done to support 'our' boys at home? At the end of the conflict there were thousands of dead and injured and Thatcher told us to 'rejoice', rejoice for what? One woman's egocentric, megalomaniac adventure over a tiny island eight thousand miles away?

"The battle for the Falklands is by no means over – since Britain 'possessed' the islands one hundred and fifty years ago, the Argentinians and incidentally all other South American countries, have disputed its right to be there. The Falklands are a colonial thorn in the side of South American dignity and will remain so as long as British governments continue to assert their arrogance over lands and peoples to which they have no moral right.

"It is obvious that few people in this country are aware of the real implications of the Falklands War. The cost in life and capital has been out of all proportion to the results. Having spent £1,600 million to stage the war, Britain is now committed to spend over £500 million a year to maintain forces on the island against inevitable future attack from Argentina; although Thatcher claimed 'victory', it is necessary to remember that Argentina has made no agreement to cease hostility. In a country as impoverished as the UK, it is hard to believe that massive outlays of capital to stage pointless wars can be justified. So far the Falklanders, many of whom are still not recognised as British citizens, have cost the British taxpayer over £1 million per head. Think what that could do for the social services, from education to health, that are being cut back because Thatcher claims that the country can't afford the money. As the old die in the UK from cold they can't afford to keep out and others die through lack of treatment in our understaffed hospitals, Thatcher kills thousands and spends billions on a sea washed lump of rock on the other side of the world.

"This year, 1983, Thatcher has given the go-ahead for the installation of American cruise missiles on several sites in the UK. These weapons, designed to fly beneath 'enemy' radar to give 'maximum surprise attack potential', will greatly increase the risk of the nuclear nightmare becoming a reality. Further to this, it was recently disclosed that America intends to set up a 'War Centre' in the UK as a fallback should 'the enemy' necessitate a retreat from the present centre in West Germany. It would appear that the US Government regards Britain as a convenient military building site and that Thatcher, in her adopted role as imperial warlord, is happy to welcome them on our behalf with open arms. The British people, however, have not been asked what they think about either the cruise missiles or the centre and in Thatcher's 'democracy' there's little chance they will be. A further even more frightening erosion of British 'democracy' is that Britain will have no say in the use of the missiles – in plainer language it means Britain has become nothing more than a convenient staging-post for the militaristic ideology of another nation. Given the volatile and pugnacious reputation as 'The Iron Lady', it is perhaps a good thing that Thatcher will not have her finger on the button, but the absorbing reality is that Reagan will. Do we really want to be the Fifty Third State with no rights of citizenship? Thatcher made a great issue of the 'right of the Falklanders to self-determination', rights that she increasingly denies the people of her own homeland.

"The Falklands debacle demonstrates how easy a slide into total war could be. If Thatcher had had her way and ordered the bombing of the Argentinian mainland, it is quite possible the ensuing escalation would have led to the holocaust. Britain and other countries in Europe are being set up by the American government as prime targets in a future war that could quite possibly have nothing to do with us. We have lost our international reputation through Thatcher's lunatic war and we are losing our national right to self-determination through her equally lunatic agreements with America. The contradictions are obvious and absurd. Are we prepared in these hideously dangerous times to sit by and let this happen?

"From its roots in the blues to Elvis' waggling hips, rock 'n' roll has sent a thousand cinema seats through the screen of middle-class complacency. It has been about rebellion, rejection and revolution, a big sod off to the grey people who make our world into a battlefield and who see us as toy soldiers with which to enact their terrifying war plans.

"*I have written this letter to ask you if you are doing enough, or indeed anything to oppose this slow, but inevitable, drift towards total war.*

"*Music is a powerful tool through which radical ideas have been expressed since time immemorial, yet at a time when the world is threatened almost daily with annihilation, rock 'n' roll appears to have increasingly concentrated on shallow fun and cretinous escapism.*

"*As rock 'n' rollers in our various roles of musicians, singers, song-writers, critics, wheelers and dealers, we work with and are supported by people who for one reason or another identify with our varied activities. It is our responsibility to warn of what is happening in this dangerous world rather than just covering up the agony with mindless entertainment.*

"*The blues weren't entertainment even if they are entertaining; they were a cry from the soul, 'stop the oppression now', the same cry that led Lennon to sing 'free the people now'. It is our responsibility as 'entertainers' to make similar demands for sanity in our songs, interviews, reviews, press releases etc... It isn't our future as successful bands and artists that matters, it is the future of the world.*

"*Please think about what this letter says and try to find it in yourself to act on behalf of the planet rather than your pocket.*

"*To quote Lennon again – 'All we are saying is give peace a chance.... What are YOU saying?*

"*Sincerely*

"*Penny Rimbaud. CRASS. Jan 12 1983.*

"*If I can't dance, it's not my revolution!*"
– Emma Goldman
"*Fuck art, Let's dance*"
T-shirt of the 80's

In 1980 agit-prop lefties Gang Of Four had called their first album *Entertainment*, with a suitable sense of irony and perhaps the merest hint of confusion about where they lay within that concept. Free festivals, especially Stonehenge, were growing at a rapid rate because as well as a sense of freedom, they offered a sense of fun. But the agit-prop bands of the time that chose the mainstream as their medium, having retreated from punk rock's innate sense of fun, were struggling with the conflict between wanting to change the world and not particularly enjoying the process. It wasn't a great advert for their projected future. In an interview with Radio Free France, members of Crass debated the concept amongst themselves, for want of anyone else to talk to:

Phil Free: "What is an entertainment band doing? A band like Abba or Bucks Fizz. They're operating in support of the status quo. Why are they pretending not to be a political band?"

Andy Palmer: "I think we are entertaining anyway ... at least I hope we are ... otherwise no-one would come to see us, would they? You've got entertainment bands who do nothing but entertain and you've got political bands who do nothing but bore the pants off most people. And you've got people in between – I think there'd be something wrong with what we put on if it wasn't entertaining."

Penny Rimbaud: "We're singing about a decent way of living and people like Abba and Mick Jagger are singing about an exclusive way of living."

Andy Palmer: "I think a lot of people don't use their imaginations to present what they have to say in a way which is effective and entertaining. To say something is entertaining isn't necessarily to say something is a piece of shit, or that it supports the status quo. You can present the most radical ideas in an entertaining and exciting way and therefore there's a chance of being effective. Like you said on the record, how many times do we need to hear rehashed versions of feeding of the five thousand? It seems to be what's happening."

Penny Rimbaud: "I'm sure to some extent we're talking about our own shortcomings and problems in pushing what we have largely been responsible for – the alternative punk movement. We have become entertainment over the last two years in the sense that all entertainment is entertainment in the sense that it was monopolised by people who identified with and vicariously lived off the energies of people like ourselves. Those who didn't were away somewhere else doing it themselves. It was increasingly becoming a gathering of people who wanted to state an identity, and very little else. It seems to me that the bands and the movement that we now criticise is just that which we want to leave behind. It doesn't mean it's not relevant, cos it is relevant, but all those bands can get on and do it."

Understandably, at the end of a gig fans wanted to talk to Crass about the politics they'd just been confronted with. The same people might equally have talked to Adam Ant about sex, Steve Strange about fashion or Sheena Easton about the weather. But Crass always provoked the same response.

Steve Ignorant: "I remember thinking that doing the gig is alright, but afterwards I want to have a bit of fun. I don't want it to be manifestos, this is the message, rehearsing answers in your mind. I remember thinking I'm getting a bit bored by this, and I don't really give a fuck and I'm not gonna lose sleep trying to work out what this guy's going on about the unions – what the fuck do I know about unions? So I didn't give a shit. Now I would – I think I'd approach it differently. I don't think I'd be that ignorant. I think it's alright to be naïve but not ignorant."

Phil Free: "Every time we did an interview it was a pretty po-faced affair."

Mick Duffield: "To be involved was good fun, enjoyable – it was a laugh, on many occasions. But that didn't mean it was casual, the aesthetic of the stage presentation was given a lot of thought. We were angry with what we were supposed to be buying in to, the blatant hypocrisies, lies and evasions."

Isn't it the politics of depression?

Mick Duffield: "No, it's not being passive and saying, 'It's all overwhelming and nothing can be done about it' but standing up and shouting 'I'm really pissed off about this it's got nothing to offer me.'"

At this time, another strand of punk – part anarcho, part reaction to the grey Crass ethic – was beginning to look very appealing. The likes of Southern Death Cult, Blood And Roses, Look Mummy Clowns, Brigandage, Hagar The Womb, Rubella Ballet, Flowers In The Dustbin and The Mob were playing punk tinged with the experience and sus of the anarcho era but with added colour, joy and pride. Though they may not have cared (and indeed may well not have even known), Crass was beginning to look very drab in comparison to a large section of their audience. Elements of this new movement would be christened positive punk (with the obvious inference that punk had got too negative) and would soon show it hadn't really learned much from the mistakes of either original or anarcho punk, but nevertheless the energy had subtly shifted away from black and white protest towards technicolour dreaming. You just knew they weren't listening to The Cramps out there in Epping.

What they *were* doing, however, was engaging in heated debate about the pros and cons of violence: from violence at their concerts to the heady thoughts of armed insurrection.

"Violence only makes disagreements worse, it works on the principle of winners and losers and both pacifists and anarchists believe that no one should have to suffer the inhuman condition of being a loser and no one should have to benefit from the inhuman condition of being a winner. We're not born that way, so why should we, or anyone else, live that way? All other forms of political thought rely on there being losers, who are exploited as slaves by the winners, who enjoy the privileges created by them. Both right and left wing states employ force to maintain power; people are reduced to simple tools servicing the machinery of the state and as such, are expected to live and, if need be, die for that state."
Penny Rimbaud – *Last Of The Hippies*

Steve Ignorant: "I remember that as being particularly dark ugly times and I don't like to dwell on them. I didn't quite understand what to do about it. In one way, we were pacifists and had that way of dealing with it, but on the other hand I always thought Conflict were right – that if they started trouble, you just trounce the fuck out of them. I would have found it easier to deal with if there'd been that definite way of dealing with things. Punks were a soft touch – the times we did gigs when you get five skinheads ruling 200 people. And what fun that must have felt like to those skinheads."

Joy De Vivre: "The band was a pacifist concept. Veering from nonviolence was maybe part of the dialogue, but it certainly wasn't part of what we were putting out. People were edgy and uncomfortable and wanted things to change."

Phil Free: "People were *desperate* for things to change. Once you realise how strong the steamroller was, it got very difficult to just sit there and say we'll chime some bells. Which is a fine Buddhist thing to do, but I was born in Essex! There'd be a lot of talk, but no-one really knew how to make a pipe bomb or whatever. No one was going to get involved in anything more radical... I think Pete let off a smoke bomb at the Henley Regatta, it came out of a life raft – floating down the river and giving off smoke. Pete was much more into *interfering* with things, to try and stop things working. There was more flamboyant talk about 'arming up'..."

Joy De Vivre: "... but it wasn't ever really more than discussion. Ideas being batted about."

Mick Duffield: "I was always comfortable with the content of the records until a very very late stage, when it seemed to be heading towards advocating armed ... using arms, questioning whether pacifism was a good idea. Then I started to feel uncomfortable."

The wider anarcho punk movement, rather than joining in this debate was busy finding its own feet. In *The Curse Of Zounds* by Zounds and *Let The Tribe Increase* by the Mob, it had two great debut albums that were truly of themselves and not simply Crass derivatives. Though both bands had released singles on the Crass label, both had been active before Crass and it showed in the maturity of their sounds and words.

Glastonbury CND Festival (as it was then known) was also growing substantially, introducing a wider range of people to the peace movement as well as the festival scene. That year, the hippy stalwarts were joined by acts as diverse as Curtis Mayfield, UB40, The Chieftains, James Brown and Dr John. Just down the road, Stonehenge Festival had changed enough to welcome a plethora of punk bands: The Mob, Poison Girls, Action Pact and Omega Tribe all played without incident.

On May 7, 1983, 40,000 people, mainly young, descended on Brockwell Park in South London for a YCND rally and/or to watch The Damned, Hazel O'Connor, Madness and The Style Council. All the usual revolutionary left groups were there, more interested in recruiting than in peace (or anything else), as ever. Records on the Crass and Corpus Christi labels from Omega Tribe, Anthrax, The Alternative, Conflict and Sleeping Dogs still regularly peppered the alternative charts. On the June 19, Gee Vaucher illustrated a review of the book *Who Killed Karen Silkwood?* by Howard Kohn, a conspiracy theory implicating US Government involvement in the death of the American anti-nuclear campaigner.

Conspiracy theories. New clear campaigns. Ch-ch-ch-ch-changes? Not likely.

After they'd recorded 'Sheep Farming', with Eve's sparkling imper-sonation of Thatcher, an idea took seed. "She sounded so much like Thatcher," remarks Penny Rimbaud, "without even trying that hard. So the initial idea was that we should get an actor who sounds like Reagan." Crass knew an American actor, John Sharian – perhaps best know for his role as the replacement robot in Red Dwarf – and per-suaded him to record a 'dialogue' with Eve as Thatcher.

Pete suggested he tried to do it as an edit. In those pre-digital days, this was a mammoth task of physically cutting and re-assembling tapes of speeches, word by word. "It was the most extraordinary piece of editing I've ever seen," remarks Rimbaud, "but obviously the sort of stuff the KGB were up to all the time, because that's what the Pentagon thought it was.

"The tape was done in absolute secrecy at Southern. We worked with one engineer – the tapes were taken to his house every night and stuck away. No-one knew about them ... it was quite a dodgy thing to be doing really."

When it was completed, Pete went off to Europe to distribute the tape in the most anonymous way possible and nothing more was heard. Then, after about six months, Dave King, designer of the Crass logo and by now resident in San Francisco, sent the band a copy of an article from the *San Francisco Chronicle*:

"Washington.

"A fake tape of a purported conversation between President Reagan and British Prime Minister Margaret Thatcher was circulated in Europe this spring, possibly by the KGB, the State Department said yesterday.

"This type of activity fits the pattern of fabrications circulated by the Soviet KGB, although usually they involve fake documents rather than tapes," the department said, in a written response to reporter's questions.

"The department said that although the recording is of 'poor quality', a technical analysis revealed that the voices were those of Reagan and Thatcher.

But the department indicated the voices were spliced together and said they were not part of an actual conversation.

"'We checked with the White House, which advised that no such conversation took place,'" the department said.

"'The President's part in the recording apparently was lifted from his November 22, 1982 speech on nuclear disarmament,'" it said. "'We are not sure where Mrs. Thatcher's remarks came from.'

"The department said a copy of the tape was received by the US embassy in the Netherlands a week before the British elections.

"'The tape dealt with the Falklands crisis and US missiles in Britain,' the department said.

"It said, 'From the drift of the tape, the evident purpose was to cause problems for Mrs. Thatcher by blaming her for the sinking of the British destroyer Sheffield and also for us by stirring trouble on the INF (Intermediate Range Nuclear Forces) issue.'

"The Sheffield was sunk by Argentine forces last year during the war with Britain over the Falkland Islands.

"Britain and the United States took part in a NATO decision to install intermediate-range nuclear missiles in Europe late this year as a counter to similar Soviet forces if an agreement on restriction such weapons is not reached.

"The State Department said the tape-recording was sent with a covering letter from an anonymous person to Dutch journalists.

"It is said an analysis by the language experts 'suggests that the author was not a native speaker.'

"The Reagan administration has contended for some time that the KGB has a forgery factory producing false documents to mislead target audiences."

One look at the transcript would seem to suggest that the speech was disjointed enough to be fairly quickly labelled a hoax:

THATCHER: . . . own business!
REAGAN: I urge restraint.
THATCHER: It's absolutely essential or the area 'be 'through the roof".
THATCHER: Look, our objectives are fundamentally different
THATCHER: Al Haig. . .

REAGAN: . . . Secretary Haig. . .

THATCHER: . . . doesn't seem to be able to find a solution.

REAGAN: Why eliminate Belgrano? You directed this. The Argentinians were then going. . . Secretary Haig reached an agreement.

THATCHER: Argentina was the invader! Force has been used. It's been used now, punishing them as quickly as possible.

REAGAN: Oh, God, it's not right! You caused the Sheffield to have been hit.

Those missiles we followed on screens. You must have too, and not let them know. What do you hope to gain?

THATCHER: What I said before – "Andrew". . . . As "cruise" go in, I want incentives at all levels. . . .

REAGAN: There's a deal . . . a third more submarine ballistic missiles, and you will see that the United States forces remain deployed. The intermediate range missiles are US defence. You proposed building them in Europe. Build up the economy. They don't work, they're social pro-grammes. . . The United Kingdom is a . . . er . . . little nation. . .

THATCHER: You still need those nations, and you're given long term international markets.

REAGAN: We are supported by our allies, whether they want, or not.

THATCHER: I, I don't understand you. . . .

REAGAN: In conflict, we will launch missiles on allies for effective limitation of the Soviet Union.

THATCHER: You mean over Germany?

REAGAN: Mrs Thatcher, if any country of ours endangered the posi-tion, we might bomb the "problem area", and correct the imbalance.

THATCHER: See, my. . . .

REAGAN: It will convince the Soviets to listen. We demonstate our strength. . . The Soviets have little incentive to launch an attack.

THATCHER: Our British people. . .

REAGAN: London! . . .

THATCHER: I think. . .

REAGAN: Let that be understood.

Penny Rimbaud: "The point was that within the tapes was a whole load of classified information that we'd got from the Falklands and didn't know how else to put out, which would have been very damaging indeed for Thatcher. The stuff about the Belgrano, but more notably stuff about the Sheffield and the Ark Royal – Prince Andrew being on the Ark Royal which is why the Sheffield had to go down. It turned nasty when *The Observer* rang us up." Crass thought they had covered their tracks completely and were shocked to be fingered.

It was arranged for a journalist from *The Observer* to come to Dial House, were Crass was "very very wary, obviously". After initial denials, a deal was struck whereby if *The Observer* was prepared to print the alleged information contained on the tape, then "maybe we could admit to having produced the tape".

Rimbaud expands: "The Sheffield stuff still hasn't been dealt with properly in the press, ever, because it was too much of a story. There was almost mutiny, which is why all of those ships were so slow coming back – because they had to quell the mutiny and de-programme everyone before they brought them back."

Sounds ran the story the next week: "They (Crass) justified their actions by saying: 'We wanted to precipitate a debate on the Falklands and nuclear weapons to damage Thatcher's position in the election. We also did it because of the appalling way Tom Dalyell (almost the only MP to raise any awkward questions over the Falklands affair) was treated over the Belgrano debate in the House of Commons.

"'We believe that although the tape is a hoax what is said in it is in effect true. We were amused and amazed that the tape had been attributed to the KGB.'"

As the band's activities – far more than their records – gained them so much attention, so the signs of a deep exhaustion were setting in. It didn't help that the bad guys were still winning the war.

Penny Rimbaud: "It was so shattering, the Falklands, and the power that Thatcher was then wielding, and what was happening with the miners. We couldn't have gone on, pretending that the possibilities that we felt were genuine ... there was a huge movement building up – the peace movement, the punk movement. It was massive, and it appeared to be having a really big social effect. And the more information we could throw into that, the better. And the information was getting gobbled up.

"But within weeks of the Falklands, people were hiding – I don't remember anyone saying anything about the Falklands – where did all the bands disappear to? They'd been shouting 'no more war' but no-one did anything. I remember feeling incredibly alone during that period. People were afraid. It was a very nasty time. It would have been very very dishonest to come out of that thinking we were still a part of what had gone before it."

Meanwhile, a general election was looming, with Margaret Thatcher poised to win. Although she had been deeply unpopular and pretty much unre-electable throughout her first years in power, the Falklands War and the jingoism that surrounded it had seen her leap up the opinion polls.

Led by Michael Foot, Labour had produced its most left wing manifesto in memory, advocating multilateral disarmament and devolution for Scotland and Wales. Despite many of the issues therein being taken up since, at the time it came to be known as 'the longest suicide note in history'. Whatever the rights and wrongs of the issues, this was a tactical disaster in a country still foaming at the mouth with post-war testosterone. Thatcher's Tories won the election by a landslide, with Labour turning in its worst performance since 1918. More than the war itself, the election result was an enormous blow to those in the 'movement' who imagined they were taking the general public with them.

Around this time, Crass was presented with a possible opportunity to bring Thatcher down, as a prostitute approached Crass to ask if they were interested in compromising pictures of Dennis Thatcher.

Penny Rimbaud: "A friend of a friend who was an upper-class retrobate knew the call girl. She told him about the pictures . . . we went into quite a serious debate: I certainly felt that what people do with their sexual lives is their business. But in this particular instance, it did give the possibility of creating a flaw in the Thatcher empire. So we looked at it as a serious option. As it turned out, the debate went on too long. By then, she'd decided to withdraw the offer, very sensibly on her behalf. Because I don't know what we could have done with it."

Eve Libertine: "I never really liked that sort of thing – whoever it is, I don't like it, and may well have said so. I find all that stuff mucky and smutty and I don't really like it, even if it's Dennis Thatcher. I'd rather not involve myself in all that, and I'd rather we as a band didn't."

Crass' woes deepened with the release of their next album, *Yes Sir I Will*, which was dreadful.

The sleeve was a visibly rushed job: an old article dug up from an old *International Anthem* sat next to hastily typed lyrics. The sleeve folded out to a blow up picture from *The Sun* of Prince Charles meeting horrifically burned soldier Simon Weston. The caption below reveals the source of the album title: "Get well soon," said the prince. And the heroic soldier replied, "Yes sir, I will."

The music was something else again. The concept of a collection of songs had been abandoned in favour of one lengthy monologue over a background that could be best described as a racket, improvised noise that slams the door shut on any attempt at communication. The lyrics were pure desperation about everything and anything. As a paradox to all this, the noise and interference is all nudged to one side for a beautiful gentle piano and vocal track with Penny Rimbaud on vocals – 'What Did You Know, What Did You Care'. In amongst the chaos also lurked a Steve Ignorant song, 'And What If I Told You To Fuck Off', a rant against all those who constantly asked questions about the viability of an anarchist state. It wasn't one of his better moments.

Overall, Crass appeared to have completely lost the plot. The album was a huge letdown, an expression of powerlessness in direct contrast to the hope that shone from their previous releases. Tellingly, although Crass sympathisers Graham Lock and Paul Du Noyer were both still writing for *NME*, neither reviewed it, and nor did anyone else at the paper.

Penny Rimbaud: "It gets very tiring the phone being tapped all the time, letters being opened before you've read them, being suspicious of people – realising that it's not just you you're talking to, it's hundreds and thousands of young kids hanging on everything you're bloody saying. That's a responsibility we took seriously. We didn't take *ourselves* seriously, but we took being Crass as a very serious responsibility. You have to look deeper into the honesty of the statements you're making. There was a lot of self-doubt in *Yes Sir I Will*. That was to say to people that they

might think we know what we're doing, but we fucking don't. We've
been caught with our trousers down here and this is what I feel about it.
There's quite a bit of self-criticism in there. At the same time, there's
quite a bit of seemingly violent polemic. But that — coupled with the
self-doubt — was the respect towards your fifteen-year-old following:
'We don't actually know — this is my bash at it'. That's how I like to think
Yes Sir comes over."

Pete Wright: "I know that, when we'd worked on Christ The Album
for months, and suddenly there was a war that needed responding to, the
Yes, Sir improvised approach grated a bit, especially when we went to
Iceland with it. Penny and I were in a privileged position in that we
come up with the core of the music — I don't think I have ever played
better (and, luckily, had just found the bass sound I had been searching
for for six months) — but poor old Phil and Andy were faced with an
impossible task to fit in with that lot."

Yes Sir . . . itself was adapted from a long and personal piece of prose
Penny had written down. As with all Crass stuff, the personal was lost
and a lot of the power of the words with it: "Everything was 'we', you
couldn't say 'I'" he says. "At the time I was very happy to do that. That
was part of the agreement. But, yes, I think it would have been considerably more powerful if it had said 'I'. Because it was very much *my*
response to what was going on, in a much more uncompromising way
than 'Banned From The Roxy' or the little songs I wrote."

Steve Ignorant: "I hate that fucking record — that and *Ten Notes On A
Summer's Day* are just two piles of garbage. The fun had gone, but I didn't
know how to say it. Because we were Crass, and because Crass lived
together, it didn't ever stop. So your personal life was part of Crass, and
Crass was part of your personal life — it's all intertwined. So the way that
you were was Crass and the way that you lived was. . ., you could never
switch off. Even if I went to the pub or to a gig, I was always careful not
to get drunk in front of people cos it might backfire, I might get seen.
So, yeah, it was quite a restriction and it stopped being fun."

The accompanying gigs weren't much fun either. Crass abandoned all
of their other songs and simply delivered *Yes Sir* in its horrible drawn out
entirety. Vocalists Steve and Eve just stood there reading the lyrics from
sheets of paper — the piece was so long that the vocalists had to read from

crib sheets – and a bad time was had by all, as Steve remembers: "We did *Yes Sir* as a complete set one day and I hated it! I looked like a lemon with that fucking bit of paper! I didn't know how to move, I didn't know where to stand. People said, 'Oh but the lyrics are great' – well, they are, but. . . I just really don't like it"

Andy Palmer, talking to Radio Free France in the eighties, was more optimistic: "I don't know of anyone who has listened to *Yes Sir I Will* and said they actually enjoyed it. Whereas I think most people now enjoy *Feeding Of The Five Thousand*, but when we put it out to begin with, nobody enjoyed that either. You can latch onto a way of doing something which is initially effective and flog it to death – which is what punk has become. Punk has become a standard – it was initially a rejection of standards – to which bands conform in the way they present themselves, the way they present their music, in the way they write their lyrics."

Penny Rimbaud, in 1984, ruminated to Radio Free France: "The boundaries increasingly ceased to have any relevance – prior to the Falklands War, one naively believed that there were separations between 'this' and 'that' and that if you dealt with 'this' then you could do 'that' . . . like songs – each song had its little separate thing to deal with and *Yes Sir I Will* is a statement about the fact that there isn't any separation – that its all one and the same thing, that there is no single cause or single idea – there's no-one else to blame but yourself. That you can't say, 'Well let's now concentrate on the Northern Ireland problem, let's now concentrate on the problem of sexual relationships . . . you can't do that – everything is now one major problem and that major problem stems from yourself."

When asked about the apparent disparity between the aggression of their music and the peacefulness of their message, Crass always responded that the anger was derived from passion rather than aggression. *Yes Sir I Will* often seemed to cross that line.

Gee told Radio Free France: "If you're going to rant and rave or be angry about anything, one does it because you have a vision of the opposite. We've worked the way we have done for the last seven years because it seemed that people weren't informed about what was happening in the world on a simple basis, especially a lot of young people.

The feeling I got off a lot of young people was that they thought there was something drastically wrong with the world – *technically* they didn't know how that was operating and obviously we've offered them information which hopefully gave them the possibility of deciding for themselves, and a broader outlook on their own lives."

In an attempt to lighten the mood and prove (to themselves?) they did still laugh occasionally, Crass put out 'Whodunnit?' a comedy single, to coincide with the General Election. The sleeve featured a soiled piece of toilet paper, while the song featured music hall piano, some very odd jokes told in the style of music hall comedians and a chorus: "Birds put the turd in custard, but who put the shit in number 10?" It came in brown vinyl.

Penny Rimbaud: "Increasingly as we became cornered in a political outlook, because we appeared to be an alternative authority, we were in the 'right' political position. And because of that we got polarised in that political position. And inevitably that position became a reformist one because we couldn't move out, because we're not revolutionaries. We knew a few days before the election that there was absolutely no chance at all of there being anything other than a Thatcher victory, so we produced 'Whodunnit' as a statement of our despair, disgust, disappointment and disinterest. And just as a sign of disrespect really. We were reduced to being naughty boys and girls in the schoolroom."

A more coherent reaction to the injustices of the time came with the first Stop The City protests in London. Organised by London Greenpeace (not Crass, as is sometimes inferred), the first demonstration took place on September 29, 1983.

"We were a growing active group involved in a wide range of radical campaigns," says Dave Morris of London Greenpeace. "We went to anti-militarist blockades of military bases some of them involving tens of thousands of people. We were inspired but frustrated and wanted to do more. We thought there must be something we can do in London. What's the point of thousands of Londoners organising coaches to the countryside when it would be easier to just hop on a bus or tube and blockade Central London – that would really ratchet up the protests!"

"At Stop The City, I collected 33 different leaflets that had been handed out in what must have been tens of thousands."

The leaflets that circulated explained the presence of hordes of anarcho-punks in the Square Mile: "The 'City' is a place where the real decisions that affect our lives (and those of people like us all over the world) are made. People once lived in the area, but now it's just packed with the headquarters of banks, companies, multinationals and places like the Stock Exchange. Billions of pounds change hands every day making profit for a few whilst millions of people all over the world are starving. Money is made from weapons dealing, destroying nature, and generally by exploiting and controlling us all."

Just in time for the first demo, an empty office block was squatted for a new Anarchy Centre (known as the Peace Centre this time round) at 99-119 Roseberry Avenue in North London.[1] It was duly raided by heavy-handed riot police the night before Stop The City. Not a good omen, but the event itself was to be a startling success in many ways.

All day the police struggled to control a new concept that had taken them by surprise. Normal demonstrations had leaders, stewards, organisation and an overload of Socialist Workers Party placards. Stop The City had kids in colourful rags forever breaking off from the main group on their own initiative to effect their own actions: graffiti, street theatre, noise free food, bank locks glued, patriot flags burned, leafleting, anti-apartheid actions against Barclays Bank, many arrests. And ultimately success, if only partial, as concluded by *The Times*: "The banking community struggled to keep money flows moving despite the unrest. They succeeded, but only just! Bank balances were £11 million below target tonight."

By virtue of about 1,500 leaderless young punks, and few older ones, the anarcho punk movement had arrived. It was no longer simply a bunch of kids who bought the same records, it was – and is – a peoples' culture.

Several more Stop The City events took place after that in London, generally with more people but less success than the first one as the

---

[1] The venue would later go on to become the British Headquarters of Amnesty International, giving this author the unusual opportunity to work in a building in which he'd previously both slept and played a concert.

police became wise to the tactics. Penny Rimbaud wrote a superb piece about it for *Punk Lives* and many people made the connections in their lives between exploitation and their own personal behaviour. Equally, a tradition had been born – a tradition that is with us today all over the world, in the anti-globalisation movement, in the animal rights movement, in the various anti-war movements and underneath the red and black flags you'll see at demonstrations from Sydney to Lodz.

1984

So it was finally upon us – the mythical 1984 – the year of the Orwell book and the year that Crass had been counting down to almost from their inception. Come midnight New Years Eve we put on 'The End' by the Doors, which feels terribly fitting. Then follow it with 'Anarchy' by the Pistols to show we hope it's not really.

After a gap of almost five years, Crass played their first gig abroad for years, in Iceland, somewhat unusually. For the second time in their career, they would use a replacement drummer as to all the time he'd spent in the studio producing other acts, Penny Rimbaud had burst an eardrum and was therefore unable to play. He was replaced by Martin, the drummer from Flux Of Pink Indians.

The occasion that tempted them out of their self-imposed embargo was news that the Americans wanted to build more bases on the north of the island. Big anti-American demonstrations ensued and Crass was invited over to play in support.

It was the first time they unveiled their new live set, which broke new ground in extremity even for them. It consisted solely of *Yes Sir I Will* with nothing else to sweeten the pill. As a noble ideal it was perhaps admirable, but as a tactic on an aesthetic level it was a disaster, seemingly designed to repel the converted rather than preach to them. Imagine being a Crass fan and waiting all your life for them to come and play in Iceland, and when they do this happens. Politically or tactically 'correct' or not, it must have been heartbreaking.

The next single indicated an even greater sense of anger at the perceived impotence of the anarcho movement. 'You're Already Dead' featured on the sleeve a picture of Margaret Thatcher with her eyes gauged out. The flip side showed Michael Heseltine with his mouth scratched away. The fold out was the usual mass of information about the peace and war movements.

The words suggested writer Penny Rimbaud was somewhere beyond despair: "If you're the passive observer, here's a message to you / You're already dead / Afraid to do what you know you should do / You're Already Dead ... 400,000 people marched for CND / They're already dead unless they're willing to act on what they see." Underneath all the shouting, the music was experimental.

Elsewhere 'Nagasaki Is Yesterday's Dog End' was an uninspired racket that like 'Yes Sir I Will' didn't even try to be anything else. 'Don't Get Caught' gave moments of light relief with Crass rocking out at the end with a guitar solo. The words were cautionary: "If you leave the path that you've been taught / Don't expect help so don't get caught." The song also captured the frustration that was threatening to boil over into political violence: "If we can't go past them, we'll have to go through" had serious undertones.

"There's a desperation there," notes Eve. "I think it's just as well it stopped! Because I'm not sure where it would have gone – it must have exploded!"

Joy De Vivre: "It was because of what was happening around us, and so we got heavier and heavier because the situation was getting nastier and nastier, and so our stuff got more and more dour. But in general, the sense of where we were going was pretty bloody heavy. We had our own kind of fun in our lives, but what we put out was more and more desperate and more and more angry. I suppose what we put out was desperately serious and earnest, and a bit funless."

Phil Free: "We were laughing around the table, laughing when we were rehearsing, even pissing ourselves when we were recording. But it just dried itself out by the time it was edited."

Joy De Vivre: "All that laughter and hysterics was our way of coping with all the shit. What we were actually saying was very dark and depressing. What we knew was frightening and depressing. So we had our laughter between ourselves. What we wanted to actually transmit was that things were serious."

Phil Free: "We started off with a Labour government, which was the sunny side of the hill, a socialist government. After our first album was out, Thatcher came in. We played a gig in Stoke and two policemen came in to make sure the kids were alright. There was a kitchen we were using and we made them tea and started chatting with them. One of them said, 'If Thatcher gets in, I'm leaving because there'll be a police state in a few years'. It was extraordinary. Then two years later, we were actually at war, and nuclear missiles were being sited in England."

Joy De Vivre: "Any sense of fun we had was for our own survival and not our output."

Far from being the advanced guard of yore, Crass had now found themselves in a situation where each artistic statement was a response to outside events.

Joy De Vivre: "I think there was a bit of the re-active all along. I just think it got stronger and stronger. We always been a reaction: to complacency, to crap music and crap culture."

In their public output, Crass had simply ceased to be fun, and in doing so were beginning to jealously guard their failure to communicate, just as Exit had done. In increasing their own awareness and that of others, they'd opened up a pandora's box of monsters that were now gnawing away at their sensitivities.

Eve Libertine: "You follow a bus and there's a huge advert with a naked woman on it. You're bombarded when you go out with all this stuff, which you (can) get used to. You've have to be really aware all the time, really telling yourself: watch that, watch that, watch that ... of course it's depressing − we weren't there to do pretty tunes, we were there to point stuff out. What was going on, what *is* going on."

Phil Free: "Certainly it seemed to become darker as the years rolled by, to the extent that you'd be going into town on the train; you'd look up and think these people don't know about the nuclear wotsit that's occurring in XYZ or the number of missiles they're building..."

Eve: 'It's very easy to say that [it's depressing] sitting at a kitchen table. If we had some of the death and destruction here on the floor on front of us, you'd probably feel very differently about the depressing nature of it. For example, *Yes Sir I Will* – it's all over there, but it's happening at this moment in Iraq, with people blown apart, families destroyed . . . *of course* it's depressing.'

"We are women, we are strong, we are fighting for our lives / Side by side with our men, who work the nations mines / United by the struggle, united by the past / And it's here we go, here we go, for the women of the working class"
North Staffs miners wives

If things were dark at Dial House, they were about to get a whole lot darker.

The miner's strike started on March 12, 1984. The trouble began after an announcement by Chairman of the Coal Board Ian MacGregor six days previously that 20 uneconomic pits would have to close, putting 20,000 miners out of work. Arthur Scargill, the National Union of Miners leader, called for flying pickets to drum up support, and one of the most violent strikes in UK history began.

Nobody on either side was under any illusions – this strike wasn't just about the miners, it was a fight for the very soul of Britain. Margaret Thatcher wanted to crush the working class ethic and was prepared to use any instrument of the state, allegedly including the army dressed as police, to do so. Arthur Scargill, the N.U.M. and all those who supported the miners wanted to bring down Thatcher before she could do any more damage. It was the nearest thing to civil war that century – and the most important.

Penny Rimbaud: "Thatcher was massively empowered by the Falklands War and then she turned in on her own. It wasn't just the miners, it was the whole alternative lifestyle. Smash the unions, smash the old British Socialist working-class ideology, smash the ideology of the alternative world. Then maybe you get the bland, fucked-up community we're now having to put up with."

Much like the early days of the Spanish Civil war, all bets were off and all differences put aside as everybody of the broad left united against the Thatcher regime. Punk bands everywhere, in fact *all* kinds of bands everywhere, played benefit gigs for the striking miners. As the anarcho punk movement got more directly involved with the miners – on the picket lines and in the kitchens – two cultures met for the first time. Despite having a solidly left-wing history, the miners – like many Labour voters – were culturally straight. Many still thought a women's place was at the sink rather than in the movement. Previously contact with punks was probably restricted to catcalls ridiculing the 'weirdo' across the street.

For the upper middle-class elements of the anarcho punk movement – and there were many, particularly in the south – this was their first real contact with working class culture. The Apostles and Living Legends aside, it seemed like the anarcho movement had studiously ignored the class war going on around them, often not even realising, in their stoned soul picnic, it was being waged.

There was precious little room left to doubt it on May 29 when police, including many on horseback, and miners fought pitched battles at Orgreave. A famous photo of the time shows a mounted policeman charging on his horse and reaching over to club a miners head. This was not serving the public, this was political. 1984 was living up to its promise.

Steve Ignorant cites the Battle Of Orgreave as a pivotal moment in peoples' minds during the miners strike. "Especially when the guy got battered and given brain damage by the police. There were people who we knew who ran a squat in Vauxhall and they had a derelict house which they turned into a bar. They'd put on benefits and have striking miners and pickets come down and stay with them. So there was all that kind of involvement...

"It was just part of what we were doing. It was like, 'Here's the next thing we have to do, to talk about'. Before that, it had been Greenham Common, then the Falklands."

Steve believes a change had taken place in Crass anyway. "By that time we were an anarchist, political-based band. It wasn't so much about being yobboes. So I don't think class even came into it. We just did it because we were Crass and that's what Crass did basically. I can't philosophise about it, I just supported the bloody miners – and their families – and now look what's happened to those towns and cities. The drug rate has gone through the roof, as everybody said it would.

"At that time it really was political because people were getting involved in politics beyond Crass – doing benefits for the miners' wives. And all of a sudden, nothing was fun anymore – it was *all* dark and depressing. How can you write a love song when there's whole communities dying?"

Phil Free: "We were driving round in a blue Sherpa, which is what the police used, and we were dressed in black. So we sort of looked like police and the police would wave us through. You'd be driving along in a convoy of thirty or forty police vans – it was quite terrifying. It was a civil war of its kind. We'd be on tour driving up the motorway and there'd be a policeman on every bridge – *every* bridge."

A final act of defiance came in the form of a banner Crass decided to hang just over the river from the houses of parliament. Andy Palmer & Pete Wright took it into the Royal Festival Hall, on the south bank of the Thames. Creeping out to the balcony, they hung it over the edge: "You picked the scabs, now the wounds will fester". A cute situationist response to a less than cute class war. Next to the phrase was a Crass symbol and the phrase "working for you", the catchphrase of the Greater London Council at the time.

The band played their final gig in July 1984 – a benefit for striking miners in Aberdare, Wales. Aberdare is in the Rhonnda Valley, a mere lump of coal's throw from Aberfan where Gee Vaucher's political awakening had been prodded into action by the disaster twenty years previously.

It was clearly all over for Penny Rimbaud: "I remember that miners' gig. My general impression of it was, 'This is a fucking pantomime'. There's all these people leaping up and down; meanwhile there's all these people having their entire lives stripped from them. Thatcher's army destroying a complete lifestyle."

After the gig, Andy Palmer announced that he wanted to leave the band. As well as the obvious sadness, there was much inner relief that the job was over.

Steve Ignorant: "I remember when Andy said he wanted to leave the band, I was thinking 'Thank fuck for that', cos I'd been dying to say that for ages, but I didn't know how to – I was too scared."

Pete Wright: "When we found ourselves in 'explaining mode' and one of us tired, another would pick up the duty seamlessly. We got very tired.

No so much 'tired of' (continuously explaining things after gigs), but 'tired'. We spent a lot of time trying to create a body of like-minded activists, and we were pulling in influences all the time. You probably know yourself, that if you are privy to specialist information, it becomes increasingly difficult to talk with people who aren't, and can become a bit manipulative."

Penny Rimbaud: "There wasn't anything else to do. Also, we were getting frankly bored with each other. The differences were manifesting. The difference in what activism means, in what commercialism means. . ."

Andy's split with the band was complete. He negotiated a payoff with the band through John Loder and effectively bought himself out. He's the only member of the band who doesn't receive ongoing royalties and the only member of the band who refused to co-operate with this book.

Penny Rimbaud: "When I see him (Andy Palmer), he's very positive about that period. He regards it as something that was of value, but he hasn't got any more to add to it. I think in a way that's more honest. . ."

No longer operating under the comfort of a collective identity, the individuals that had for seven years hidden (even from each other) behind the banner of Crass, suddenly found themselves staring in the mirror at themselves again. Alone and with a newly singular responsibility and face.

Eve Libertine: "I did feel towards the end that we'd lost that feeling. I didn't like a lot of the songs we were doing. I think it was losing that love and I think it was very sensible that we stopped when we did. It went overtly political – *Penis Envy* was political but it was about *personal* politics, because I actually believe that is the only way change can happen. I don't believe in (party) political change. You can't just tell everyone what to do – it has to come from each individual person seeing that possibility within themselves beyond their idea of who they are. With the miner's strike and the Falklands, it all seemed to be . . . 'anti-' again. I think it was good that we did the Falklands things because it was outrageous and nobody was really saying anything. But it did change – the message was kind of different – there was a rigidity to it."

Phil Free: "There comes a point where without the band, why are you together? There are a lot of different people who've maintained a situation above and beyond, in quite extreme situations. It had kept the group cohesive because there was a group necessity to go through them – having two thousand Italians walk through the door or going to grimy skinhead-filled places, which was not my media, or even just being onstage, which is not my media either."

Gee, talking to Richie Unterberger for the book *Unknown Legends of Rock'n'Roll*, posted at the Perfect Sound Forever website: "I think the most significant change you can hear, really, is the total desperation about the Tory government. I think you can really hear it in *Yes Sir I Will*, the black one. I mean, that's pretty heavy, that one. I think it's not disillusioned as such. But you can see what's really going on. I for one, when she [Thatcher] got in the third time, I thought that's it. I'm not prepared keep making videos, keep doing illustrations, that are really concerned with her shit. I just thought, enough, there's another life outside of this. You can only take so much. Unless you really live here and you've known the English sort of spirit and seen it really crushed through what happened with the miners, what happened with the newspapers here, what happened with the women at Greenham, it just took its toll on all of us. We just thought, well, we're not giving up. We're gonna have to change tactics. I suppose that's what's happened."

Penny Rimbaud: "Splitting wasn't a problem for me. I'd always been creative, I'd always been an artist, it didn't matter to me whether it was Exit or Crass. I knew I'd always be involved in something and I always have been. I can't not be. The more autonomous the individuals as creative artists were, the less it mattered to them that nothing was happening."

Andy Palmer moved out of Dial House and went to live in London in the Black Sheep Housing Co-Op set up by members of the Puppy Collective. The atmosphere at Dial House was changing once again.

Steve Ignorant: "Andy Palmer wasn't living at Crass mansions anymore – he was living with his partner. Then Penny's dad got ill. In fact, that's really weird – peoples' parents started dying, so that took up a lot of time."

256

Joy De Vivre: "I've always likened the band to one of those cubic puzzles – once you took one bit out, it didn't work anymore. Andy went and the brew of people stopped being that particular brew."

The brew of people had curdled and become individuals once more. Stripped of their anonymity, they were free to reflect on everything that had happened since Penny & Steve started playing together in 1977; free to find themselves again and see what they looked like.

The anonymity the band had chosen for themselves when everything started getting serious had been for specific reasons. "I suppose it boiled down to a lack of artistic confidence," says Penny. "Because we weren't individually able to take responsibility for any particular aspect of what we were doing, we were sometimes defending things that weren't actually anything to do with us. I might be defending a song that someone else had actually done – you're always on slightly dodgy ground there. The relationship between me and Steve was very very deep – it was an incredibly intimate and personal relationship. I came from an utterly different background to him, a totally different age group, but we were able to work together in a really fine way, a precious way.

"Had there been endless attacks, it would have probably been 'svengali exploiting poor working class boy' sort of thing. Like it or not, those things hit. If you are in public life you have to understand that that's what's going to happen. What we did with Crass was to produce as fierce a Berlin Wall against that sort of intrusion as we could. We were willing to talk about what we wanted to talk about, and we were willing to be very very open about 'Crass' – what we weren't willing to do was talk about our individual position within that. Because that wasn't relevant."

There was a deliberate policy to minimise the cult of personality. "When we performed we worked as a group," says Eve. "We decided that we'd put aside all personal differences, and it was a conscious decision that we'd go onstage and be one body. What we were saying was what was important, not our own personal feelings. It's very easy for audiences to pick up on (individuals) and they do it all the time – they pick people out of groups. In my mind, it was to stop that happening."

The band effectively finished in 1984, just as their records had suggested. It was a neat touch (if you ignore *Acts Of Love* in '85 of course), but opinions are split regarding whether this was always the plan:

Joy De Vivre: "Yes, that was the idea."

Steve Ignorant: "It's crap. I thought it would go on forever. I thought we'd end up supporting, in my wildest dreams, Frank Sinatra or the Dead Kennedys. I thought we'd go on and on."

Phil Free: "No, I don't think we were always going to stop. The countdown was just a literary reference, to the extent that I didn't understand what it was for the first couple of months. So, no it wasn't. But you've been to war, you've planted nuclear devices all over England, we were now taking out the miners, decimating the mining communities. The Government was hell-bent on destroying another aspect of English society as we knew it. I think by that time we just ran out of steam."

If all that wasn't tiring enough, Crass was finally taken to court. The police had raided a record shop near Manchester, confiscating an array of records under the Obscene Publications Act, including *Penis Envy*. Maybe the police were Orwell fans too.

Eve Libertine: "Someone in Chester complained about 'Bata Motel'. They played that in court and everyone was told they mustn't laugh. They said it was sado-masochistic – they took it completely the wrong way. It was about high heels, and the fact you can't run because you're strapped into these things. And they didn't get the point, so they banned it. So it was banned in Chester – maybe it still is!"

Penny Rimbaud takes up the story: "We could have had it heard in the High Court, but if we had have done, it would have set precedent. If we had lost it, that would have meant there would have been a ban across Britain. Whereas if we had it heard in Chester, it would only be that specific area where our records would be banned.

"Our defence was that there was far more blasphemous and obscene material commonly available for sale. The two things we played were Derek & Clive – the one about Christ wanking – and Alexie Sayle's 'Hello John Got A New Motor', the B-side that goes 'you cunt, you cunt, you fucking fucking cunt' etc. In truth, one of them was using obscene language and the other one was being much more blasphemous than we'd ever been.

"They hadn't got a record player in the court room, so the first hour was spent with various members of the constabulary driving home to bring back their stereo. In the end, we were listening to stereo records on one speaker, so we were losing half of everything we were listening to – it was so bodged up.

"There were these three very serious looking magistrates sitting on the bench, all with their pens ready. Whenever there was a 'fuck' or 'shit' or any swear words, they'd all look at each other to confirm they'd heard what they thought they heard and then tick it off. But not once was there any question of the subject matter because they couldn't understand it.

"We then played the other records as our defence and the whole court started cracking up. There were punks in the back who'd come along because they'd heard about the case. As we started Derek & Clive, there was uncontrollable laughter ... in that particular situation, it seemed so good. One of the magistrates said that people weren't taking the case seriously. Anyone laughing to this material will be spending the night in jail for contempt of court."

"Then the Alexei Sayle record was put on – I had my head down and my mouth was literally bleeding as I bit into it. I knew if my mouth opened I'd start giggling – it was even worse having been told we musn't laugh. Everyone in the court was the same – even the police, all trying not to laugh.

"Then I had to get in the dock. Because they couldn't hear the context of the records, because they couldn't hear the lyrics properly, they were just saying, 'Why are you so angry?' It just seemed so silly. I remember I was so bored with it. I sort of lost the plot – sort of went to sleep but I could still here my voice rambling on. I was thinking, 'What *is* going on here?' So had to sort of draw myself back from this dream I was in into the body that was talking about 'well this is passion, it's not anger, blah blah'. I came back round and there were these three sober sombre looking figures sitting on the bench, staring at me with porky eyes."

The case was adjourned while the magistrates considered the verdict and the Crass contingent felt sure of victory. But they lost. The record was banned, but the band weren't fined or otherwise punished. Nonetheless, they weren't happy. Penny chatted with their solicitor, who was also shocked at the verdict, and then joked that, "The bomb was going off in three minutes. And for a moment, he took it seriously. Which indicated to me how frightened people were of what we were doing."

An appeal was heard in Liverpool. Sensing the potential importance, and still expecting promised financial help from certain independent labels, Crass spent a fortune on a top barrister. "He was always employed to defend soft-porn people like *Playboy* and *Penthouse*," says Penny. "That cost us big money. And we thought we were still working in the remit of being helped out by all these other labels."

The appeal was lost and 'Bata Motel' was banned, the judge ruling that the song was sexually provocative and obscene. "Clearly he was looking thorough all the tracks," ruminates Penny Rimbaud, "looking for something that was obscene. They weren't obscene at all. They might use a bit of street language, but street language isn't obscene. So he had to find something he could pin it on. Maybe if he'd had a copy of *Asylum*, he could have pinned it on that.

"Eve was absolutely overjoyed when she heard the result – she was uncontrollably laughing, saying all these years I'd been desperately trying to get done for obscenity and it was *her* who'd done it. She was very very pleased with herself for that – she liked the irony. Whereas I'd always set out to be offensive to bourgeois taste, she was always much more considered in her lyrics. They weren't just polemic, they were normally quite well studied arguments.

"It as good as busted us. We'd spent an awful lot of money on various productions from Hit Parade, Kukl ... we'd been overspending... *I'd* been overspending trying to do splendid productions. So we weren't that well-off anyway. Andy had left and we'd given him a golden handshake."

The labels who had promised help never came through. "I don't think we got a penny," says Penny. "Had it gone another way, it would have affected all those labels. As it was, they pinned it onto us. Effectively we won the appeal, because it was just this one track.

Whereas if the magistrates ruling had been accepted, I think all of those records would have been banned. It would have also given the authorities carte-blanche to pick off areas one by one. In terms of the freedom to say what you want through vinyl, it was a very important case. And it cost us dearly."

It cost Crass dearly in the sense that it changed their financial outlook – no longer were they in the position to produce other acts in the way to which they had become accustomed.

TO INFINITY AND BEYOND

"Death in rebellion is the only proof / That I was alive in 1985"
1985 – The Apostles

The final album released under the moniker Crass was *Acts Of Love*, in 1985. Although attributed to Crass, it would be more accurate to see it as a Penny Rimbaud record with contributions from other Crass people. It consisted of fifty short poems set to quirky discordant music that owed more – much more – to free jazz than punk rock.

Penny Rimbaud: "I remember when we were recording *Acts Of Love* – Andy coming into the studio and saying he'd like to do something like that himself, meaning he understood that I was trying to make a personal expression within the framework of where we were. I think that was a seed for him. He was a painter before he got involved with the band, and I think that's how he saw he might be able to express himself, which is what he's done."

Eve told Radio Free France in 1984: "The stuff we've done before may not have seemed to be offering something of beauty, but we were shouting about what was preventing that beauty. The beauty was there as something intangible at the end of all the shouting. I think it possibly got a bit obliterated at times although I think people did seem to understand what we were getting at."

RFF: Is acts of love punk?

"If punk is about throwing something out from a different angle, about something new, then I think it still is in the spirit of so-called punk."

Gee Vaucher: "For me, *Acts Of Love* was the starting point anyway – the poems and the original illustrations were done a long time before Crass. They were part of the inspiration, part of the source of going on to say what we did. For me, it's a return to those roots – not going backwards, but the source of inspiration within oneself. It's a very natural extension of what we've done with Crass.

"It seemed to be going in the direction of causes. Young people would get caught up in causes and the whole barbaric nature of the cause that they were trying to confront. What we've tried to do is remind people of why they were putting themselves in a very dangerous position socially and personally, by making a beautiful record really."

Joy De Vivre: "I think Pen was pretty devastated by Andy leaving and I think maybe *Acts Of Love* was something that came out of that sorrow. That he needed to get back in touch with a part of him that the band hadn't necessarily included. And to include the band in it."

Eve Libertine: "I think in a way it's a cleansing. I think we got bogged down sometimes in the anger and could almost forget in the misty haze why the anger was there."

In 1985, Pete Wright told *Mucilage* fanzine: "I think it's two things, one side allowed ourselves space to try and discover and develop certain areas, we are still in the process of doing so, like launching ourselves into the dark with this new LP. On the other hand we do tend to withdraw occasionally from the arena to allow other people to get on with things. We don't want to end up monopolising everything by continuously instituting moves. You have to stand back and clear the floor for people.

"Some people in the band have done an album set of fifty poems, it's sort of classical and hasn't gone out as Crass. We felt we'd been jumping and shouting about things for quite a few years, we tried to see what positive contributions had been . . . a demonstration of our own positive side . . . we wanted to produce something of beauty, quality and vision. Although all that has been underneath Crass from the start it hasn't always been clear that Crass itself is trying to push things onto a different stage."

In the same interview, Penny Rimbaud offered further: "I imagine most grannies would prefer it to most so called punks. I should think a lot of punks will be thoroughly pissed off, cos it doesn't say fuck in every song. It will be interesting to see what happens, to see how many people reject it in the same way their parents reject punk."

It seems curious and perhaps illuminating to note that Rimbaud's view of punks – once so hopeful and optimistic – had by this point been reduced to the idea that they simply wanted to hear swearing. Of course, back at the time of their first recordings, it was true – albeit for more subtle reasons – but by now this could reasonably be interpreted as a sign that a tired cynicism about 'punk' had set in in the Crass camp, or at least in the Rimbaud head.

Phil Free: "It was words he'd written before Crass, but Pete did the bass lines – some of the greatest bass lines ever. Pen would hum a tune, Paul (Ellis) would work it out on the keyboard. Pete then did the bass and I did the guitar. It took a long time to do because it didn't have the same relevance or the same urgency."

Penny Rimbaud: "The things that have inspired me are not political works in the sense that Crass' earlier works were. What has inspired me are the poems and paintings and pieces of music that have been left which are statements of that which is beyond the human spirit. In Monet's Water Lillies, Brahm's symphonies and Walt Whitman's poetry, I see expressions of the unbeaten human spirit that has existed throughout history and despite history. One could reasonably say that throughout history, the powerful and the wealthy and the evil and malicious have conspired to destroy the human spirit. One could quite reasonably say that in modern society, everything is designed to destroy the human spirit. I would hope that *Acts Of Love* is a contribution to the documentation of the spirit.

"I would hope also that beyond and above the seven years that we were Crass the punk band that some spirit rose above all that. I believe that was the case – I believe the reason for our enormous popularity has been that people recognise the spiritual value of what we have tried to offer. The contribution of *Acts Of Love* is possibly nothing compared to some of the greater contributions but nonetheless I hope to throw another drop into the ocean. Van Gogh was a punk, Beethoven was a punk, Mozart was a punk. Throughout history, these people have contributed.

"Possibly Crass as a band made some mistakes in creating a sense of fear. Unwittingly and unintentionally but I think there are occasions in our work where we created fear and that's a negative feeling, it's a negative force. People should be aware, people should be informed. They should know what happened at Hiroshima and at the Nazi concentration camps – but if they live in *fear* of that then they live limited lives. We have to find that balance. All too often what appears to be informed opinion, what appears to be offering information is simply being used to intimidate, enormously to the advantage of the state. CND, for example, promotes fear because it isn't an organisation attempting to look at vision, to offer some real tangible future, because it's basically a negative force which is simply saying, 'We're afraid of being bombed'. It's having the reverse effect of the one it wants. So inadvertently and unintentionally it's serving the interests of the state.

"When creativity is in opposition to destruction, inevitably destruction prevails. To a very small degree, that was one of the things that we initially didn't realise. The moment creativity falls into the trap of being in opposition, it's becoming defined – the whole purpose of creativity is that it's channelling and describing undefined areas – its bringing form from formlessness. The moment the form is defined (by the authorities, by the state, by the schools, by parents, by the church) then we're no longer in a creative situation. We have to be aware of the political and social conditions and we have to side-step them to allow our creativity to be free. Because if our creativity isn't free, then we're not actually offering anything positive – we're not offering vision."

Acts Of Love also put Crass where you'd least expect them – on Radio Two. Peter Clayton and Brian Matthews allowed themselves a moment of amusement on the *Around Midnight* show: "Now the next thing is quite the oddest record to have come my way for ages. You get in touch with a Penny Rimbaud, and when you phone her up it turns out to be a fella. Penny is a nickname because he was always thought to have slightly, er lavatorial thoughts."

PC: "Well, as far as I can see that's an Edith Sidwell poem produced accidentally by a self-confessed violent punk rocker. . ."

BM: "Oh yes, who's been listening to Aubade."

PC: "But probably not you see,"

BM: "Oh come on, it's the same rhythm and everything."

PC: "I don't. . ."

BM: "Oh give over Peter, you're being gulled and gecked."

PC: "Well perhaps I'm being too nice but I think he did it by accident because I think nobody could come that close and *know* that he was coming that close. I think he'd be ashamed or startled. . ."

BM: "Well he's not ashamed to work in a band called Crass and call himself Penny Rimbaud . . . where does shame come into it?"

PC: "I was absolutely amazed. It's John Peel territory this!"

BM: "Ha ha! Yes, it is."

As a swansong, Crass recorded the oddity *10 Notes On A Summers Day*. The sleeve announced the band's demise: "*10 Notes* represents Crass's last formal recording. We shall continue to make statements both individually and as a group, yet no longer feel obliged to be limited by the inward looking format of the 'band'."

10 Notes was written, appropriately enough, in the summer of 1984, while Penny Rimbaud was at Summerhill School, 'working' as the pool attendant. "It was written as a poem," he says. "It describes where we'd ended up after all those years of frenzy and madness. You've put everything you've got into something, you've shouted and screamed; and then you suddenly find yourself on your own sitting under an oak tree, and you think, 'Fucking hell, what was that about?'"

10 Notes was bereft of chainsaw guitars, shouting and swearing, again closer to Penny Rimbaud's free jazz roots than anything remotely to do with punk rock. "I went in and said we're going to do it completely the wrong way round. The drum track was put on last. The first track put down was the piano track, which I played. I can't play piano but I just went in and played about 20 minutes worth of piano. The whole thing was based around that."

It was an improvisatory process that Eve in particular felt suited to and enjoyed, unlike Steve. "I approached *Ten Notes* as 'I'll just be an instrument'," he says. "That shouldn't have been called Crass, that should have been Crass performing with Penny Rimbaud, because that's his record . . . I just think it's rubbish."

George Mackay is equally forthright in his opinions on the piece: "It was just crap. When they tried to be positive, utopian even, it just wasn't as powerful."

Penny Rimbaud: "It was a parting shot – all very self-referential. It was obviously not something we could develop. Steve didn't like it at all, Eve hated it till she got stoned one night and suddenly realised it was fucking brilliant. I think to say they were humouring me by doing it is a bit unreasonable, but I think there's a certain element of that. It's how I'd like to have gone. . ."

. . . and, of course, it is how Penny Rimbaud *has* gone, only this time with musicians who both understand and enjoy that kind of music.

On March 3, 1985, the miners called off their year long strike and Thatcher emerged victorious. It had been a desperately close battle, as might have been expected with so much more than the mining communities involved at stake. The working class had tried to break her but instead she had broken the working class, albeit temporarily.

After defeating a foreign enemy in the Falklands War, Thatcher had now slain what she called "the enemy within". It was time to turn her steely death-stare onto other 'enemies within' who had to be unethically cleansed. The class war was in full flow and middle-England was on the lookout for new victims.

Stonehenge Festival, now including a plethora of new-age travellers, found itself high on the hit list. Glastonbury Festival grew more and more mainstream over the years – dropping the CND connection, embracing capitalism and eventually erecting a Berlin/Gaza wall around it to keep out undesirables. But Stonehenge was still free and growing each year at a rate that clearly alarmed the powers that be. As a yearly living advert for the viability of alternative lifestyles, the Festival was a startling success – an ideal roam exhibition.

The 'Peace Convoy' was a group of new age travellers so named because they'd gone down to visit the peace camp at Greenham Common one year after Stonehenge. On their way to Stonehenge

Festival in 1985, they were ambushed by the police, who forced them all – men, women and children – into a bean field and dealt all there vicious beatings, destroying their homes in the process. Home affairs correspondent for the *Guardian* Nick Davies wrote the following day:

"There was glass breaking, people screaming, black smoke towering out of burning caravans and everywhere there seemed to be people being bashed and flattened and pulled by the hair ... men, women and children were led away, shivering, swearing, crying, bleeding, leaving their homes in pieces... Over the years I had seen all kinds of horrible and frightening things and always managed to grin and write it. But as I left the Beanfield, for the first time, I felt sick enough to cry."

ITN news man Kim Sabido concurred, speaking to the camera: "What we, the ITN camera crew and myself as a reporter, have seen in the last 30 minutes here in this field has been some of the most brutal police treatment of people that I've witnessed in my entire career as a journalist. The number of people who have been hit by policemen, who have been clubbed whilst holding babies in their arms in coaches around this field, is yet to be counted... There must surely be an enquiry."

There had been an enquiry after the police violence at Windsor Free Festival in the seventies, but the Thatcher Government evidently felt no need for such frivolities.

As a result, Crass almost played a final, post-Andy Palmer gig. After the police had run riot at the Battle Of The Beanfield, the travellers regrouped elsewhere for a reconvened festival and Crass decided to go down to play a gig as a show of solidarity. If the police could act like that, pacifism was clearly out of the window. "We took some shovel handles, just in case," recalls Penny Rimbaud. When they arrived, however, in an echo of their attempt to play the effort to revive Windsor Free Festival at the start of their time together as a band, there was no generator.

After the noise, silence...

Penny Rimbaud: "As long as we were operating as Crass, as a corporate body – and we were one of the first great corporations in that sense – we even had a better logo than most corporations – everything was fine. But as that stopped, things started becoming thornier.

"There was an awful lot of personal things that had to be put aside through being a band – we'd made this agreement, we were very committed and very honest within that commitment. But what we weren't looking at was ourselves. And basically I think we were waking up one-by-one and thinking, 'Who the fuck are you?' Because it wasn't any longer Phil the guitarist and Pete the bassist, it was *Phil* and *Pete* and I was thinking, 'Do I like Pete? Do I like where he stands now?' I think there was a very distinct divide between possibilities, futures. You could almost bring that down to an activist divide between the pacifist and the non-pacifist element – that was under question. Different forms of honesty? Different approaches to what one believes is honest? Different aspirations? All sorts of things were coming forward and we weren't very well equipped for that. We could deal endlessly with 'what do we do if the police come out tomorrow?' We were brilliant at that, we'd learnt how to do that as a group of people; we were so fast. When we arrived at a gig, Joy would go and do the cooking, Pete would be putting up the stacks, everyone knew what they were doing. So the fact that we might not like one another didn't even enter the equation."

Steve Ignorant: "You've got Pete Wright going off on his tangent; Phil Free saying fuck-all; Joy de Vivre saying whatever Phil Free says is right; Eve Libertine out there on her own, like me; Pen & Gee rowing and Andy Palmer wanting to go off and have a relationship with Lou (his girlfriend). And it all broke down in the end. Then you end up with Penny Rimbaud writing these obscure leaflets about 'would I pick up a gun and pull the trigger?' and Pete Wright saying 'either we get really radical or we don't' ... what are you on about, you arseholes? We are in a punk band. We ain't gonna change the fucking world."

Only they did. Well, sort of.

Steve Ignorant: "Once the band wasn't there, everybody looked at each other and thought, 'Well, if it wasn't for the band, would I be living with you?' It got really personal. What bugs me is that I don't remember too much about it. I was quite happily – naively – going on my merry little way, thinking it was still alright. It wasn't until people were walking out the door and actually leaving that I realised there was all this stuff going on. I thought it was all things that could be resolved around the dinner table like they used to be. But of course it was more than that, and there seems to be this resentment ... things were said that were really painful and which each individual in the band still feels – it still hurts really. So it changed in that way. Although we still had punk rockers turning up from Italy, wanting to stay at Crass mansions and all that.

"It was really weird for me to see Dial House change like that. Before it had been so involved with Crass and it felt ... different: what's going on? What do we do? Then people started leaving. It's odd, you've had something for going on ten years then it all falls apart, splitting at the seams."

One way Steve dealt with his confusion was to write songs about the situation, songs that would surface later with his post-Crass band Schwarzeneggar as 'Goodbye To All That' and 'Too Much Too Little Too Late'.

With more time on his hands, Steve "panicked a bit. I was in my early thirties and I thought, what do I do now? Because the only job I'd had was working in a supermaket and one year in a hospital. But apart from that, just being in a punk rock band. I thought the day was going to come when I'd have to get a job. So I looked in the paper and even back then there were no opportunities for me – it was all things like 'lathe operator' and 'capstan setters', whatever that is. So that was certainly an incentive to get off my arse and get in another band.

"When Crass finished, I didn't have to worry about being on tour, about writing songs, about being nervous to be onstage. I could just do whatever I wanted to do, but what the fuck do you do when all the qualifications you've got is being a lead shouter in a punk rock band? And then suddenly I realised I'm not Paul Weller, who could just phone up whatsit from The Ruts and say, 'I've got an idea for this single.' There wasn't that network for me so I had to start right from the beginning."

As the band discovered their individual selves again, so the black uniform began morphing into more colourful garb. It wasn't easy though. Penny Rimbaud recalls venturing out in a white top and being so uncomfortable that he actually went into a shop to buy something black to wear instead.

Steve Ignorant bought some "rockabilly peg trousers, like Madness" and "those short-sleeved American shirts with the nice little turn-up. And a nice little James Dean quiff". He also remembers a Penny

Rimbaud visit to India as a moment of sartorial awakening. "He came back wearing white..."

Joy DeVivre: "I probably made the worst fashion choices of my entire life during that time! The things I chose from jumble sales were pretty awful! When you take off your black..."

Phil Free: "I had no idea what the hell you could wear! I mean, wearing black is quite easy. You might like this colour or that colour, but how the hell do you choose? And also it was still strong that we couldn't wear denim."

Joy DeVivre: "The band had finished. It had ceased to exist and what was left was people still trying to do that kind of life together. It was quite hard trying to find our feet without the band as it had been."

Phil Free: "It was a massive social bond. I kept a diary one time where we had two thousand visitors in one year..."

Joy DeVivre: "I did a lot of cooking — made a lot of bread!"

Phil Free: "I suppose there came a point when you were living on understood shared experiences, if not necessarily what you think now. So how are you going to suddenly say I don't want to do this?"

Joy DeVivre: "Also I think, trying to retrieve the information and the emotional tenures of the time, there was a feeling that one needed to do something terribly different. And if somebody, like Pen, wanted to do that, then we'd all be behind him."

Phil Free: "There was also a huge amount of stuff going on. Gee's mum died — she lived in the house while she was dying; Pen's mum died; Pen's father had died; Eve's mum died; the kids were leaving school."

Phil Free: "One of the things about the band is that Pen is quite fundamental to it. I remember at one stage him saying that it was all between Steve and him, and nobody else was really that important. But the thing that kept it going for seven years was everybody else. Otherwise it would have just lasted a couple of months. Pen certainly drove things. He always had ideas, never stopped having them. But he always needed people to bounce them off, to work with him and carry him through the ideas.

"Realistically, a lot of times the ideas were as untenable for him as they were for the rest of the world. We can all draw a house, but we can't necessarily put the bricks in place or dig the foundations or supply the power. And one of the functions within the band was maintaining the band, otherwise it wouldn't have lasted."

Joy De Vivre: "When you get a group of people together, you may have one person who's particularly vocal and eloquent. But in the group, you do affect each other, and Pen's ideas were no more stable than anyone else's."

Steve Ignorant continued writing songs, including 'Happy Hour', which he would perform with both Conflict and later The Stratford Mercenaries. He felt free to start enjoying life a bit more. "It was brilliant because I wasn't questioned any more; I was just left alone. I could look at the barmaid's arse without being branded sexist. I could have milk in my tea without being called a bastard cos I wasn't a vegan. By that time, it had got really extreme. To get out of that was such a relief cos it was such a fucking headache, you know?

"I went to an anarchist book fair and I thought what's the lowest of the low that 'Steve Ignorant from Crass' could do? I'll be a shoeshine boy. So I shined shoes. People were saying the shoe polish had meat in it. 'Haven't you read your multinational corporation booklet?' I did a pretty good job as it goes – I might do it again someday."

On New Years Day 1989, the remaining members of Crass who were still living at Dial House had the mother of all rows. It started with an innocuous conversation about smoking, but ended up with all the personal differences that had been "put aside" when Crass made their decision to get serious, coming home to roost. Over ten years of suppressed frustration and communication exploded into a vicious row, the effects of which still seem to ripple today, over 15 years later.

Penny recalls: "One of the band had just stopped smoking, and he was trying to persuade his partner to give up smoking. I just rather innocently said 'Well, statistics don't mean anything. More people are killed on the road every year than die of smoking-related diseases etc etc.' I was bullshitting as much as he was. It was some stupid little thing. There was a terrific difference at the end between the direct violent action and the direct non-violent action. We'd managed to hold that one at bay for seven years. I couldn't go on pretending that I still believed in the ethic that we'd been promoting for all those years. I was a profound pacifist and I'd still like to be."

"It seemed to get unnecessarily aggressive", remembers Eve. "Whereas other times someone would say 'I don't think smoking is good' and someone would say 'Well I'm smoking anyway' and you let it go. But it seemed to be a reason for saying something else."

Phil Free: "It wasn't an enormous row, it was just a strong conversation. People wanted space. People didn't need to be there but didn't know how not to be there. When you've lived in a place for ten years, where do you go? I'd moved in there because I had nowhere else to go. The last cottage I'd lived in was £2.50 a week! And I'd got no means of income."

Joy De Vivre: "Which is quite frightening, leaving without anything. We left with two chairs and a table and a mattress."

Pete Wright, Joy de Vivre and Phil Free all left Dial House. Luckily, Mick Duffield helped Phil and Joy out – he was doing well in the film business and had bought himself a flat in which they stayed. Mick was still actually living in a squat, hanging on till the bitter end.

AFTER THE FACT

With his new threads, Steve Ignorant spent a couple of years playing with Conflict, who to all intents and purposes filled the space that Crass had vacated as the leading lights of the anarcho-punk movement. Conflict's politics roughly mirrored Crass, but with a far greater emphasis on the animal rights movement and far less on pacifism. Steve would also form his own bands, first Schwarzenegger and then Stratford Mercenaries, returning to punk rock.

Steve also got into Punch & Judy: "I got this old book, *Mayhew's London*, written by a Victorian, or pre-Victorian statistician, about Punch & Judy. It used to give me the creeps as a kid. It had an old script in it so I wrote it as a radio play. To give myself inspiration, I made a Mr. Punch figure out of wood, which used to sit on my desk. Then I thought it would be nice to make a set of these characters. Then I thought a lot of kids come to visit the house, so it would be nice to make a little booth. Then I thought, I've got all the figures, I might as well try doing it. So I got a swozzle..."

And after an initial performance in Dial House, Steve Ignorant became perhaps the most unlikely (to those who've never met him) children's performer. Another early performance was at a Blyth Power concert, but before long Steve was playing children's concerts as a bona-fide entertainer, agent and all. One gig has a special place in his heart. "For three weeks, every Sunday, I did four shows a day for £75 a show in this bar at the Hilton by Heathrow airport. It was meant to be entertaining rich Saudi Arabians' kids while their parents had board meetings. The only people I performed to for the whole three weeks were the bar staff."

Despite assurances from the bar people that they'd say Steve had performed even if he hadn't, Mr. Ignorant played Mr. Punch with diligence to an audience that may have reminded him of the early Crass gigs.

Pete Wright returned to his pre-Crass acoustic music with Judas II, a 'Mad In England' duo with Martin Wilson who've so far released one album, *s/t*, including a couple of songs co-written with John Arthur Hewson from the Friends Of Wensleydale Jasper days.

Penny Rimbaud, Eve Libertine and Gee Vaucher continue to work together. Under the name Last Amendment, they play regularly at the Vortex jazz club in Dalston, London, performing poetry to free jazz backing.

Following in the footsteps of many leftists, in the eighties original Crass guitarist Steve Herman moved to Nicaragua, where the Sandanista movement had thrown out the US-backed Somoza dictatorship, to contribute to what was seen as a great beacon of hope for the future – which was precisely the reason Ronald Reagan reacted so violently against it. On February 45, 1989, Steve died there.

In August 2005, John Loder passed away. Penny Rimbaud wrote his obituary for the *Guardian*, recalling their first meeting: "I first met the sound engineer and record producer John Loder in about 1968. He was on an acid trip and seemed to be talking out of the top of his head. The next time I met him he was straight and made a lot more sense. We soon found that we shared. a common interest in Jimi Hendrix, Frank Zappa, John Coltrane, and KarlHeinz Stockhausen. When we got bored with them, we would play birdsong forwards and Bach backwards."

He recalls John Loder spending a brief time as a mini-cab driver, then building Southern Studios in his garage. As Rimbaud recalls: "And it was John's managerial, production and engineering skills which were to assist the likes of Crass, Bjork, Chumbawamba, Fugazi, Shellac, The Jesus And Mary Chain, Slint and Babes In Toyland into the public domain."

John Loder built up Southern to incorporate several labels and Southern Distribution, now an international force.

Just as it seemed the remaining residents of Dial House could rest and enjoy the beauty of their surroundings, the very existence of the place itself was threatened. Initially, Penny Rimbaud had sublet the house from a farmer who in turn rented the land from the Post Office. It was then owned by British Telecom who sold it on to the Peer Group. They planned to sell it for development. Penny and Gee formed the North Weald Action Group with other concerned local residents and used all their rabble-rousing experience from the Crass years to best effect.

"It was horrible, really horrible" remembers Steve Ignorant. "It had been going on for ten years. First it started with BT – our original land-lords – being really arrogant. Then, by the time it got to court, Peer Group, who were now the landlords of the land and wanted to sell it off for a golf course, were super-arrogant. It was really scary because it came down to the decision of the judge: if he said the landlord was right, Dial House wouldn't be there anymore – Penny and Gee would be living somewhere else."

Penny, speaking in 2000 while the case was ongoing, was in defiant mood: "Maybe like all empires, it's going to crumble into dust. But it's not going to crumble into fucking gold dust. If I'm going to close down thirty years commitment, it's not going to be because some yuppie bastard has decided to make my house into a gold mine. What they'll get is a burned-down ruin.

"It's been a home to over a hundred people. It's been saving hundreds of lives, not just through what goes out of the place, but also what goes on within it. It would be a total tragedy."

His defiance was tempered by an overwhelming exhaustion at the endless hours of work that had to be put in to save the place: "It will always be what it is if I've got anything to do with it, which is the open house it always has been. But whether I've got the strength to still be behind the open door, I don't know."

The court case was found in favour of the Dial House residents.

Steve Ignorant: "Basically, they couldn't get us out and the case actu-ally set a precedent whereby if you've been living together for a number of years, you don't have to be married or related to be living as a family. So they couldn't split us up, which meant we could stay there. Plus the organic garden, which takes nine years to do and all that doo-dah.

"So Peer Group said they were going to sell the house. And the only way they could do it, with us as sitting tenants, was send it to auction. And who the fuck is going to buy that place with us sitting in it? So we got a load of friends to sit in the auction room and buy the place for us. . ."

They also went to the Guardian, where they issued a plea for help via a sympathetic article entitled 'Country House Anarchy': "The Grade 2 listed 16th-century cottage on the outskirts of North Weald was set up as a commune by artists, and later Crass mainstays, Penny Rimbaud and Gee Vaucher in 1967, and it has since become a punk equivalent of the Bloomsbury set's Charleston House. The similarity is not lost on Rimbaud, who managed to persuade the courts of the cottage's significance as a cultural outpost. The house was the birthplace of the Stonehenge festival and the base from which Crass rejuvenated the peace movement and created the blueprint for the kind of anti-globalisation protests seen in London and Seattle in recent years. It was also a temporary home to many of the bands who recorded for Crass' eponymous record label. One such visitor was Bjork, who stayed in 1984 when she was recording an LP for the label with Sugarcubes predecessors, Kukl.

"The appeal for funds is an ideological struggle as much as a financial one. After all, the four, Rimbaud, Vaucher, Eve Libertine and Steve Ignorant (to give them their 'punk names;), have breached the old anarchist 'all property is theft' maxim. 'It was very, very difficult indeed for us to decide to go ahead with the appeal, because in a way even that is contradictory to our ethos,' says the commune's founder, Rimbaud. 'If it hadn't been for the fact that that idea was so wholeheartedly supported and even to some extent initiated by people outside of here, then I don't think it could be tolerable.'"

Around the same time as the court case, Steve Ignorant finally left Dial House to move in to a house nearby with his girlfriend Jona. "It just wasn't for me anymore," he says. "The thing I found difficult about moving out was that I'd made a commitment to the place, through thick and thin. Pen and Gee were caught right in the middle of [the court case] and for me to leave at that time, I really had to steel myself and say no, this really is the right time to go.

"It took me about three and a half years to stop missing it, even though I was just down the road. I think when I first moved in with Jona she found it a bit difficult because it was almost like I missed those people more than I was happy living with her. It wasn't like that at all – it wasn't the people I missed so much, it was little things like the way the door latch opens when you go in the back door, or a certain tree or a bush ... it was the actual house I missed and it took me three and a half years to get over that."

To this day, Steve still feels "odd" when he goes back to visit Dial House. "I still feel I've got the right to put my tuppence-worth in even though I don't live there. I spoke about that to Pen and Gee recently and they agreed that, because I was such a part of the place that I have got the right to say if I feel uncomfortable about something. It's odd because now there are people there that I don't know and things going on that I'm not a part of. I tend to look round to make sure nothing's missing, and nothings been moved."

With the battle to save Dial House won, its new owners found themselves saddled with a huge debt. It must have felt supremely ironic to think that the royalties from the band that the house spawned could have sorted out this debt with ease once upon a time, had they not been so adept at giving it all 'back' in one way or another.

One remedy was to hold an auction – the Dial House Art Auction – of works of art from ex-members and friends of the band, as well as old original artwork from Crass Records releases, featuring material from over 100 bands and artists. Steve Ignorant contributed his standing figure of Mr Punch. "But even at the time," Steve muses, "I was thinking that if we got our heads together about Crass merchandise and all these people ripping us off..."

The closest Crass came to reforming – and the closest they will come – occurred when a punk retrospective festival was held at the National Film Theatre on London's South Bank. Sandwiched in among punk ephemera and nostalgia films from the seventies, Crass was offered an evening to themselves. "They got in touch with Gee, as the Crass movie maker," remembers Penny Rimbaud, "probably thinking they were going to get reels of Crass jumping up and down on a stage. Gee, being who she is, said, 'I'm not going to do that unless I can make it into an event.'"

It was indeed an event.

Crass – or members of Crass – would perform a second time on the South Bank, this time at the Queen Elizabeth Hall as they organised an anti-war event at which almost all the band would make individual contributions as well as a swathe of sympathetic artists. "I think the guy who approached us about doing it was hoping that he was offering such a big platform that the band would reform."

These days, as in those days, all the members of Crass live relatively frugal existences, certainly compared to their peers. Andy Palmer aside, the members of Crass still get royalties as their records – like many punk records – are being bought by subsequent generations.

"I can *just about* live off them," says Steve, emphasising the 'just about', before revealing figures that he quite rightly pre-empts with "a lot of people won't believe this, but me and Jona have got our budget down to £20 a week shopping and I get about £30 a week pocket money." This puts Steve way below the poverty line. "Those royalty cheques pay for my board and lodging basically – anything else I want, I have to go out and work for it. Digging holes in the ground and doing shit stuff like that."

"Authority does not exist without the value and support that we give it. As long as we, the people, bow down to the system, authority will exist and so will the system. Either we accept that we are to live as mindless robots in a world that is walking the tightrope of nuclear war, where security checks will become a way of life, where the streets are patrolled by tanks and the skies by helicopters, where people no longer dare speak of what they feel and believe for fear of those who might be listening, where love is a memory, peace is a dream and freedom simply does not exist – or we demand our rights, refuse to be a part of the authority that denies them and recognise that the system is nothing but a small handful of ruling elites who are powerless without our support. We have the strength, but do we have the courage?

"We must learn to live with our own weakness, hatred, prejudice, and to reject theirs.

"We must learn to live with our own fears, doubts, inadequacies, and to reject theirs.

"We must learn to live with our own love, passion, desire, and to reject theirs.

"We must learn to live with our own conscience, awareness, certainty, and to reject theirs.

"We must learn to live with our own moralities, values, standards, and to reject theirs.

"We must learn to live with our own principles, ethics, philosophies, and to reject theirs.

"Above all, we must learn to live with our own strength and learn how to use it against 'them', as they have used it against 'us'. It is our strength that they have used against us throughout history to maintain their privileged positions. It is up to me, alone, and you, alone, to bite the hand that bleeds us. THERE IS NO FUTURE BUT OUR OWN BECAUSE THERE IS NO AUTHORITY BUT OUR OWN, YOU AND I, WHO LOVE THIS PLANET 'EARTH', ARE ITS RIGHTFUL INHERITORS – IT IS TIME TO STAKE OUR CLAIM.

"Throughout the 'hippy era', we had championed the cause of peace, some of us had been on the first CND marches and, with sadness, had watched the movement being eroded by political greed. Throughout the 'drop out and cop out' period we hung on to the belief that 'real' change can only come about through personal example, because of this we rejected much of hippy culture, notably the emphasis on drugs, as being nothing but escapism. It is sad that many punks appear to be resorting to the same means of escape while in their blind hypocrisy they accuse hippies of never having 'got it together' – neither will these new prophets of the pipe dream.

"We had hoped that through a practical demonstration of peace and love, we would be able to paint the grey world in new colours; it is strange that it took a man called Hope, the only 'real' hippy with whom we ever directly became creatively involved, to show us that that particular form of hope was a dream. The experiences to which our short friendship led made us realise that it was time to have a rethink about the way in which we should pursue our vision of peace. Wally's death showed us that we could not afford to 'sit by and let it happen again'. In part, his death was our responsibility and although we did everything that we could, it was not enough.

"Desire for change had to be coupled with the desire to work for it, if it was worth opposing the system, it was worth opposing it totally. It was no longer good enough to take what we wanted and to reject the rest, it was time to get back into the streets and attack, to get back and share our experiences and learn from the experiences of others.

"A year after Wally's death, the Pistols released 'Anarchy In The UK,' maybe they didn't really mean it ma'am, but to us it was a battle cry. When Rotten proclaimed that there was 'no future', we saw it as a challenge to our creativity – we knew that there was a future if we were prepared to work for it.

"It is our world, it is ours and it has been stolen from us. We set out to demand it back, only this time round they didn't call us 'hippies' they called us 'punks.'

Penny Rimbaud – *Last Of The Hippies*

EPILOGUE

In 2007 it will be 30 years since Crass got together for a bit of a laugh and something to do. In the years since they split, having evolved into a genuine force for social change, so much has changed and so much has stayed the same.

Penny Rimbaud has taken of late to complaining at every given opportunity about how Crass have been airbrushed out of punk histories. In this, he has a fair point, but he then goes on to needlessly deride the Pistols, The Clash and others as mere puppets, claiming the movement started by Crass was the only one to effect any lasting change. This is a disappointingly narrow, even curmudgeonly, vision. While Crass was by far the most important political band (and, yes, that includes The Clash), punk changed a great deal more than that. Fashion, design, architechture and art were all irredeemably changed by the punk explosion. Oh, and music.

Is it shallow to mention clothes? Nobody seems to make any new statements with clothes any more – if they're not busy looking 'normal', they're busy buying into retro fashions – plastic safe impressions of the rebellions of bygone years. Where has all the 'danger gear' The Clash sung of gone? I guess to all the punks in eighties Eastern Europe and other countries where punk was a step further down rebellion road, that complaint would look shallow indeed.

But this book is necessarily from a UK perspective. I'm aware that a lot of what Crass said is relevant globally but as they stopped playing abroad because they couldn't be sure they'd put their message over correctly, so I too must assume at least the humility to know I don't know what it's like growing up in Michigan, or Moscow, for that matter. As the past is a different country, so different countries have different pasts, different contexts and different perspectives.

And what of the letter written to me by Pete Wright as I set out on this project, imploring me to consider that this could be more than a coffee table book? Well, I'd like to think it is Pete; I'd like to think I've left a fair few signposts and clues for those who'd like to take things further. But I'll let you in on a little secret. I always thought The Poison Girls were a far better band than Crass, and it puzzled me that Crass was so much bigger and more influential. In the course of writing this book, it struck me that Crass – by accident or design – always hit the populist button more accurately than the Poisons. So I hope you'll understand the inclusion of things like discographies and discussion about the music. You were a band, after all.

On a personal level, revisiting those years has been a strange experience. They were the punk years – years when we could be heroes, just like the Bowie song. And we were heroes. The stared-at years, where every venture outside the house was a gentle confrontation just because of the way you dressed. There was always an element of danger, but far outweighing it was the buzz you got from being stared at for all the right reasons. But these were also the Thatcher years – it's not healthy to hate but that woman really did personify evil. I refer you to 'Tramp The Dirt Down' by Elvis Costello (and also 'Shipbuilding' while we're at it, the finest anti-war song ever). We're still living with her legacy and many are still dying with it.

Those who think things can never change ignore the scientific fact the everything is in a constant state of flux – change is always happening to everything, from the cells in your body (which renew every three months, making you a new person four times a year) to political change to social change. The question is not whether things are moving, but in which direction. The anarcho punk movement, of which Crass was a part, helped; certainly not musically, but politically and culturally. Were Crass its leaders? To the elements who could tie their own shoelaces, certainly not. To others, certainly.

In 1989, Cruise Missiles began to leave Greenham Common as the Cold War ended in a victory for the forces of capitalism. In 2000, the Greenham women were invited to symbolically remove the last piece of the fence.

As the third world war continues unannounced, the message of the peace movement is struggling to be heard. But for the first time – because of the nature of the war – that same peace movement is for the first time drawn from all classes, creeds and colours. Greenham mobilised women, but it was middle class and whiter than white.

Christ The Album should have been the last Crass record, and but for the untimely intervention of the Falklands War it might well have been. As good a place to any to sign off is the end of that record, where the band sample E.P. Thompson addressing one of the big CND rallies in Trafalgar Square. It still seems pertinent – one day we'll be back.

"Looking at you, I know one thing. We can win. I want you to ... I want you to SENSE YOUR OWN STRENGTH."

DISCOGRAPHY OF RECORDS MADE AND PRODUCED BY CRASS, & OTHER OUTPUT

CRASS RECORDS

Alternative
'In Nomine Patri' (1982)

Andy T.
Weary Of The Flesh E.P. (1982)

Anthrax
Capitalism Is Cannibalism E.P. (1982)

Annie Anxiety
'Barbed Wire Halo' (1981)

Bullshit Detector
Bullshit Detector, Volume 1, Various Artists (80)
Bullshit Detector, Volume 2, Various Artists (1982)
Bullshit Detector, Volume 3, Various Artists (1984)

Captain Sensible
This Is Your Captain Speaking E.P. (1981)

Conflict
The House That Man Built E.P. (1981)

Crass
'Reality Asylum' (1978)
'The Feeding Of The 5000' EP (1978)
Stations Of The Crass (1979)
'Bloody Revolutions' (1980)
'Nagasaki Nightmare' (1980)
'Rival Tribal Rebel Revel' (1980)
'Toxic Graffiti 'Zine Flexi' (1980)
'Our Wedding Flexi' (1981)
Penis Envy (1981)
'Merry Crassmass' (1981)
Christ – The Album (1982)
'How Does It Feel?' (1982)
Yes Sir, I Will (1983)
'Sheep Farming In The Falklands' (1982 Flexi; 1983 7″)
'Whodunnit?' (1983)
'You're Already Dead' (1984)
Acts Of Love (1984)
Best Before (1984)
Ten Notes On A Summers Day (1984)
Penny Rimbaud Reads From Christ's Reality Asylum (1992)

Cravats
'Rub Me Out' (1982)

Dirt
'Death Is Reality Today' (1981)
Never Mind Dirt, Here's The Bollocks... (1982)

Donna & The Kebabs
You Can Be You E.P. (1979)

D & V
'The Nearest Door' EP (1983)
D & V (1984)

Flux Of Pink Indians
'Neu Smell' EP (1981)

Jane Gregory
'After A Dream' (1984)

Hit Parade
'Bad News' EP (1982)
Plastic Culture (1984)
Nick Nack Paddy Wack (1986)

Kukl
The Eye (1984)
Holidays In Europe (1984)

Lack Of Knowledge
'Grey' EP (1983)

Mdc
'Multi Death Corporations' EP (1983)

Mob
'No Doves Fly Here' (1981)

Omega Tribe
'Angry Songs' EP (1982)

Poison Girls
Chappaquidick Bridge (1980)
'Statement' (1980)
'Promenade Immortelle' (1980)
Hex (1980)

Rudimentary Peni
'Farce' EP (1982)

Sleeping Dogs
'Beware Sleeping Dogs' EP (1982)

Snipers
'Three Peace Suit' EP (1981)

Zounds
'Can't Cheat Karma' EP (1980)

OTHER LABELS

Christ: The Bootleg (LP recorded live in Nottingham, 1984, released 1989 on Allied Records)

'The Unelected President' – track on Peace Not War anti-war CD compilation. (This track is actually a remix of 1982's 'Major General Despair', with new lyrics and additional instrumentation provided by Dylan Bates, 2003.)

You'll Ruin It For Everyone (LP recorded live in Perth, Scotland, 1981, released 1993 on Pomona Records)

VIDEO

Christ: The Movie (a series of short films by Mick Duffield that were shown at *Crass Performances* (VHS, released 1990)

Semi-Detached (video collages by Gee Vaucher, 1978-1984, VHS, 2001)
The Eklektic 1 & 2, by A. Palmer & S. Stockton

BIBLIOGRAPHY

Hippie/Alternative Culture

Beam, Alan. *Rehearsal For The Year 2000* (Revelation Press)

Clerk, Carol. *The Saga Of Hawkwind* (Omnibus Press)

Farren, Mick. *Give The Anarchist A Cigarette* (Pimlico)

Green, Jonathan. *All Dressed Up* (Jonathan Cape)

Mackay, George. *Senseless Acts Of Beauty – Cultures Of Resistance Since the Sixties* (Verso)

Miles, Barry. *Hippie* (Cassell Ilustrated)

Neville, Richard. Hippie Hippie Shake (Bloomsbury)

Varon, Jeremy. *Bringing The War Home (The Weather Underground, The Red Army Faction And Revolutionary Violence in the Sixties and Seventies)* (University Of California Press, 2004)

Worthington, Andy. *Stonehenge – Celebration & Subversion* (Alternative Albion)

Punk

Colegrave, Stephen & Sullivan, Chris. *Punk* (Cassell)

Diggle, Steve. *Harmony In My Head* (Helter Skelter)

Garrett, Nicky. *UK Subs, The Early Years*

Hebdige, Dick. *Subculture: The Meaning Of Style* (Routledge)

Marcus, Greil. *Lipstick Traces* (Faber & Faber)

McNeil, Legs & McCain, Gillian. *Please Kill Me* (Abacus)

O'Neill, Sean & Trelford, Guy. *It Makes You Want To Spit – An Alternative Ulster 1977 – 1982* (Reekus)

Raha, Maria. *Cinderella's Big Score, Women Of The Punk And Indie Underground* – (Seal)

Reynold, Simon. *Rip It Up And Start Again – Postpunk 1978-1984* (Faber & Faber)

Robb, John. *Punk Rock – An Oral History* (Ebury)

Savage, Jon. *Englands Dreaming* (Faber & Faber)

Stevenson, Nils & Stevenson, Ray. *Vacant* (Thames & Hudson)

Crass and Anarcho Punk

International Anthem: A Nihilist Newspaper For The Living issues 1-3 (Exitstencil Press, 1977–81)

The Eklektic 1 & 2 3 (Exitstencil Press), by A. Palmer & S. Stockton

McKay, George. *Senseless Acts of Beauty* (Verso)

O'Hara, Craig. *The Philosophy Of Punk – More Than Noise* (AK Press)

Ratter, JJ. *Dancing With Francoise Sagan* (Penny Rimbaud's 'other' autobiography, unpublished)

Rimbaud, Penny (introduction). *Love Songs* (collected lyrics of Crass) (Pomona Books)

Rimbaud, Penny. *Exit, A History – On Out, In Out, Shake It All About* (sleeve notes to the [as yet unreleased] Exit CD of their performance at the Roundhouse, August 20th 1972)

Rimbaud, Penny. *Christ's Reality Asylum* (Exitstencil Press)

Rimbaud, Penny. *Life Amongst The Little People* – Written, silk-screened and bound by Crass in 1978 (Exitstencil Press)

Rimbaud, Penny. *Shibboleth- My Revolting Life* (AK Press)

Rimbaud, Penny. *The Diamond Signature* (AK Press)

Vaucher, Gee. *Crass Art and other Post Modern Monsters* (AK Press)

Whalley, Boff. *Footnote* (Pomona)

Rimbaud, Penny. *A Series Of Shock Slogans And Mindless Token Tantrums* (Exitstencil Press) (Originally issued as a pamphlet with the LP *Christ The Album*, much of the 'Last Of The Hippies' section of the text is now published online, and quoted from liberally in this book.) Within this pamphlet is a list of books and pamphlets dealing with pacifism:

Le Guin, Ursula. *The Dispossessed* (Granada/Panther)

Mayer, Peter (ed). *The Pacifist Conscience* (Pelican)

Piercy, Marge. *Woman On The Edge Of Time* (Womens Press)

Sampson, Ronald. *Society Without The State* (Peace Pledge Union)

Sharp, Gene. Making The Abolition Of War A Realistic Goal (World Policy Institute)

Tolstoy, Leo. *The Inevitable Revolution* (Housemans)

Tolstoy, Leo. *The Kingdom Of Gold And Peace Essays* (Oxford University Press)

Tolstoy, Leo. *The Law Of Love & The Law Of Violence* (Anthony Blond)

Various. *Non-Violent Action, A Selected Biography* (Housemans)

Miscellaneous

Manco, Tristan. *Stencil Graffiti* (Thames & Hudson)

McCall, Anthony & Eamon, Christopher (ed). *The Solid Light Films and Related Works* (Steidl)

Vague, Tom. *Anarchy In The UK – The Angry Brigade* (AK Press)

Webber, Andrew J., *The European Avant Garde* (Polity Press)

Wheen, Francis. *How Mumbo Jumbo Conquered The World* (Harper Perennial)

Websites

All these have contributed, either by quotes or inspiration, to the writing of this book:

Alistair Livingstone (ex-KYPP) http://greengalloway.blogspot.com/

Perfect Sound Forever http://www.furious.com/Perfect/

Mucilage http://www.uncarved.org/music/apunk/crass.html

The Commune Movement: http://www.diggersanddreamers.org.uk/

The History Of Squatting: http://www.squat.freeserve.co.uk/story/contents.htm

The Harry Cowley Club, Brighton, UK http://www.cowleyclub.org.uk/

Fluxus: http://www.fluxus.org/

ACKNOWLEDGEMENTS

Thanks to (in order of appearance) to me, my mum, dad and brother, Mark Edmonson, Penny Rimbaud, Pete Wright, Gee Vaucher, Eve Libertine, Steve Ignorant, Mike Clarke, Gordon Wilkins, Mick Duffield, Mickey Howard, Sean McGhee, Honey Bane, Annie Anxiety, Mark Brennan, Sean Forbes, Pete Sutton, David Tibet, Graham Burnett, Genesis P Orridge, Warren Carter, Colin Chalmers, Pete Sutton, Suzie Box, George Mackay, Anna Caswell, Dave Morris, Bernard Chandler, Jan & Ella, Charlie Harper, Anthony McCall, Richard Cross, Ian Glasper, Dawn Matthews, Dave King, Simon Reynolds, Radio Free France (and all who sail in her), Chris Low, Dave Morley, Tom Vague, Andrew Gallix, Guy Trelford, Joy De Vivre, Phil Free, Tony D, Alistair Livingstone and Bob Short.

And thanks to the following records for getting me through this book (relatively) sane, headphones securely clipped on while I wrote: Mozart, Scott Walker, Matt Monro, Roxy Music, Aswad, Can, Dr Alimintado, Richard Hawley, Flowers In The Dustbin, Adam & The Ants and David Bowie.

THE ANGRY BRIGADE
The Spectacular Rise and Fall of Britain's First Urban Guerilla Group
DVD I 60 minutes I $19.95 I SKU: 760137482093

"You can't reform profit capitalism and inhumanity. Just kick it till it breaks."
— Angry Brigade, communiqué no. 8

Between 1970 and 1972 the Angry Brigade used guns and bombs in a series of symbolic attacks against property. A series of communiqués accompanied the actions, explaining the choice of targets and the Angry Brigade philosophy: autonomous organization and attacks on property alongside other forms of militant working class action. Targets included the embassies of repressive regimes, police stations and army barracks, boutiques and factories, government departments and the homes of Cabinet ministers, the Attorney General and the Commissioner of the Metropolitan Police. These attacks on the homes of senior political figures increased the pressure for results and brought an avalanche of police raids. From the start the police were faced with the difficulty of getting to grips with a section of society they found totally alien. And were they facing an organization—or an idea?

This documentary, produced by Gordon Carr for the BBC (and first shown in January 1973, shortly after the trial), covers the roots of the Angry Brigade in the revolutionary ferment of the 1960s, and follows their campaign and the police investigation to its culmination in the "Stoke Newington 8" conspiracy trial at the Old Bailey—the longest criminal trial in British legal history. Produced after extensive research—among both the libertarian opposition and the police—it remains the essential study of Britain's first urban guerilla group.

DVD Extra: **THE PERSONS UNKNOWN** (1980, 22 minutes)
The so-called "Persons Unknown" trial (hence the title of the Poison Girls/Crass benefit record *Persons Unknown/Bloody Revolutions*) in which members of the Anarchist Black Cross were tried (and later acquitted) at the Old Bailey on charges of "conspiring with persons unknown, at places unknown, to cause explosions and to overthrow society." This film contains the only known footage of Crass performing live. Also, interviews with Stuart Christie, Nicholas Walter, and many other UK anarchist activists and propagandists of the time.

PM Press
PO Box 23912
Oakland, CA 94623
www.pmpress.org

FRIENDS OF PM PRESS

These are indisputably momentous times—the financial system is melting down globally and the Empire is stumbling. Now more than ever there is a vital need for radical ideas.

In the year since its founding—and on a mere shoestring—PM Press has risen to the formidable challenge of publishing and distributing knowledge and entertainment for the struggles ahead. We have published an impressive and stimulating array of literature, art, music, politics, and culture. Using every available medium, we've succeeded in connecting those hungry for ideas and information to those putting them into practice.

Friends of PM allows you to directly help impact, amplify, and revitalize the discourse and actions of radical writers, filmmakers, and artists. It provides us with a stable foundation from which we can build upon our early successes and provides a much-needed subsidy for the materials that can't necessarily pay their own way.

It's a bargain for you too. For a minimum of $25 a month, you'll get all the audio and video (over a dozen CDs and DVDs in our first year) or all of the print releases (also over a dozen in our first year). For $40 you'll get everything that is published in hard copy. Friends also have the ability to purchase any/all items from our webstore at a 50% discount. And what could be better than the thrill of receiving a monthly package of cutting edge political theory, art, literature, ideas and practice delivered to your door?

Your card will be billed once a month, until you tell us to stop. Or until our efforts succeed in bringing the revolution around. Or the financial meltdown of Capital makes plastic redundant. Whichever comes first.

For more information on the Friends of PM, and about sponsoring particular projects, please go to www.pmpress.org, or contact us at info@pmpress.org.

ABOUT PM PRESS

PM Press was founded at the end of 2007 by a small collection of folks with decades of publishing, media, and organizing experience. PM co-founder Ramsey Kanaan started AK Press as a young teenager in Scotland almost 30 years ago and, together with his fellow PM Press co-conspirators, has published and distributed hundreds of books, pamphlets, CDs, and DVDs. Members of PM have founded enduring book fairs, spearheaded victorious tenant organizing campaigns, and worked closely with bookstores, academic conferences, and even rock bands to deliver political and challenging ideas to all walks of life. We're old enough to know what we're doing and young enough to know what's at stake.

We seek to create radical and stimulating fiction and non-fiction books, pamphlets, t-shirts, visual and audio materials to entertain, educate and inspire you. We aim to distribute these through every available channel with every available technology—whether that means you are seeing anarchist classics at our bookfair stalls; reading our latest vegan cookbook at the café; downloading geeky fiction e-books; or digging new music and timely videos from our website.

PM Press is always on the lookout for talented and skilled volunteers, artists, activists and writers to work with. If you have a great idea for a project or can contribute in some way, please get in touch.

PM Press
PO Box 23912
Oakland, CA 94623
www.pmpress.org